Energy Law in Finland

Energy Law in Finland

Second Edition

Laura Huomo
Kaisa Huhta
Petri Vesa
Alice Guimaraes-Purokoski
Jaakko Klemettilä
Arto Rajala
Leea Salminen

This book was originally published as a monograph in the International Encyclopaedia of Laws/Energy Law.

Founding Editor: Roger Blanpain
General Editor: Frank Hendrickx
Volume Editors: Kurt Deketelaere & Bram Delvaux

Wolters Kluwer

Published by:
Kluwer Law International B.V.
PO Box 316
2400 AH Alphen aan den Rijn
The Netherlands
E-mail: international-sales@wolterskluwer.com
Website: lrus.wolterskluwer.com

Sold and distributed in North, Central and South America by:
Wolters Kluwer Legal & Regulatory U.S.
7201 McKinney Circle
Frederick, MD 21704
United States of America
Email: customer.service@wolterskluwer.com

Sold and distributed in all other countries by:
Air Business Subscriptions
Rockwood House
Haywards Heath
West Sussex
RH16 3DH
United Kingdom
Email: international-customerservice@wolterskluwer.com

ISBN 978-94-035-0503-9

e-Book: ISBN 978-94-035-0504-6
web-PDF: ISBN 978-94-035-0505-3

The Authors

Laura Huomo has extensive experience in energy-related transactions both from the regulatory and from the financing side. She is specialized in natural gas. She has published internationally, mainly on issues related to project financing of energy projects. She holds a PhD. from the Faculty of Law, University of Helsinki, Finland (topic: Project Financing of Natural Gas Pipelines – A Study on Natural Gas Pipeline Project Financing under Financial Law and Law of Security Interests). In addition; she was one of the two specialist secretaries in the committee of the Ministry of Economic Affairs and Employment preparing the complete reformation of the Finnish Natural Gas Market Act and she continued to be part of the working group putting together the rules for the natural gas markets (market model rules and virtual trading place structure). Laura Huomo works as an Energy and Capital Markets Counsel at Roschier, Attorneys Ltd. She can be contacted via email at laura.huomo@roschier.com.

Kaisa Huhta is a researcher in international and European energy law at the University of Eastern Finland (UEF) Law School – Centre for Climate Change, Energy and Environmental Law (CCEEL) and a lecturer in European Union (EU) energy law. She has also been a visiting researcher in the Institute of European and Comparative Law at the University of Oxford, UK. Her research focuses on EU energy law and particularly on EU electricity markets. She actively contributes to leading international publications and carries out consultancy work in the field of energy law. She can be contacted via email at kaisa.huhta@uef.fi.

The Authors

Petri Vesa is an attorney-at-law and a member of the Finnish Bar Association, and practices law in Attorney-at-Law Petri Vesa Ltd. His practice areas include environmental law and energy law, and he acts for clients, *inter alia*, on environmental and water permits and emissions trading as well as contaminated soil cases. Previously he has been working in other law firms and as an in-house counsel for one of the leading energy companies in Finland. He graduated from Helsinki University of Technology in 1998 (MSc, Energy and Environmental Technology) and from the University of Helsinki in 2000 (LLM).

Alice Guimaraes-Purokoski is Justice of the Finnish Supreme Administrative Court (SAC). She is currently a member of the 3rd Chamber of the SAC where cases concerning, e.g., public procurement, municipalities, energy and telecommunications, competition and social affairs are being dealt with. Before joining the SAC, Guimaraes-Purokoski worked as director of the unit for EU litigation at the Finnish Ministry for Foreign Affairs. As a state agent before the European Court of Justice, she has represented Finland in several court cases since 2003, including cases with energy aspects. She has previously worked with energy issues at the Finnish Ministry for Trade and Industry and at the European Commission DG TREN as a national expert. Guimaraes-Purokoski was trained on the bench in 1996–1997 (Helsinki District Court). Her PhD thesis examined the vertical division of competence in EU law and used the development of European Community (EC) energy policy and the regulation of public service obligations as examples.

Jaakko Klemettilä is a counsel at DLA Piper Attorneys Ltd, Helsinki office. Jaakko graduated from the University of Helsinki in 2000 (LLM) and has been practising tax law since 2001 with the Finnish tax authorities and two large accounting firms. Jaakko has also gained experience in energy taxation while working as a tax director with a listed Finnish multinational enterprise, which is one of the major energy consumers in Finland.

Arto Rajala is a Ministerial Counsellor in the Energy Department (Energy Market Division) of the Ministry of Economic Affairs and Employment in Finland. He is responsible for law drafting projects in the energy market sector as well as electricity and natural gas market regulation. He has worked on energy markets since 1995 as the Chief Legal Officer and the Director of the Energy Market Authority and a Chief Counsellor of the Ministry. Since 1996, he has participated in most of the government law drafting projects in the sectors of electricity and natural gas markets as well as several processes for establishing EU energy market legislation. He also has experience as a City Court Judge and as a Chairman for a division of the Consumer Disputes Board. Rajala graduated from Helsinki University in 1986 (LLM) and trained on the bench in 1992–1993.

The Authors

Leea Salminen is the former General Counsel of the Finnish subsidiary of the Exxon Mobil Corporation group of companies. She has extensive practical experience for several years in the oil sector of Finland from a global point of view. She is recognized as an expert in legal questions of oil in Finland. As Chairman of the Legal Committee of the Finnish Oil and Gas Federation for more than ten years, Leea Salminen has been following closely the development of the European and Finnish legislation and jurisprudence in energy matters. Leea Salminen is a member of the Finnish Bar Association´s group of experts on environmental law. Currently, Leea Salminen advises clients on various energy matters as well as competition issues and commercial contracts at Procopé & Hornborg, Attorneys at Law in Helsinki.

Table of Contents

Table of Contents

List of Abbreviations

AC	Alternating Current
ACER	Agency for the Cooperation of Energy Regulators
ADR	European Agreement Concerning the International Carriage of Dangerous Goods by Road
BWR	Boiling Water Reactor
CDM	Clean Development Mechanism
CER	Certified Emission Reduction
CHP	Combined Heat and Power
CO2	Carbon Dioxide
DC	Direct Current
EC	European Community
EEA	European Economic Area
EEZ	Exclusive Economic Zone
EIA	Environmental Impact Assessment
EA	Energy Authority
EMAS	Eco-Management and Audit Scheme
EPW	European Pressurized Water Reactor
ERU	Emission Reduction Unit
ETSO	European Network of Transmission System Operators
EU	European Union
FCCA	Finnish Competition and Consumer Authority
GW	Gigawatt
HVDC	High-Voltage Direct Current
IEA	International Energy Agency
IPPC	Integrated Pollution Prevention and Control
kV	Kilovolt
LCP	Large Combustion Plant
LNG	Liquefied Natural Gas
LPG	Liquefied Petroleum Gas
MW	Megawatt

List of Abbreviations

PVO	Pohjolan Voima Oy
PWR	Pressurized Water Reactor
RID	Regulations Concerning the International Carriage of Dangerous Goods by Rail
TEN-E	Trans-European Network for Energy
TSO	Transmission System Operator
TVO	Teollisuuden Voima Oyj
TWh	Terawatt-Hour
VAT	Value Added Tax

General Introduction

1. The aim of this introductory chapter is to give an overview of the Finnish legal system, its latest developments and of energy law as a part of it. Given this purpose, it will not go in depth into any of the areas covered but instead will explain the context of the subsequent substantive chapters contained in the book. The introduction will start with a short overview of the general constitutional structure of Finland and move then to other issues such as the principles and development of the Finnish energy law. This country review will also introduce various governmental or public actors in the energy field, and the chapter will end with a brief discussion of the sources of Finnish energy law.

§1. General Background

2. Under the Constitution of Finland (731/1999, as amended), Finland is a sovereign republic. It has a statutory legal system, but with the notable difference that it has not been codified in the same way as the legal systems of Germany, France and many other continental European countries. The Finnish constitutional system is, as in most European countries, a tripartite system: The legislative powers are exercised by the Parliament (*Eduskunta*). The government submits government bills[1] to the Parliament for approval, and, when adopted, they become 'Acts of Parliament'. The executive powers are exercised by the President of the Republic and the government, and the judicial powers are exercised by independent courts of law, with the Supreme Court and the Supreme Administrative Court as the highest instances.[2] The role of the government has grown in substance vis-à-vis the role of the President of the Republic due to the provisions of the Finnish Constitution (section 93) allocating the executive functions relating to European Union (EU) affairs to the government. Since the Lisbon Treaty has modified the status of the European Council, transforming it from a non-decisive high-level colloquium to one of the most powerful EU institutions, and has decreased the number of ministers allowed to participate in its meetings, the relative importance of the Prime Minister has increased.

3. The Finnish judiciary system is divided into two lines: the general courts and the administrative courts. The general courts have jurisdiction in civil, commercial

1. The Parliament can also act on its own motion. Section 39 of the Constitution.
2. Section 3 of the Constitution.

and criminal law cases. The general court system is composed of twenty-seven District Courts, five Courts of Appeal and the Supreme Court as the final instance. The Supreme Court establishes judicial precedents in leading cases and it thus ensures uniformity in the administration of justice by the lower general courts. The Supreme Court gives some 100 precedents annually. The administrative courts have general jurisdiction in administrative law cases. The system is composed of six regional administrative courts and the administrative court of the Aland Island. The Supreme Administrative Court is the Court of last resort in administrative law cases. It decides normally some 4,000–5,000 cases per year. Some 200 of these are published as yearbook decisions. Both the Supreme Court and the Supreme Administrative Court were established in 1918, soon after Finland gained its independence from the Russian Empire. The court lines are independent of one another. The general courts apply in their proceedings Code of Judicial Procedure that although being amended on several occasions dates back to 1734 along with the special procedural rules applicable to criminal proceedings whereas the administrative courts apply in their proceedings mainly Administrative Judicial Procedure Act that was enacted in 1996.

4. Appeal to the Supreme Court is limited to certain specific grounds (significance of a judgment on the issue, errors in handling the case and other significant grounds for granting an appeal). Leave to appeal is currently required in more than half of the cases handled by the Supreme Administrative Court. Since the Constitutional Committee of the Parliament was revised in 2012, its earlier reserved position towards introducing a more substantial general leave to appeal system to the Supreme Administrative Court and direct appeals to the Supreme Administrative Court are becoming ever more exceptional in the future. Since administrative decisions may be appealed against by a direct appeal to the regional administrative court, the requirement of the European Human Rights Convention, of which Finland has been a member since the 1990s, to provide at least one opportunity to appeal a case, is fulfilled.

5. There are also certain special administrative courts, the Market Court being the most pertinent in the energy law context. The Market Court has a dual role: First, in competition matters, for example, the Market Court issues decisions prohibiting competition restrictions, mergers and acquisitions and imposing fines. The Market Court is also competent to handle cases on public procurement. The above decisions are based on proposals made by the Finnish Competition and Consumers Authority (FCCA). Second, the Market Court is the first level of appeal for decisions made by the FCCA or the Energy Authority (EA). The decisions of the Market Court may, with certain limitations, be appealed to the Supreme Administrative Court. With the exception of certain competition and public procurement cases where sanctions are at stake, as a rule, the case may be appealed against provided that the Supreme Administrative Court grants a leave to appeal.[3]

3. For a more detailed overview of the institutional framework for competition issues, *see* Kim Talus, 'Competition Law Country Report' (Finland) at www.concurrences.com.

§2. Basic Principles of Energy Law

6. Much like in most EU Member States, energy law as a separate legal discipline is a very recent phenomenon. However, the regulation of energy markets is not in itself a recent innovation, and the energy law that is now considered a separate discipline or area of law is a product of the two last centuries. As such, it is still possible to pose the question whether energy law should be understood as a separate area of law or just an application of general competition law and environmental law – both of which are themselves rather new sectors of law – in combination with a specific regulatory framework intended to address certain particularities of that sector of the economy. Without taking a definite stand on this question, the interdisciplinary character of energy law can hardly be questioned. First, much like environmental law, it contains elements from various legal disciplines.[4] Second, it is very much interlinked with energy economics and, in parts, (geo)politics.

7. Energy law has only started to emerge as a university discipline in Finland. The first lecture series dedicated to this topic was introduced in 2008–2009, and a chair of energy and environmental law was created at the University of Helsinki in 2009. Mirroring this trend, the first PhD studies focusing or touching on this area were completed in 2008–2009.[5] Instead, much like environmental law, energy law should primarily be placed in the field of administrative law.[6]

8. If energy law is approached as a part of general administrative law, then the emphasis is placed on regulation of markets, including new generation capacity, energy networks and climate change-related issues. With this kind of approach, less emphasis is put on the private law aspects of energy, which would include compensation for nuisance, disturbance and contractual questions. However, even in these areas, the administrative law affects the private law sphere. Issues relating to expropriation and end-customer contracts are also affected by acts that would fall within the sphere of administrative law. Given the administrative law character of energy law in Finland, many administrative law principles are applicable to this field of law.[7]

---

4. Anne Kumpula, 'Environmental Law', in *An Introduction to Finnish Law*, ed. Juha Pöyhönen (Helsinki: Kauppakaari, 2002), 503.
5. The first study touching this topic was Jurgen Poesche, *Ökologisches Energierecht in der Europaischen Union* (Helsinki: Helsinki University Press, 2008). However, this study is a collection of articles and relates largely to environmental law. It was also defended as an environmental PhD The second book to appear was Alice Guimaraes-Purokoski, *Vertikaalinen toimivallanjako EU-oikeudessa – Tutkimus yhteisön toimivallan kehittymisestä energia-alalla sekä julkisen palvelun velvoitteiden ja yleispalvelun sääntelystä sähkön sisämarkkinoilla* (Helsinki: Suomalainen Lakimiesyhdistys, 2009). This study focuses on the vertical division of competences within the EU and uses the energy policy as the example and application of the general framework. This PhD was defended under the EU law discipline.
6. The precise placement of energy law in the private or public law depends on the definition of 'energy law'.
7. For these principles, *see* Juha Pöyhönen (ed.), *An Introduction to Finnish Law* (Helsinki: Kauppakaari 2002).

9. In addition to this administrative law character, Finnish energy law is closely linked to EU energy law. Because of this, in addition to the EU energy law acquis, the general EU law affects the interpretation and application of energy laws in Finland. This is also apparent from the substantive sections of this study. The discussion regarding electricity and natural gas market regulation makes frequent references to the EU energy laws. Finally, many elements of the wider energy regulation, including regulation of nuclear power and climate change regulation, are connected with the international treaty arrangements in these areas.

§3. Historical Background

10. While the regulation of water resources and the use of land, although lacking energy policy, specific grounds, can arguably be seen as directing the way energy markets are regulated in a wider sense and while this type of regulation predates the modern energy market regulation in Finland, this short introduction will focus on the historical developments in the energy market regulation during the period starting with the 1928 Act on Power Plants (Laki sähkölaitoksista; 167/1928). The intention here is not to engage in a detailed overview of the progress in the energy markets and their regulation. Instead, this section will cover only the most basic changes in order to give the reader an overview on how the regulation has changed. The changes that can be detected are, among others, a movement from a state-centred system towards a market-based system and a change of scope from regulation of certain narrowly defined issues – safety, in particular – to regulation of markets more generally.

I. Electricity Market Regulation

11. The above-mentioned Act on Power Plants (167/1928) was not concerned with larger energy market questions but was primarily geared towards the safety aspects of electricity generation. However, with the rapid development of the economy and industrialization,[8] a need to coordinate both power generation and distribution emerged. This was carried out through the Electricity Act of 1979 (Sähkölaki; 319/1979), which replaced and repealed the 1928 regime. The 1979 Act regulated electricity markets much more widely and covered issues such as construction of additional generation capacity, supply obligations and distribution areas. The intention of the new Act was to further develop the electricity markets in Finland through increased planning and efficiency. It made both the generation and the transmission activities subject to a licence.

12. The system created, based on public planning and licensing, was quickly perceived as too heavy and cumbersome. As such, the Act was modified to simplify

---

8. Like in neighbouring Sweden, the industrialization process was supported by the existence of hydropower. *See* Tore Wiwen-Nilsson, Malin Håkansson & Mikael Wärnsby, *Sweden – Energy Law* (The Hague: Kluwer, 2005).

the planning schemes. In a similar fashion, the licences to construct generation capacity and transmission lines were abolished save for some larger units. These changes came into force in 1989.

13. By 1992, changes in the energy markets had again created a need to adapt and modernize electricity regulation. A committee that was set up to examine the situation and to propose necessary changes submitted its report in the spring of 1992.[9] Based on this report, the government set a goal to adopt a new Electricity Market Act by 1995.

14. Like the 1979 Electricity Market Act, a 1957 act that regulated cross-border transmission of electricity (Laki sähköenergian siirtämisestä yli maan rajojen; 410/1957) was abolished by the 1995 Electricity Market Act.[10] According to the 1957 act, transmission of electricity across the borders was subject to permission from the Council of State. The permission was subject to public interest, and the transmission could not harm the national balance or the development of the power sector. In practice, all the applicants had received permission for transmission, and the significance of the system was negligible. As such, it was only natural that the law was abolished. Another factor was, of course, that EU membership came to require this for intra-EU situations.[11]

15. As can easily be detected from the above, the legal framework for the Finnish electricity markets prior to the 1995 Electricity Market Act was not geared towards allowing free and efficient competition. As such, the markets before 1995 were marked by limited competition in the wholesale and generation markets and no competition in the retail markets. As the producers and the generators had the control of the networks, they could effectively block competition. The producer could pass on the risks involved in power generation to the purchaser and could apply differentiated tariffs. With the change in the underlying paradigm – from state to market – and a strong belief that markets could deliver more efficient outcomes, the 1995 Act aimed at providing non-discriminatory access to all parties. This, in turn, would foster competition and provide freedom of choice for the customer.[12] In addition to this, the main change brought by the 1995 Act was the abolishment of a centralized scheme to license generation capacity. While a licence would still be required for transmission and distribution of electricity, generation or supply would no longer be subject to permission from the State, save for certain types of generation. Similarly, the abolishment of central planning and all unnecessary obstacles to free trade for competitive segments of the electricity markets brought significant changes in the regulation. The third energy package has brought great benefits to

9. *See* Sähkölaitostoimikunnan mietintö; KTM 15/1992.
10. Article 56 of the 1995 Electricity Market Act.
11. Finland joined the EU in 1995, and this was one of the factors considered when the new legislation was drafted.
12. Seppo Kärkkäinen & Arto Rajala, *Pitkien tukkusähkösopimusten vaikutukset sähkön vähittäismyynnin kilpailutilanteeseen* (Helsinki: Edita, 1999), 14.

the consumers. It has increased the liquidity of the electricity markets and cross-border trade. Consumers have more choice. This has also assisted in maintaining the level of wholesale prices.

II. Natural Gas Market Regulation

16. In the natural gas markets, the progress, though very different in many details, was similar to that of electricity: from regulation of safety aspects to regulation of a 'market'.[13] Here, the initial act, the Act on Explosive Substances (Räjähdysvaarallisista aineista annettu laki; 263/1953) was not intended to regulate a market in natural gas. Instead, it was a general act that encompassed, among many other things, natural gas as an explosive substance. It made the importation, possession, use, sales, and transportation of natural gas subject to a licence scheme. The Act also created a government authority to oversee the licencees' activities. The supervisory authority had the right to obtain information on all aspects of the licensed business, including samples of the substance itself.[14]

17. The first attempt to regulate the natural gas market structure was made in 1993. Using the Act on Explosive Substances as the legal base, a Decree on Natural Gas (Maakaasuasetus; 1058/1993) was adopted. According to this Decree, natural gas pipelines could be constructed only with a specific construction licence.[15] The Decree also contained detailed provisions on inspections, safety aspects and various prohibitions. The 1990s also saw the enactment of other decisions and decrees covering various aspects of the natural gas business.[16] The first natural gas market act was adopted on 31 May 2000 (Maakaasumarkkinalaki; 508/2000).

18. A new Natural Gas Markets act (Maakaasumarkkinalaki; 587/2017) has entered into force on 1 January 2018. The Act includes clauses which will enter into force on 1 January 2020 when the construction of the Balticconnector–pipeline will be completed.

19. Subsequent changes in natural gas market regulation in Finland have been largely brought about by the progress in EU energy law acquis and will be examined in more detail in the chapter on natural gas market regulation.

20. The third energy package has brought great changes to the consumers in the natural gas markets of the EU. Once the third energy package will be completely implemented in the Finnish legislation on 1 January 2020, these benefits will

---

13. As will be seen in the chapter on natural gas regulation, the Finnish gas markets are still dominated by a single monopolistic company. As such, it is questionable whether we can talk about a 'market' in the sense used in modern energy law.
14. Government Bill for the Natural Gas Market Act (HE 134/1999).
15. Sections 2 and 7 of the Decree on Natural Gas.
16. Such as the Decision on the Application of the Natural Gas (1059/1993), the Decree on Construction and Usage of Natural Gas Pipelines (among many other things) and the Decree on Natural Gas Equipment (1434/1993), covering CE-labelling of natural gas equipment.

become available also to the Finnish natural gas users and foreign and domestic competition can enter the newly opened markets.

§4. Role of Government Institutions in the Shaping and Administration of Energy Law and Policy

21. This section will present the main public actors that are active in some aspects of the energy markets. In addition to the most obvious government authorities such as the EA, the Finnish Competition Authority (FCA) and the relevant courts and ministries responsible for energy issues, the less obvious institutions, active in areas such as innovation or energy auditing, will be examined.

22. Ministry of Economic Affairs and Employment: The main government body responsible for the Finnish energy markets is the Ministry of Economic Affairs and Employment. It has the leading role in terms of planning future energy and climate change policy. Responsibility regarding the latter is shared with the Ministry of the Environment. While international cooperation is within the responsibility of the Ministry of the Environment, the Energy Department of the Ministry of the Economic Affairs and Employment is responsible for coordinating and leading the implementation of national climate policy in the government, together with the other ministries involved in the energy sector. These include the Ministries for Taxation, Transport and Communications, Agriculture and Forestry and Foreign Affairs. In addition to steering and planning the energy policies, the Ministry of Employment and the Economy prepares government bills that reflect the policy choices and submits them to the Parliament for approval. Within the Ministry, the Energy Department is divided into four subdivisions with different responsibilities: energy markets, energy efficiency and technology, renewable energy and base production of energy.

23. Unlike in many other countries, there is no government agency that has centralized responsibility for implementing the energy policy tasks set by the government. Instead, there are several government agencies that play different roles in the energy sector. These include the agencies described below.

24. EA: The EA is the national regulatory authority for electricity and natural gas markets. It began operation as the Electricity Market Authority on 1 June 1995, with the entering into force of the Electricity Market Act. Its name was changed to the EMA on 1 August 2000, at the time when the Natural Gas Market Act entered into force and further to EA on 1 January 2014 when the Ministry of Economic Affairs and Employment gave EA certain tasks related to the advancement of renewable energy and energy efficiency.

25. The principal task of the EA is to regulate the pricing and the terms of transmission, distribution and other network services in both the electricity and the natural gas markets. The actions to regulate transmission and distribution system operators take place mainly on *ex ante* basis. In addition to this, the EA supervises the generation and supply sectors. This supervision of markets, including supply prices, takes place mainly *ex post*. Where necessary, cases of possible non-compliance are brought up either through complaints or on the initiative of the EA itself. The EA also promotes efficient competition in both the electricity and the natural gas trade – for example, by intervening with respect to terms and prices of network services that are considered to restrict competition. To enhance the transparency and availability of information, prerequisites for competition, the EA also produces and publishes real-time information on the pricing of both electricity and its distribution.

26. As will be seen in more detail in the subsequent chapters, electricity and natural gas network operations are subject to licence. The EA grants network licences to organizations and utilities engaged in network operation and building permits to companies constructing power lines carrying voltages of 110 kilovolts (kV) or more.

27. Finally, since August 2004, the EA has been the National Emissions Trading Authority in Finland. The EA grants the emissions permits that give installations the right to emit carbon dioxide (CO_2) into atmosphere, supervises the monitoring and reporting of emissions data and maintains the Emissions Trading Registry of Finland.[17]

28. Tekes – Finnish Funding Agency for Technology and Innovation: This agency, among many other things, finances research and development and innovation projects by universities and private companies. These include projects relating to clean energy such as renewables and biofuels and to energy savings.[18]

29. VTT: Much like Tekes, VTT is a part of the Finnish innovation system under the domain of the Ministry of Employment and the Economy. It conducts research in all areas of energy including developing sustainable, safe and efficient energy, process and plant technologies. It also focuses on areas such as energy economy, transmission and storage as well as the efficient use of energy and the management of emissions.[19]

30. Motiva Oy: This government agency is active in promoting the efficient and sustainable use of energy and materials. Its main areas of operation include energy efficiency agreements (relating to Directive 2006/32/EC on the promotion of end-use efficiency and energy services), energy auditing, material efficiency and renewable energy.[20]

31. STUK – Radiation and Nuclear Safety Authority: Unlike the above-mentioned agencies operating under the Ministry of Employment and the Economy,

17. www.energiamarkkinavirasto.fi.
18. For more detailed information, *see* www.tekes.fi.
19. For more detailed information, *see* www.vtt.fi.
20. For more detailed information, *see* www.motiva.fi.

STUK operates under the Ministry of Social Affairs and Health. It has various tasks under both the Nuclear Energy Act (Ydinenergialaki; 990/1987) and the Radiation Act (Säteilylaki; 592/1991). For example, according to section 6 of the Radiation Act (592/1991), STUK is in charge of ensuring 'Compliance with this Act and with the provisions and regulations issued pursuant thereto.' STUK formulates detailed safety requirements concerning the use of nuclear energy. As an independent regulator, it also ascertains that the nuclear power plants produce energy according to these requirements. Its role has been particularly visible in the construction process for Finland's new nuclear power plant, Olkiluoto 3.

32. In addition to these regulatory functions, STUK is active in research in related areas, including the biological effects of radiation, levels and prevention of natural radiation, radiation hygiene, radioactive substances in the environment and food, medical doses, methods of measuring radiation and non-ionizing radiation (radar, lasers, ultraviolet radiation, mobile telephones, etc.).[21]

33. FCA: The functions and jurisdiction of the FCA will be examined in more detail in Part VI: Interaction between Energy Law and Competition Law. In general terms, its objectives are to promote and protect sound and effective economic competition and to increase economic efficiency in both private- and public-sector activities. In the energy markets more specifically, the objective of the FCA is to ensure fair and equal entry conditions for both domestic and foreign undertakings. The tools used include intervention when competition restraints are detected and actions to influence the development of legislation and regulation. In competition control, for example, the FCA reviews the national grid tariffs for electricity to ensure that there are no elements of foreclosure or discrimination in the pricing of the national grid.[22]

34. On 29 January 2009, a working group under the auspices of the Ministry of Employment and the Economy proposed several significant modifications to the current Act on Competition Restrictions. That proposal included no major institutional changes, but the responsibilities of the FCA would be enlarged. Under the new law, the FCA would, for example, have the right to carry out inspections in certain private homes.

35. Market Court: As mentioned above, the Market Court is one of the specialist courts in Finland. It began operation only in 2002 and can hear cases that come under its jurisdiction as set out in: (1) the Competition Act (kilpailulaki; 948/2011), (2) the Public Procurement and Commissions Act (Laki julkisista hankinnoista ja käyttöoikeussopimuksista; 1397/2016), (3) the Act on Proceedings before the Market Court (Laki oikeudenkäynnistä markkinaoikeudessa); 100/2013) and (4) certain other legislation, including the Electricity and Gas Market Acts, Act on the Supervision of Electricity and Gas Markets (590/2013) as well as Trademark and Patent

21. For more detailed information, *see* www.stuk.fi.
22. *FCA's Yearbook 2009*, 26.

Act. The Market Court has handed down numerous decisions in cases relating to regulatory pricing in electricity transmission and distribution.

36. The Supreme Administrative Court: As noted above, the Supreme Administrative Court is the court of last resort in administrative cases. Its jurisdiction is relates to questions of law and fact arising in administrative decisions, such as those issued by the EA and FCCA. An example of a high-profile case decided by the Supreme Administrative Court is the United Power case.[23] Here, the Court rejected the company's appeal, which asked the Court to overturn the decision by the Ministry of Trade and Industry (today, the Ministry of Employment and the Economy) not to allow the construction of a 1,000 megawatt (MW) undersea cable between Russia and Finland.[24]

§5. Sources of Energy Law

I. Legislation

37. Much like in the other Nordic states, the Finnish doctrine on sources of law emphasizes the significance of the written law and the *travaux préparatoires*, the government bills. In addition, the decisions of the Supreme Court and the Supreme Administrative Court have a strong persuasive force, but are not binding precedents analogous to common law.

38. Within the written law, the general hierarchy among the various national statutes is: (1) the Constitution, (2) ordinary laws, (3) decrees, (4) regulations of the Council of State, (5) regulations of a ministry and (6) other authoritative instructions.[25] According to the Constitution, if, in a matter being tried by a court of law, the application of an act would be in evident conflict with the Constitution, the court must give primacy to the provision in the Constitution.[26] If a provision in a decree or another statute of a lower level than an act is in conflict with the Constitution or another act, it cannot be applied by a court of law or by any other public authority.[27]

39. The *travaux préparatoires* or government bills are a central source of law in Finland. A government bill explains the grounds for the proposed new law. It describes the goals and the purpose of the legislation as well as the relationship between the new legislative act and the pre-existing law. The underlying idea is that the government bill, with possible discussions during the Parliamentary proceedings, will indicate the intention of the legislature.[28]

---

23. Judgment of the Supreme Administrative Court of 20 Nov. 2007 (D No. 315/2/2007).
24. *See also* Vesa Lappalainen, 'Proposed Finland-Russia Interconnector Rejected', *OGEL* 1 (2007), www.ogel.org.
25. *See* Juha Pöyhönen (ed.), *An Introduction to Finnish Law* (Helsinki: Kauppakaari 2002), 26.
26. Section 106 of the Constitution.
27. Section 107 of the Constitution.
28. *See* Juha Pöyhönen (ed.), *An Introduction to Finnish Law* (Helsinki: Kauppakaari 2002), 26.

40. The general EU law is an increasingly significant source of law in Finland. This is the situation not only where the national law is based on a directive, but also where the act is of national origin. In the first option mentioned, a directive having been implemented in the national law, the interpretative effect of the directive is of paramount significance. In addition to this scenario, there are numerous instances where, for example, the general principles or the case law of the European Court of Justice affects the interpretation of national laws.

41. The sources of energy law in Finland follow the general scheme outlined above. Most national energy law is currently based on EU law, and, as such, EU law affects its interpretation. This is very much evident in the substantive chapters of this book.

II. Case Law

General

42. In the Finnish judicial system, regulatory decisions of the national regulatory authority, the EA, may be appealed against by transmission or distribution system operator to the Market Court. Market Court functions as a special court of first degree in energy regulatory, competition and public procurement cases. Regulatory decisions that may be appealed against contain decisions of the EA approving *ex ante* methodologies for defining reasonable profit and charges for transmission or distribution system operation (*confirmatory decision*) during a monitoring period of two consecutive four years. Transmission or distribution system operator may also bring an action against a decision of the EA issued after the expiry of the monitoring period (*monitoring decision*) by which the Authority defines whether the profit gained by the transmission or distribution system operator has exceeded or went below reasonable profit level and whether the transmission or distribution operator thus has the right to either reduce or increase the level of its transmission or distribution charges during the following monitoring period.

43. Also, decisions of the EA addressed to transmission or distribution system operator on compensation to be paid by these to the final customers due to considerable power cuts where there is a causal link between the fault of the network operator and the power cut may be appealed against to the Market Court.

44. The Market Court has the competence to handle the facts and merits of cases brought before it. The Market Court is composed of both professional judges and an expert member. In general, administrative court procedure is written but the Market Court may organize an oral hearing upon request of the parties or on its own motion.

45. Both the transmission or distribution system operator party to the case and the EA may make an appeal against the decision of the Market Court directly to the Supreme Administrative Court. Leave to appeal is thus not required.

46. In the following, a succinct review is made of the recent case law of the Supreme Administrative Court. Cases dealt with are mainly published i.e., yearbook decisions.

Rental Arrangements

47. There have been several cases before the Supreme Administrative Court where the margin of manoeuvre of the national regulatory authority has been at stake.

48. In its yearbook decision (KHO 2017:124), the Supreme Administrative Court examined a case where the distribution system operator had rented the distribution network it operated from its parent company. The distribution system operator claimed that it had the right to subtract from its profit and loss account the investment costs it had allocated to the distribution network although these costs had been taken into consideration in the network rent it paid to its parent company.

49. The EA considered in its monitoring decision made after the expiry of the second monitoring period (2008–2011) that subtraction of the investment cost from the profit and loss account of the operator was inconsistent with network rent arrangements confirmed by the EA.

50. The Market Court quashed the decision of the EA and decided the case in accordance with the argumentation of the distribution system operator. The Market Court grounded its decision to the predictability of the regulatory system and pointed out three separate reasons for this. First, the Market Court deduced from CJEU's judgment in case C-274/08 *Commission v. Sweden* that according to EU law the national regulatory authorities were under the obligation to follow similar regulatory methodologies from one regulatory period to another. Second, the Market Court found that in its earlier, final judgment it had already made similar interpretation regarding subtraction of investment costs of a distribution system operator operating in a rented distribution network. Third, the Market Court gave importance to the fact that the EA had accepted during the first year of the same monitoring period, 2008, the methodology of handling the investment costs to network proposed by the distribution system operator that had rented the network from its parent company.

51. The Supreme Administrative Court quashed the decision of the Market Court and validated the disputed monitoring decision of the EA. The Supreme Administrative Court noted that case C-274/08 concerned an infringement action of the European Commission against Sweden on the transposition of the *ex ante* regulatory provisions (Article 23.2.a) of the electricity market directive 2003/54/EC into Swedish national legislation. The CJEU found that Sweden had not properly implemented the *ex ante* regulatory provisions of the Directive 2003/54/EC into its national legislation since there were no specific provisions corresponding to the provisions of the directive in Swedish national law and since the national praxis Sweden claimed to be in accordance with the requirements of the directive was not such.

Therefore, the Swedish regulatory system was not predictable as required by the Directive 2003/54/EC. The Supreme Administrative Court deduced that case C-274/08 *Commission v. Sweden* concerned a situation different from the one at hand. The Supreme Administrative Court also found that the Market Court had not, in its earlier final decision, taken a stance on specifically similar situation that was at stake in the case before the Supreme Administrative Court. The Supreme Administrative Court also found that notwithstanding the fact that the EA had accepted certain trances of network investment costs in the distribution system operator's profit and loss account during the first year of the monitoring period, this did not prejudice how the EA should manage these trances during the rest of the monitoring period. The Supreme Administrative Court considered, contrary to the Market Court that the decision of the EA was not to be quashed as being against the principle of predictability. The EA had not exceeded its discretionary powers whilst confirming the monitoring decision.

Standard Compensation for the End User

52. The Electricity Market Act contains provisions concerning standard compensations to be paid by a distribution system operator for an end user whose electricity supply is interrupted where the interruption is caused by the distribution system operator. The distribution system operator may be released from the obligation to pay compensation if it proves that the interruption is caused by an obstacle that is beyond the sphere of its influence that it cannot reasonably be required to take into consideration in its operation and the consequences it could not have avoided or overcome when acting with due diligence. The level of standard compensation is schematically linked with the length of interruption. The threshold for compensation is an interruption of twelve hours in which case the end user is entitled to a standard compensation equal to 10% of the end user's annual electricity distribution tariff. Where the interruption time exceeds 288 hours, the end user is entitled to a standard compensation equal to 200% of its annual electricity distribution tariff.

53. Yearbook decision of the Supreme Administrative Court (KHO 2016:2) concerned the calculation of the length of electricity supply interruption and thus the level of standard compensation in a situation where the distribution system operator claimed that the total time of electricity distribution interruption suffered by the end user was not caused by an event that was within the sphere of its influence. The distribution system operator claimed that the interruption in electricity supply was partly caused by an interruption in the regional network and was thus beyond the sphere of its influence. In the case at hand, the interruption of electricity supply commenced in the distribution system operator's distribution network some forty minutes before an interruption occurred in the network of the regional distribution network. The regional distribution network did not operate for some seven hours whereas the total length of the interruption in the distribution network lasted for almost seventy-seven hours.

54. The Supreme Administrative Court noted at the outset that the EA did not have a large margin of discretion regarding the calculation of the length of the electricity supply interruption.

55. The Supreme Administrative Court then stated that the distribution system operator is relieved to pay standard compensation for the end user once the interruption in electricity supply is caused solely by an interruption in operation of the transmission or regional network. Such an interruption may be regarded as having been caused by an obstacle that is beyond the sphere of distribution system operator´s influence.

56. The Supreme Administrative Court found that this was not the case in the preceding case. In this case, the interruption in the electricity supply commenced first in the distribution system operator's network. The interruption of electricity supply occurred during a heavy storm and it was caused by trees that fell in the distribution network thus crushing several points in the network. The distribution system operator was immediately informed of the interruption of electricity supply in its network. Interruption in the regional network occurred some forty minutes after the interruption in the distribution network commenced and it was repaired some seven hours after the occurrence of the interruption. The Supreme Administrative Court stated that the interruption in the distribution network was caused by the distribution system operator. The distribution system operator could have started immediately after having been informed of the interruption in its network measures to localize the crushed points in the network. The distribution network operator neither did give any evidence of such measures nor did it give evidence on attempts to repair the network during the interruption in the regional network. The Supreme Administrative Court further found that storms cannot be considered to be exceptional circumstances that the distribution system operator cannot reasonably be required to take into consideration in its operation and the consequences were not such that it could not have avoided or overcome when acting with due diligence. On the contrary, it was noted to be rather typical that the network needs to be repaired in circumstances where the supply of electricity is interrupted.

57. The Supreme Administrative Court concluded that there were no grounds for limiting the amount of standard compensation the distribution system operator was due to pay to the end user.

58. In yearbook decision KHO 2015:105, the transmission system operator (TSO) (appellant) claimed that the methodologies confirmed by the EA were not predictable and lacked reasoning as regards the way the inflation rate was to be taken into consideration whilst defining reasonable rate of return to the network investment. The appellant considered that this caused unpredictability and thus a regulatory risk.

Reasonable Rate of Return

59. The Supreme Administrative Court stated that the EA had the right to take into consideration when drafting *ex ante* methodologies, the experience it had gained from earlier monitoring periods as well as errors and malfunctions perceived in these methodologies. This may lead to the need to amend and modify methodologies applied earlier. It is characteristic of *ex ante* regulation that the methodologies may be amended from one monitoring period to the other. The Supreme Administrative Court noted that the TSO had the right to be heard of the new methodologies prior to them being confirmed. Methodologies shall also need to be duly reasoned.

60. The appellant also claimed that when approving the methodologies, the EA had not duly incorporated in these the obligation to grant appropriate incentive to the TSO over both short and long term, to foster market integration deriving from Article 37 paragraph 8 of the Directive 2009/72/EC concerning common rules for the internal market in electricity. The Supreme Administrative Court stated that although the methodologies contained incentive to develop the network, to improve the quality of electricity transmission and distribution and the efficiency of the network, they did not contain any specific incentive to improve the integration of the market. Notwithstanding this, other incentives of the methodologies contained elements that stimulated investment which consequently enhanced integration of the market.

Amending Confirmatory Decision of the EA

61. The decision of the EA confirming the methodologies for the monitoring period of four years may be amended by request of the transmission or distribution system operator concerned or by the initiative of the EA. It is provided in the Electricity Market Act that the EA may amend the decision, e.g., if the network operator has given erroneous or incomplete information that has influenced the contents of the decision; if this is deemed necessary due to a pertinent reason that has occurred after the decision was approved or if there are other weighty reasons to modify the decision.

62. Yearbook decision KHO 2014:81 concerned a case where the TSO had made a request to the EA to amend the monitoring decision due to heavy storms that had caused extraordinary repair costs to the operator as well as compensation claims from end users. The EA had declined to amend the decision since the monitoring period the decision covered had already expired as the request was made.

63. The Market Court considered that the decision of the EA could be amended notwithstanding the expiry of the monitoring period. It quashed the decision of the EA but did not return the case for the scrutiny of the Authority and instead scrutinized the case materially on its own motion without giving the parties the right to be heard of the merits.

64. The TSO appealed against the decision of the Market Court to the Supreme Administrative Court. The Supreme Administrative Court found that the TSO was entitled to make an application to the EA after the expiry of the monitoring period. Although this was not specifically stipulated in the Electricity Market Act, the interpretation was coherent with the national regulatory system. Notwithstanding the fact that the monitoring period covered by the decision had expired, the decision at stake was found to bind the EA once it makes its surveillance decision defining the net profit or loss of the network operator during the monitoring period that had expired. The EA should thus have scrutinized the request to amend the confirmatory decision.

Ex ante Regulation of Security-of-Supply Natural Gas Products

65. The Supreme Administrative Court considered in its yearbook decision KHO 2011:109 the competence of the EA to *ex ante* regulate the pricing of natural gas market products transmitted, distributed and submitted by the sole importer and supplier. The EA had decided that the natural gas supplier needed to modify its pricing relating to security-of-supply obligations binding the supplier. The EA ordered that the supplier's net operating profit should not exceed 2.5% during the next monitoring period of three years.

66. The natural gas supplier claimed that in order to define whether the price of natural gas it supplied was reasonable, differentiation would need to be made between different gas products. The Supreme Administrative Court did not accept this argument and instead stated that obligation to supply is by its very nature general and not limited to certain method of supply or natural gas product or overall use of natural gas. The Supreme Administrative Court recognized that the EA had large discretionary powers to define as when the price of natural gas supply (security of supply) is reasonable.

Obligation of the Network Operator to Develop the Network

67. According to the Electricity Market Act, a transmission and distribution system operator is under an obligation to develop its network. The Supreme Administrative Court estimated whether this obligation was fulfilled in its decision of 14.1.2016 N:o 72. The case concerned the consequences of the same heavy storm to the regional network that caused electricity supply interruptions to the end clients of the distribution system operator in the case that was discussed earlier (KHO 2016:2). In this case, the pertinent question was whether the EA was entitled to order the regional network operator to rectify the error or wilfully neglect the cause of the network not being at a reliable level during the heavy storm.

68. The EA considered that the regional network operator was under the obligation to maintain the outskirts of the network tidy of trees in order that falling trees would not cause disruption to the operation of the network. The regional network operator was also liable to carry out regular field investigations. Since the regional network operator had not fulfilled these obligations, the EA considered that the disruption in electricity transmission resulted from an error or wilful neglect on the side of the regional network operator.

69. The Supreme Administrative Court found that although the obligation to keep the outskirts of the networks tidy of trees was not specifically stipulated in the Electricity Market Act, it was a prevailing practice among high-voltage network operators and should have been followed by the regional network operator as well. It also found that the regional network operator had not duly carried out regular field investigation or had not taken the necessary steps to rectify the defects it had found during such investigation.

Procedural Issues: Capability of Being Party

70. According to the Electricity Market Act, a project authorization of the EA is required for the construction of a new high-voltage (minimum 110 kV) transmission network. Should the network cross borders, the project authorization is granted by the Ministry of Labour and the Economy.

71. The Supreme Administrative Court confirmed in its decision 29.1.2016 N:o 231 the decision of the regional Administrative Court dismissing an appeal against such project authorization brought by a group of residents of a municipality where the transmission network was to be constructed. The decision to dismiss the action was based upon the fact that the route of the transmission against such project authorization network was not defined in the authorization nor was there need for a reservation of the area needed for the transmission network. Furthermore, the project authorization did not establish concession right, right of redemption or any other rights to utilize land owned by others. Hence, the court found that the project authorization did not constitute a decision directly affecting appellants' rights, obligations or interests in the sense of section 6(1) of the Administrative Procedure Act.

Oral Hearing

72. In yearbook decision KHO 2015:105, the Supreme Administrative estimated whether the right to fair trial required that an oral hearing should be organized at the Supreme Administrative Court although the Market Court had already held an oral hearing in the case. The appellant requested a new oral hearing to be organized since it considered that the Market Court had misinterpreted the opinions expressed by expert witnesses and furthermore it proposed a new expert to be heard as a witness in oral hearing.

73. The Supreme Administrative Court rejected the request for a new oral hearing. It reasoned its rejection by noting that the recordings, including transcriptions, of the Market Court's oral hearing were at its disposal and therefore there was no ambiguity of what the expert witnesses had stated at the Market Court. The appellant did not claim that it had not had the opportunity to put forward all the questions it deemed necessary already at the Market Court. The appellant could have nominated the expert witness it wished to be heard by the Supreme Administrative

Court already at the Market Court. Furthermore, the opinion of the new expert witness nominee had been submitted to the Supreme Administrative Court in writing. The Supreme Administrative Court concluded that the appellant's right to fair trial was not violated although the oral hearing was not organized at the Supreme Administrative Court.

Right to Be Heard

74. In the yearbook decision KHO 2014:81 (*see* above) the Supreme Administrative Court stated that the Market Court had acted against the rules of the general administrative procedural law system when it had scrutinized and decided the request of the TSO to amend the regulatory decision directly without respecting the TSO's right to be heard.

75. Furthermore, the Supreme Administrative Court found that deciding upon the request of the TSO addressed to the EA required that the EA utilizes its independent margin of manoeuvre as national regulatory authority. The Market Court did not have the competence to decide the request at a first degree without the EA first using its regulatory powers and deliberation.

76. The Supreme Administrative Court concluded that even if the Market Court had had the competence to decide the case at a first degree (*quad non*) the Market Court would have been under the duty to respect the procedural right to be heard of the parties. A pertinent fair trial rule had therefore been breached. The Supreme Administrative Court quashed the decision of the Market Court and returned the case to the EA for handling.

Part I. Electricity

Chapter 1. General Overview of the Legal Framework for the Electricity Sector

§1. Electricity Market Act

77. The Finnish electricity market legislation is based on Directive 2009/72/EC of the European Parliament and of the Council of 13 July 2009 concerning common rules for the internal market in electricity and repealing Directive 2003/54/EC.[29] The legislation aims at fully implementing the Directive in Finland.

78. The general provisions and the fundamentals of the Finnish electricity market legislation have been enacted in the Electricity Market Act of 2013 (Sähkömarkkinalaki; SäädK 588/2013), which entered into force on 1 September 2013. Since then, the Electricity Market Act has also been supplemented with some amendments.[30] The most important reforms among these amendments have been the provisions for consideration of energy efficiency, demand response and demand side management in system operation pricing (SäädK 1430/2014) and additional provision which sets a ceiling on transmission and distribution tariff increases (SäädK 590/2017).

79. The national electricity market legislation is not applicable in the autonomous area of Åland Islands, which has adopted its own legislation for electricity market.

80. The Electricity Market Act of 2013 replaced the first Electricity Market Act of 1995 (Sähkömarkkinalaki; SäädK 386/1995), which reformed Finland's electricity market in 1995. The electricity market liberalization was among the first countries in the world during 1995–1999 in a stepwise process which set all the connected customers eligible.

81. The objective of the Electricity Market Act of 2013 is to ensure that preconditions exist for an efficient, reliable and environmentally sustainable functioning national and regional electricity market as well as an internal electricity market for the EU so as to secure a sufficient supply of high-standard electricity at competitive

29. Official Journal L 211, 14.8.2009, 55–93.
30. *See* SäädK 1212/2013, 685/2014, 1430/2014, 266/2017 and 590/2017.

prices and reasonable service standards for end users. The primary means to do this is to secure sound and well-functioning economic competition in electricity generation and supply as well as reasonable and equitable service standards in the operation of electricity networks. The Electricity Market Act of 2013 is based on the principle of free competition in generation and supply activities. There is no price regulation for these activities. However, mechanisms for consumer protection and for systems responsibilities have been established. On the other hand, transmission and distribution activities have remained regulated national and regional monopolies, supervised by the Finnish energy regulator, the EA.

82. The Electricity Market Act of 2013 includes provisions covering following subjects:

- network concessions for the operation of transmission and distribution systems and for the construction of new power lines;
- general obligations and pricing principles for system operation – that is, provisions for third-party access, including connections and principles for tariffs for transmission, distribution and connections;
- provisions for transmission systems and TSOs including effective unbundling;
- provisions for distribution systems and distribution system operators;
- systems obligations for the transmission and distribution operators and other parties – that is, balancing the electricity systems and balance settlement;
- unbundling of operations;
- consumer protection in electricity supply and in distribution system operation including the obligation to supply and provisions for electricity contracts;
- supplementary provisions with regard to generation;
- supplementary provisions for the Law on Supervision of Electricity and Natural Gas Markets (Laki sähkö- ja maakaasumarkkinoiden valvonnasta; SäädK 590/2013) with regard to supervision, penal provisions and appeals; and
- transitional provisions.

83. The Electricity Market Act does not contain any provisions on the technical safety of electrical installations. This subject is regulated by the Electrical Safety Act of 2016 (Sähköturvallisuuslaki; SäädK 1135/2016).

84. The Electricity Market Act of 2013 is supplemented by a secondary legislation, which is composed of numerous decrees issued by the government or the ministry and by a number of regulations[31] issued by the EA. The secondary legislation contains detailed provisions on various themes that have to be regulated in an exact manner. The most important decrees and regulations issued by virtue of the Electricity Market Act are:

31. *See* www.finlex.fi/fi/viranomaiset/normi/500013/.

- the Government Decree on the Electricity Market (Valtioneuvoston asetus sähkömarkkinoista; SäädK 65/2009), which includes detailed provisions regarding network concessions and provisions on distribution tariffs for small-scale generation;
- the Government Decree on Measuring and Settlement of Electricity Deliveries (Valtioneuvoston asetus sähköntoimitusten mittauksesta ja selvityksestä; SäädK 66/2009), which sets detailed rules for measuring and settlement of electricity deliveries;
- the Decree of the Ministry of Economic Affairs and Employment on Communication for Trade in Electricity and Settlement of Electricity Deliveries (Työ-ja elinkeinoministeriön asetus sähkökaupassa ja sähköntoimitusten selvityksessä noudatettavasta tiedonvaihdosta; SäädK 273/2016), which sets detailed rules for the form and the schedule for communication for trade in electricity and settlement of electricity deliveries;
- the Decree of the Ministry of Economic Affairs and Employment on Systems Responsibility for the Electricity TSO (Työ- ja elinkeinoministeriön asetus kantaverkonhaltijan järjestelmävastuusta; SäädK 635/2013);
- the Decree of the Ministry of Trade and Industry on Operative Unbundling Requirements for the Electricity Distribution System Operators (Kauppa- ja teollisuusministeriön asetus sähkönjakeluverkonhaltijan toiminnallisista eriyttämisvaatimuksista; SäädK 922/2006), which includes provisions on operative unbundling requirements for the distribution operators having at least 50,000 customers; and
- the Decree of the Ministry of Trade and Industry on Unbundling of Electricity Operations (Kauppa- ja teollisuusministeriön asetus sähköliiketoimintojen eriyttämisestä; SäädK 79/2005), which sets rules on unbundling in accounts for electricity undertakings.

85. Regulation (EU) No. 1227/2011 of the European Parliament and of the Council on the wholesale energy market integrity and transparency (REMIT) sets up a legal framework for the monitoring of wholesale energy markets of electricity, natural gas and derivative products. The Regulation has been applicable since 28 December 2011. The Agency for the Cooperation of Energy Regulators (ACER) enforces REMIT by identifying and penalizing insider trading and market manipulation, to prevent such abuses from affecting the European wholesale markets. Market participants on the wholesale market, including TSOs (in Finland, Fingrid), suppliers, traders, producers, brokers and large users trading wholesale energy products, are required to register with the European Register of Market participants through their National Regulatory Authority (NRA); in Finland – the EA. Market participants must report their wholesale energy market transactions and orders to trade in detail to the ACER. The ACER will publish information in the interest of improving transparency of wholesale energy markets insofar it is not commercially sensitive or likely to create distortions in competition on the energy markets. Lastly, market participants must themselves publish, in a timely and efficient manner, inside information likely to have an effect on the prices of wholesale energy products, such as information related to the capacity and utilization of facilities, production, storage, consumption and transmission of electricity, including planned or unplanned unavailability of the facilities.

§2. EU Legislation on the Internal Market in Electricity

86. The legal framework for the electricity sector also includes the EU legislation on the internal market in electricity which is also directly applicable in Finland. Thus, the legal framework for the electricity market is a mixture of the national and EU legislation where the EU legislation forms a central and integrated part of the legislative framework regarding the electricity market.[32]

87. The Regulation (EC) 714/2009 of the European Parliament and the Council on conditions for access to the network for cross-border exchanges in electricity and repealing Regulation (EC) No. 1228/2003 and the Commission regulations issued by virtue of it include the regulations for the internal market in electricity in the EU Member States. The Regulation aims to set fair rules for cross-border exchanges in electricity, thus, enhancing competition within the internal market in electricity, taking into account the particular characteristics of national and regional markets. This will involve the establishment of a compensation mechanism for cross-border flow of electricity and the setting of harmonized principles on cross-border transmission charges and the allocation of available capacities of interconnections between national transmission systems. The Regulation also aims at facilitating the emergence of a well-functioning and transparent wholesale market with a high level of security of supply in electricity. It provides for mechanisms to harmonize the rules for cross-border exchanges in electricity. The Regulation has been supplemented by a number of Commission regulations, namely:

- Commission Regulation (EU) No. 838/2010 on laying down guidelines relating to the inter-TSO compensation mechanism and a common regulatory approach to transmission charging.
- Commission Regulation (EU) No. 543/2013 on submission and publication of data in electricity markets and amending Annex I to Regulation (EC) No. 714/2009 of the European Parliament and of the Council.
- Commission Regulation (EU) 2015/1222 establishing a guideline on capacity allocation and congestion management.
- Commission Regulation (EU) 2016/631 establishing a network code on requirements for grid connection of generators.
- Commission Regulation (EU) 2016/1388 establishing a network code on demand connection.
- Commission Regulation (EU) 2016/1447 establishing a network code on requirements for grid connection of high-voltage direct current (HVDC) systems and direct current-connected power park modules.

---

32. For the EU internal electricity market legislation, *see* EU Energy Law – Volume 1, The Internal Energy Market. 4th edn Claeys & Casteels 2016.

- Commission Regulation (EU) 2016/1719 establishing a guideline on forward capacity allocation.
- Commission Regulation (EU) 2017/1485 establishing a guideline on electricity transmission system operation.
- Commission Regulation (EU) 2017/2195 establishing a guideline on electricity balancing.
- Commission Regulation (EU) 2017/2196 establishing a network code on electricity emergency and restoration.

88. The Regulation (EU) No. 1227/2011 of the European Parliament and of the Council on wholesale energy market integrity and transparency establishes rules prohibiting abusive practices affecting wholesale energy markets which are coherent with the rules applicable in financial markets and with the proper functioning of those wholesale energy markets whilst taking into account their specific characteristics. It provides for the monitoring of wholesale energy markets by the ACER in close collaboration with national regulatory authorities and taking into account the interactions between the Emissions Trading Scheme and wholesale energy markets. The Regulation has been supplemented by the Commission Implementing Regulation (EU) No. 1348/2014 on data reporting implementing Article 8(2) and Article 8(6) of Regulation (EU) No. 1227/2011 of the European Parliament and of the Council on wholesale energy market integrity and transparency.

§3. Legislation on the National Regulatory Authority and Penalties

89. The legislative reform of 2013 also included a reform of regulatory powers for the national regulatory authority, the EA. The EA statutes have been enacted in the Law on the EA of 2013 (Laki Energiavirastosta; SäädK 870/2013). However, the provisions for regulatory powers of the EA and penalties are currently enacted in the Law on Supervision of Electricity and Natural Gas Markets (Laki sähkö- ja maakaasumarkkinoiden valvonnasta; SäädK 590/2013).

§4. Legislation on Construction and Operation of Power Plants

90. Since the establishment of the Electricity Market Act of 1995, there have not been any general energy-related authorization procedures for construction and operation of power stations. However, general concession procedures, which are linked with land use planning and environmental protection, are applied. The Land Use and Building Act of 1999 (Maankäyttö- ja rakennuslaki; SäädK 132/1999) is applied to construction of all kinds of power stations. Nuclear power stations and power stations using combustible substances and exceeding a certain size are a target group for the further concession procedures under the Environmental Protection Act of 2014 (Ympäristönsuojelulaki; SäädK 527/2014). The operators of the power stations are, in addition, obliged to notify the EA of plans to construct a power station, commission a power station and decommission a power station in order to allow the regulator to monitor national generation capacity.

91. Finland also applies special concession procedures for nuclear power stations under the Nuclear Energy Act of 1987 (Ydinenergialaki; SäädK 990/1987) and for exploitation of hydropower under the Water Act of 2011 (Vesilaki; SäädK 587/2011). The concession procedures under these acts contain a means test for licensing the construction of such power stations.

92. It is also important to note that the EU's emissions trading scheme[33] has a significant impact on the operation of combustion power stations. According to the Emissions Trading Act of 2011 (Päästökauppalaki; SäädK 311/2011), combustion power stations, excluding waste burning plants, with a nominal heat effect exceeding 20 MW need to apply for an emissions concession for greenhouse gas emissions.

§5. Legislation on Support Mechanisms for Electricity Generation

93. With regard to electricity generation, the Finnish government published in November 2017 a proposal for the legislative changes required for implementing a new support scheme for renewable energy. This new scheme is meant to replace the current Finnish feed-in tariff scheme for renewables, and it will be based on technology-neutral tendering processes. Wind power, combined heat and power (CHP), biogas, solar power and wave power plant projects are, according to the proposed legislation, eligible to participate in the tendering rounds. The aim is to organize tendering rounds in 2018 and 2019 for a total of 2 TWh annual renewable energy production, once the legislation is adopted. The scheme would be a so-called *pay-as-bid* support scheme with each tenderer approved to the scheme receiving the premium offered in its tender, and the premium paid to the energy producer would be a combination of a fixed and flexible premium added on top of the electricity market price. The proposed scheme is meant to create a temporary support scheme, while the Finnish government has set the ultimate target at renewables being produced on a market basis without separate support schemes in the future.

§6. Legislation on Securing the Adequacy of the Electricity System

94. In order to secure the electricity supply in peak load situations, a peak load capacity reserve has been established, and is governed by the Act on Peak Load Capacity of 2011 (Laki sähköntuotannon ja -kulutuksen välistä tasapainoa varmistavasta tehoreservistä; SäädK 117/2011) The EA shall determine the required capacity of the peak load capacity reserve at least every four years, and it has the

33. *See* Directive 2003/87/EC of the European Parliament and of the Council of 13 Oct. 2003 establishing a scheme for greenhouse gas emission allowance trading within the Community and amending Council Directive 96/61/EC, and Directive 2009/29/EC of the European Parliament and of the Council of 23 Apr. 2009 amending Directive 2003/87/EC so as to improve and extend the greenhouse gas emission allowance trading scheme of the Community.

authority to include power plants to the reserve based on a tender process. The current peak load capacity period runs from 1 July 2017 to 30 June 2020 and the reserve includes six power plants with a total capacity of 729 MW. The power plants included in the peak load capacity reserve have entered into agreements with the Finnish TSO (Fingrid Oyj) concerning the use of the power plant as a plant included in the peak load capacity reserve. Plants included in the reserve have a duty to be prepared to be taken into use within twelve hours from an order by the TSO during the winter months December–February, and within one month from such order during other months.

95. Due to shortages in generation capacity during peak load situations, Finland has also included in the Electricity Market Act an obligation for power plant operators to provide notification of the dates of overhaul outages at their power plants during the winter peak load period. The EA may order that an overhaul outage at a power plant be rescheduled if it is reasonable to suspect that the electricity supply will not be enough to meet the electricity demand in Finland during the notified overhaul outage.

Chapter 2. System Operation

§1. The Finnish Electricity System

96. The Finnish electricity system is based on what were once two transmission grids, the larger of which was owned by the former state-owned power company Imatran Voima Oy (IVO). However, there was also a competing grid, which was owned by the private Finnish energy-intensive industries. The grid of IVO was originally built for large-scale power generation as well as electricity distribution all over the country. The purpose of the industrial grid was originally to transmit electricity from the large-capacity industry-owned nuclear power stations on the western coast and the large-capacity hydropower stations in northern Finland to the factories located in southern Finland and along the Gulf of Bothnia. These two grids were united in 1996 when the Finnish TSO Fingrid Oyj was established. Currently, there is no significant congestion in the Finnish transmission grid because of the former structure of two separate grids competing with each other. Due to this, the mainland Finland forms only one price area in the Nordic power market, Nordpool.

97. The national transmission grid is currently owned and operated by the TSO Fingrid Oyj. The national transmission grid includes all the 220 kV–400 kV high-voltage lines and the most important 110 kV high-voltage lines serving regions and communities in sparsely populated areas of the country as well as the interconnectors connecting the Finnish power system to the Swedish, Norwegian, Estonian and Russian power systems. Fingrid also owns the most important power reserves needed for system operations of the national power system – altogether 929 MW.

98. Fingrid Oyj has been certified as a TSO according to Article 9 of the Directive 2009/72/EC, i.e., according to the principles of effective unbundling.[34] Fingrid Oyj is owned by the State (including the National Emergency Supply Agency, NESA) and some financial and insurance institutions (the State 28.24%, National Emergency Supply Agency 24.90% and institutional investors 46.83%, with corresponding voting rights for the State of 37.66%, NESA 33.20% and institutional investors 29.13%). Rights to sell TSO shares to outsiders are restricted by the articles of association and the shareholder agreement.

99. The national electricity system is operated as a part of the Nordic Power System, NORDEL. The system has strong interconnections to the neighbouring systems. Finland's main grid is connected to the Swedish grid via two 400 kV AC connections in northern Finland. Finland also has a 220 kV AC connection to Norway. In addition to the AC connections, DC links Fenno-Skan 1 (400 MW) and Fenno-Skan 2 (800 MW) interconnect the system to Sweden. There is also a 100 MW DC connection from the continent to the Åland Islands which is operated by Kraftnät Åland. The system is also interconnected to the Estonian and Russian grids with DC connections. Finland and Estonia are connected by the DC links Estlink 1

34. *See* Commission opinion on 17 Jan. 2014 C(2014) 329 final and EA decision on 14 Mar. 2014.

(350 MW) and Estlink 2 (650 MW). There are three 400 kV transmission links from Finland to Vyborg, Russia. Russia and Finland are also connected by two 110 kV connections. These enable the connection of hydropower plants in Russia to the Finnish grid.

100. According to section 3(2) of the Electricity Market Act of 2013, electricity systems with a nominal voltage of less than 110 kV are classified as distribution systems. It is one of the main characteristics of the Finnish power system that many communities have their own CHP power stations[35] for local heat generation and electricity distribution. Thus, the power system has been built to also distribute power generated locally. This characteristic of the Finnish power system has also had a significant influence on the structure of the Finnish electricity network as well as on the structure of the electricity distribution industry. Currently, there are seventy-five distribution system operators. Most of the operators are owned by local communities or their joint ventures. There are also two large regional distribution systems owned by Caruna Oy and Elenia Oy.

101. The Finnish power system includes a large number of regional high-voltage grids, the so-called *high-voltage distribution systems* serving only individual distribution systems, industrial customers or power stations. Typically, a high-voltage distribution system is an interconnection between an individual distribution system and the national transmission grid. Because of this, most of the high-voltage distribution systems are operated by local distribution system operators. However, there are also eleven operators specialized in operating a high-voltage distribution system.

102. In the Electricity Market Act of 2013, Finland also adopted a concept of a closed distribution system according to the Article 28 of the Directive 2009/72/EC. Currently, there also are two operators of a closed distribution system.

§2. Network Concessions

I. Concessions for System Operation

A. Electricity System Licence

103. Electricity system operation calls for an electricity system licence. It is not possible to operate an electricity system without such a licence. However, no licence is needed for the operation of an electricity distribution system inside a property or a group of properties.

104. According to Chapter 2 of the Electricity Market Act of 2013, there are five types of electricity system licences for different systems, classified according to the requirements and responsibilities set to the operator:

35. Power stations for CHP generation.

(1) an electricity system licence for operators of a transmission system (section 7);
(2) an electricity system licence for the operator of a transmission system with the systems responsibility (sections 7 and 8);
(3) an electricity system licence for distribution system operators with responsibility for ensuring distribution to a region specified in the licence (sections 9 and 10);
(4) an electricity system licence for operators of a closed distribution system (section 11); and
(5) an electricity system licence for operators of a high-voltage distribution system (where only general requirements of section 6 apply).

105. In addition to this, the EA may in individual cases allow operation of an interconnector without an electricity system licence if an exemption according to Article 17 of the Regulation (EC) No. 714/2009 has been granted to the interconnector.

106. The most important types of electricity system licences are those mentioned in items (2) and (3). The electricity system licence granted to a distribution system operator always specifies the licensee's geographical area of responsibility insofar as the distribution system is concerned, but it also allows for system operation in high-voltage distribution systems. The systems responsibility is determined by the EA, which has to order one TSO to be responsible for the technical operability and reliability of Finland's electricity system and to take care of the duties involved in the national balance responsibility, which is the responsibility for maintaining the balance between electricity generation and use in the whole country during each hour as well as the responsibility for national balance settlement.

107. The electricity system licence is issued by the EA. The licence is granted on a continuous basis or, on special grounds, for a specified period. The licence may be granted to an establishment as well as a communal body or a state body, but not to a natural person.

108. The purpose of an electricity system licence is to establish a foundation for network regulation directed to an individual system operator. The electricity system licence is a means for the government to select the system operators, to supervise their efforts to carry out their duties and to regulate their tariffs and terms. The licensing system may in extreme situations also be used as a means to implement actions to secure the electricity supply if the system operator has totally failed in its duties. However, the general obligations of a system operator are usually set out not in the electricity system licence,[36] but in the legislation and in separate confirmation decisions by the EA. Because of this nature, the licence is not transferable to another body or establishment.

36. There is a remarkable derogation of this principle – that is, the electricity system licence for the TSO with the systems responsibility, which includes a detailed regulation on the duties of a TSO with the systems responsibility.

109. According to section 6 of the Electricity Market Act of 2013, an electricity system licence is always granted if the applicant has the technical, economic and organizational capabilities needed for conducting its electricity system operations. These preconditions are met if:

(1) the organization of the applicant is appropriate to the scope and nature of its system operations;
(2) the applicant has a sufficient staff to the scope and nature of its system operations in its service;
(3) the applicant has in its service an operating manager and, if the applicant carries out electrical works, a manager of electrical works that meet the eligibility requirements laid down in or by virtue of the Electrical Safety Act;
(4) the applicant has the economic conditions necessary for profitable electricity system operations;
(5) the applicant has the right to decide on the resources needed for the operation, maintenance and development of an electricity system as well as the right to conclude connection agreements and transmission or distribution agreements with system users; and
(6) the applicant has demonstrated it has separated its business operations as laid down in Chapter 12 of the Electricity Market Act.

110. Any conditions necessary to meet these preconditions can be imposed in the licence. The licence or its conditions can be amended with the consent of the licensee, or otherwise, if the amendment is based on an amendment in legislation or a decision of a Court of Appeal or if the amendment is necessary due to essential changes in the operating conditions.

111. The electricity system licence granted to a distribution system operator specifies the licensee's geographical area of responsibility insofar as the distribution system is concerned. At the same time, the distribution system operator is granted a monopoly to maintain electricity distribution within this geographical area. The licensee may agree with another licensee on changes concerning the area of responsibility. For sufficiently weighty reason, the EA may also make changes in the area of responsibility.

112. While the Electricity Market Act of 2013 regulates granting of electricity system licences, supervision of licences and their conditions is regulated in Chapter 5 of the Law on Supervision of Electricity and Natural Gas Markets.

113. According to section 23, the EA may withdraw the electricity system licence if the licensee:

(1) terminates its electricity system operation;
(2) no longer meets the prerequisites required for the granting of the license;
(3) repeatedly and essentially violates the Electricity Market Act or the statutes or regulations issued under it; or

(4) repeatedly and essentially violates the Regulation (EC) No. 714/2009 or the network codes issued under it.

However, a precondition for withdrawal is that the licensee has neglected to comply with a warning for withdrawal by the EA.

114. If the electricity system licence is withdrawn, the EA has a right to decide on the measures to be taken to uphold the system operation concerned. Unless a system operator, whose licence has been withdrawn, has not carried out a voluntary transaction of the system with another system operator, the EA may decide on the transfer of the system concerned against compensation to another system operator. In this case, the EA first decides whether there are justified reasons for the withdrawal of the licence and second what conditions are necessary to implement the decision. The criteria for compensation and the determination of compensation must comply with the Act on the Redemption of Immoveable Property and Special Rights (Laki kiinteän omaisuuden ja erityisten oikeuksien lunastuksesta; SäädK 603/1977). The compensation is determined by a special commission set up for the redemption. Its decision can be appealed to the Land Court. The compensation is assessed to the full value of the assets.

B. Electricity System Licence for the TSO with the Systems Responsibility

115. The electricity system licence for the TSO with the systems responsibility is a special type of electricity system licence that can be granted to only one TSO. Thus, the systems responsibility for the national power system[37] is a legal monopoly granted to the national TSO Fingrid Oyj. The licensee's geographical area of responsibility covers the territory of Finland excluding the autonomous area of Åland Islands.

116. According to section 45 of Electricity Market Act of 2013, the EA orders one TSO in the electricity system to be responsible for the technical operability and reliability of Finland's electricity system and to take care of the duties involved in the national balance responsibility and the responsibility for national balance settlement in a manner that is equitable and non-discriminatory for all electricity market participants (*systems responsibility*). National balance responsibility means responsibility for maintaining the balance between electricity generation and use in the whole country during each balance settlement period (currently an hour).

117. The TSO with the systems responsibility is tied to the ownership unbundling requirement that forms a precondition for granting the electricity system licence. The TSO must delegate the functions related to the national balance responsibility to its separate operational entity or its wholly owned subsidiary. The TSO

37. Read more about the systems responsibility for the national power system in §5 *infra*.

must also delegate the functions related to responsibility for national balance settlement to its balance unit or an associated company owned with some TSOs from EU and European Economic Area (EEA) Member States. Currently, the responsibility for national balance settlement is carried out by eSett Oy, an associated company for three Nordic TSOs, i.e., Fingrid, Swedish Svenska Kraftnät and Norwegian Statnett.

C. Derogation under Article 17 of Regulation (EC) No. 714/2009

118. Article 17 of the Regulation (EC) No. 714/2009 of the European Parliament and of the Council of 13 July 2009 on conditions for access to the network for cross-border exchanges in electricity and repealing Regulation (EC) No. 1228/2003 includes a procedure according to which new DC interconnectors, significant increases of capacity in existing interconnectors and, in exceptional cases, new AC interconnectors may be exempted from certain provisions of the EU electricity market regulation. A decision for derogation may include exemptions from the provisions of Article 16(6) (the use of the revenues resulting from the allocation of capacity of the interconnection) of Regulation No. 714/2009 and Articles 9 (ownership unbundling), 32 (third party access to the transmission systems) and 37(6) and (10) (fixing or approving the methodologies used to calculate the terms and conditions for connection and access to systems) of Directive 2009/72/EC.

119. A derogation may be granted only under the following conditions:

(1) The investment enhances competition in providing electricity.
(2) The level of risk attached to the investment is such that the investment would not take place unless an exemption is granted.
(3) The interconnector is owned by a person that is separate, at least in terms of its legal form, from the system operators in whose systems that interconnector will be built.
(4) Charges are levied on users of that interconnector.
(5) Since the partial market opening referred to in Article 19 of Directive 96/92/EC, no part of the capital or operating costs of the interconnector has been recovered from any charges made for the use of transmission or distribution systems linked by the interconnector.
(6) The exemption is not to the detriment of competition or the effective functioning of the internal electricity market or to the efficient functioning of the regulated system to which the interconnector is linked.

120. The EA has the authority in Finland to decide on derogations under Article 17 of Regulation No. 714/2009. Although a decision on derogation may exempt a TSO of a so-called *merchant line* from that operator's most important obligations, there is still a need to regulate that operator's business operations. Thus, section 12 of the Electricity Market Act of 2013 requires the system operator to apply for an exemption for an electricity system licence. In its decision on an exemption, the EA may set the operating conditions regarding capacity allocation, congestion management and transmission charges.

121. Currently, no derogations are in force in the Finnish electricity system under Article 17 of Regulation No. 714/2009.

II. Concessions for Construction of Power Lines

A. Construction of High-Voltage Power Lines

122. According to section 14 of the Electricity Market Act of 2013, the construction of a power line with a nominal voltage of 110 kV or above calls for a project licence. No project licence is needed, however, for the construction of an internal power line inside a property. In the case of a domestic high-voltage power line, the project licence is obtained from the EA and, in the case of a cross-border power line, from the Ministry of Economic Affairs and Employment.

123. The primary purpose of the project licensing procedure for construction of high-voltage power lines is to assess whether the new power line is needed for the purposes of the power system. In the Finnish system, the project licence does not specify the course of the power line. Instead, the exact course of the power line is determined by a separate redemption procedure based on the Act on the Redemption of Immoveable Property and Special Rights or, in certain cases, by bilateral land use agreements between the system operator and the landowner(s). Usually, the applicant must apply for a separate licence for redemption from the Council of State in order to obtain the necessary land use rights for the power line project. In this context, an environmental impact assessment (EIA) is required in certain situations. Also, no area reservation or consent by the municipality needs to be obtained for the proposed course of the line prior to the granting of the project licence. Thus, a project licence for a high-voltage power line under section 14 of the Electricity Market Act of 2013 is a licence to carry out a certain construction project of a high-voltage power line in the Finnish power system rather than an actual licence to construct a power line. Several permissions might be needed even though the project licence has been granted.

124. A precondition for granting a project licence is that construction of the power line is necessary in order to secure electricity transmission. Another precondition for granting a project licence for construction of a cross-border line is that its construction is otherwise appropriate in terms of the development of the electricity market and of mutuality. Notwithstanding these preconditions, a project licence will always be granted for a service line that connects an electricity consumption site or one or several power stations to the nearest electricity system with a minimum rated voltage of 110 kV. Also, a project licence will always be granted for a power line built by a distribution system operator in its area of responsibility or, from its area of responsibility if the power line interconnects its distribution systems with each other or with a system of another system operator. Terms considered necessary for the conditions of the licence can be included in the project licence.

125. If a high-voltage power line is built outside the area reserved for it in the physical plans or if no such area reservation exists in the physical plans or without redemption procedure, the consent of the municipality concerned must be obtained for the course to be followed. This consent for the proposed course of the line need not be obtained prior to granting the project licence. The consent will not be refused, nor will conditions be set for its granting, without valid reasons based on the planned use of the area, on environmental considerations or on other aspects if the refusal or the conditions would unreasonably impair the security of electricity transmission or unreasonably inconvenience the applicant.

126. A project licence does not authorize an applicant to operate an electricity system. An electricity system licence is always needed for that purpose.

B. Construction of a Distribution System

127. The construction of a distribution system does not call for a special licence. The distribution system operator has been granted a geographical area of responsibility in which it has sole right to construct a distribution system. There are only a few statutory derogations from this monopoly.

128. According to section 13 of the Electricity Market Act of 2013, a third party is entitled to construct a distribution system within the distribution system operator's area of responsibility only if:

(1) the system to be built is an electricity consumer's service line or a backup service line that connects an electricity consumption site to the distribution system operator's electricity system;
(2) the system to be built is a service line or a backup service line that connects one or several power stations to the electricity system of either the distribution system operator or another system operator;
(3) the system to be built is an internal system for a property or a group of properties; or
(4) the distribution system operator permits another system operator to construct the system.

129. According to section 161 of the Land Use and Building Act, property owners and titleholders must allow the location of power lines serving the community or the property in the area they own or hold the title to unless these power lines can be located elsewhere satisfactorily by some other means and at a reasonable cost. However, power lines may not be built so that development or implementation of a plan for the area is hindered. If an agreement has not been reached on the location with the affected property owner or titleholder, the location decision is made by the local building supervision authority – that is, the construction board of the local municipality. The owner or titleholder of a property is entitled to be paid compensation for harm and damage caused. If an agreement is not reached on such compensation, the matter is settled according to provisions in the Act on the Redemption of Immoveable Property and Special Rights.

§3. General Obligations of System Operation

130. Finland has adopted a regulated third-party access regime in line with Article 32 of Directive 2009/72/EC. This regime is based on three general principles: (1) guaranteed access to electricity systems, (2) provision of all services by the customer's system operator and (3) wide transparency in system operation. The general obligations in Chapter 4 of the Electricity Market Act of 2013 that apply to all system operators are derived from these principles. These general obligations are complemented by more detailed provisions for TSOs in Chapter 5 and for distribution system operators in Chapter 6.

I. Guaranteed Access to Electricity Systems

131. Access to networks is guaranteed by means of three general statutory obligations that apply to all system operators, including TSO Fingrid Oyj: (1) the obligation to connect customers to the electricity system, (2) the obligation to develop the electricity system and (3) the obligation to transmit electricity in the electricity system. These three statutory obligations are supplemented with a general service obligation to provide system services in an impartial and non-discriminatory way. The general service obligation also prohibits system operators to set any unfounded terms or restrictions obviously limiting competition within the electricity trade in their system services.

132. The obligation of the system operator to connect customers to the electricity system is enacted in section 20 of the Electricity Market Act of 2013. According to this provision, the system operator must connect to its system those electricity consumption sites and power-generating installations that meet the required technical specifications within its area of operation upon the customer's request and for reasonable compensation. The connection conditions and technical requirements of each system operator must be impartial and non-discriminatory and they must take note of the conditions relating to the reliability and efficiency of the electricity system. It is important to note that the obligation to connect means the potential customer has a right to be connected to the electricity system concerned. However, as a precondition, the customer must meet the technical specifications required by the system operator. These technical specifications may be established to avoid the possibility of inadequate transmission capacity in the electricity system concerned as well as to ensure technical safety and establish the minimum technical design and operational requirements for the connection. For example, technical specifications are typically set so as to ensure that the new subscriber will not negatively affect the quality of electricity in the electricity system concerned.

133. The obligation of the system operator to develop its electricity system in section 19 of the Electricity Market Act means that the system operator must maintain, operate and develop its electricity system and the connections to other systems in accordance with operational standards laid down to electricity systems as well as in accordance with the operator´s customers' reasonable needs. The obligation to develop operator's electricity system provides that an electricity system must be planned and built and it must be maintained so that: (1) it fulfils the operational standards laid down in the Electricity Market Act and meets in other ways a good technical quality in transmission and distribution of electricity, (2) an electricity system and system services operate reliably when they are targeted by normally expected climate-based, mechanical or other external disturbances, (3) an electricity system and system services operate as reliably as possible under normal disturbance conditions and in emergency situations meant by the National Preparedness Act (Valmiuslaki; SäädK 1552/2011), (4) an electricity system operates compatibly with the Finnish electricity system and, if necessary, be interconnected to other systems, (5) eligible consumption sites and power stations can be connected to an electricity system and (6) the system operator is capable to fulfil its other obligations laid down in the Electricity Market Act. More detailed operational standards have been laid down to system operators in Chapters 5 and 6 of the Electricity Market Act.

134. The obligation to develop the operator´s electricity system is an essential part of the Finnish regulatory system for electricity system operation. It requires each system operator to actively take measures to maintain and develop sufficient transmission capacity and quality of electricity in its system as well as to develop interconnections with other systems. However, it should be noted that if the system operator fulfils the general legal standards for system operation, the obligation covers only the reasonable needs of customers. In other words, the benefits to customers and other market participants of investment in the system to meet the specific needs of a customer have to be compared with the costs and other negative impacts of that investment on the system operator and its customers. Where the benefits of the investment under this obligation outweigh the investment costs, these costs are shared among all the customers of the system operator. However, if the investment costs outweigh the benefits, the costs of the additional service will be allocated to the customer that caused the need for the investment. It is also important to note that the investments and investment plans of the system operators are not approved *ex ante* by the EA. On the contrary, the system operators decide on their investments and investment plans on the basis of the obligation to develop their electricity systems. However, the EA has an *ex post* power to require system operators to correct mistakes or omissions that infringe this obligation. Thus, investments in electricity systems are the responsibility of the system operators, not the EA. Additionally, there are elements in the tariff regulation that favour investments.

135. The third essential element in the guaranteed access to electricity systems is the obligation of the system operator to transmit electricity in its system. This obligation, set out in section 21 of the Electricity Market Act of 2013, includes two elements necessary for access. First, the system operator must sell electricity transmission services to those that need them within the limits of its system transmission capacity. Second, the system operator is responsible for metering the electricity supplied in an appropriate manner.

136. The guaranteed access regime and the transmission of electricity in the system operator's system are guaranteed to all customers connected to the system of the operator concerned as well as to electricity traders and retailers willing to sell electricity in each electricity system that operates under a licence. The system operator is obliged to transmit electricity both for consumption to consumption sites and produced electricity to the marketplace in the transmission grid. Transmission and distribution contracts are typically entered into by electricity end users and system operators. The practice of electricity suppliers and retailers contracting to buy transmission and distribution service from system operators has not become common in Finland. The legal provisions on electricity contracts do not support this kind of practice either. Only end users covered by the obligation to deliver (*see* paragraph 282) are provided the opportunity to agree with retailers that the contract includes not only the supply of electricity, but also the system service required by electricity transmission.

137. The obligation to transmit electricity binds system operators only within the limits of their system transmission capacity. This means that system operators have a right to carry out congestion management methods. Commission Regulation (EU) 2015/1222, established a guideline on capacity allocation and congestion management; these guidelines on the management and allocation of available transfer capacity of interconnections between national systems are applied to congestion management. Additionally, a system operator has to consider its obligation to develop its system if congestion occurs in that system. This obligation may require the system operator to take measures to develop sufficient transmission capacity in the system.

138. The obligation to transmit electricity includes the system operator's responsibility to measure the electricity in its system. The rules for measuring are provided in more detail in the Government Decree on Measuring and Settlement of Electricity Deliveries (Valtioneuvoston asetus sähköntoimitusten mittauksesta ja selvityksestä; SäädK 66/2009), which came into force on 1 May 2009. The Decree provides for a smart metering policy for Finland and aims to have electricity consumption measured hourly no later than the end of 2013. The Decree also requires at least an 80% rollout of automatic meter reading equipment for consumption sites in distribution networks by the end of the transitional period. At the same time, advanced metering systems that facilitate demand response and allow customers to make use of their own consumption data have been installed. System operators are given a monopoly for metering in their systems to make possible this large-scale technology transformation. Currently, the rollout level of smart meters in the Finnish distribution systems is approximately 99.6%.

II. Provision of All Services by the Customer's System Operator

139. The second important principle of the third-party access regime is the provision of all services by the customer's system operator. First, it means that each system operator must, for its own part, create the preconditions that permit the customer to contract for all system services with the operator of the system to which he is directly connected as a subscriber. Second, each system operator must create the preconditions that permit the customer to be granted the right, in return for payment of the appropriate fees, to use from its connection point, the electricity system of the entire country; foreign connections excluded. This is called the spot pricing principle.

140. The provision of all services by the customer's system operator and the spot pricing principle are the key elements in creating a liberalized electricity market. To make competition possible in the electricity market, the parties must have access to a marketplace, which is formed by a complex of electricity systems connected to each other. When this complex of electricity systems is viewed as a number of separate systems operated by different owners, difficulties in negotiating necessary services and pricing with several operators can significantly hamper trade. Thus, these electricity systems have come to be seen as a complex that allows each system operator to offer its customers the variety of system services available through the complex. Customers get access to the entire electricity system from their connection point by entering into a contract with a single system operator. Additionally, the price for these system services is determined on the basis of the types of services the customer needs, and geographical distances lose their importance as a cost factor.

141. According to section 25 of the Electricity Market Act of 2013, the spot pricing principle is not generally applied to foreign interconnectors. Rather, Finland has adopted a reciprocity principle in regulating access to foreign interconnectors. According to this principle, enacted in section 43 of the Electricity Market Act, the TSO collects transmission fees on the cross-border import or export of electricity unless otherwise provided in the international obligations binding on Finland in the mutual contracts based on the reliability and efficiency of the electricity system and on the market conditions concluded by the TSO or in other arrangements. The regulatory regime for the foreign interconnectors aims at ensuring that all market actors importing or exporting electricity pay their share of costs that their actions cause Finnish power system to incur. However, a foreign interconnector may be considered equal to the Finnish power system when the competition conditions are reciprocal in the two countries. This is what happened in the late 1990s in the Nordic power market as well as in the 2010s when implementing the EU internal energy market in the Baltic States. Also, Regulation (EC) No. 714/2009 provides for the abolition of transaction-based transmission fees between the Member States. Despite section 25 of the Electricity Market Act of 2013, the spot pricing principle is applied to the interconnectors in Estonia, Sweden and Norway. However, because competition conditions in Russia, and in Finland and the EU lack reciprocity, the spot pricing principle is not applied to Russian interconnections.[38] Unfortunately, there is no likelihood that fees for Russian interconnections will be abolished in the foreseeable future.

142. The obligation for system operators to acquire energy to cover transmission and distribution losses and reserve power needed to operate their electricity systems by following open, non-discriminatory and market-based procedures can also be included in the concept of the guaranteed access regime.

III. Wide Transparency in Electricity System Operation

143. A wide transparency in electricity system operation is the third important element of the Finnish regulatory system. The regulated third-party access regime itself provides for system operators to publish their fees, tariffs and other terms. Thus, the Electricity Market Act of 2013 orders system operators to publish their tariffs and terms for transmission, distribution and connection services as well as other systems services. Technical specifications set for subscribers are included among these terms. System operators are also obliged to give their subscribers a comprehensive and sufficiently detailed estimate of their connection costs. Additionally, Article 15 of the Regulation (EC) No. 714/2009 requires TSOs to publish their safety, operational and planning standards and estimates of available transmission capacity.

144. The transparency provisions in the Electricity Market Act of 2013 require all system operators to publish the price level of their services and economic indicators depicting the efficiency, quality and profitability of the system operations. In addition to this, distribution system operators are obliged to give an itemized account of how the price of the system service has been determined in the invoices submitted to their customers.

145. The EA has issued more detailed regulations on the publication of tariffs and indicators as well as on the content of invoices.

IV. Operational Standards for Electricity Systems

146. In the twenty-first century, extensive disturbances in electricity distribution have been experienced in Finland in spite of the fact that the level of security of supply of Finnish electricity systems is at a good level when compared internationally. Major disturbances have been caused by the overhead line networks in sparsely

38. For the reciprocity requirement in the EU legislation, *see* Commission Regulation (EU) No. 838/2010 on laying down guidelines relating to the inter-transmission system operator compensation mechanism and a common regulatory approach to transmission charging.

populated areas, which were built along the forests in connection with the electrification of rural areas after World War II. Medium and low voltage overhead lines are susceptible to damage caused by wind-toppled trees and heavy snow loads.

147. Because of the problems caused by power outages, the provisions of the Electricity Market Act of 2013 were supplemented by provisions on the security of transmission and distribution. They aim, in particular, was to prevent and control the storm and heavy snow load problems in rural and remote areas. The objective is to substantially increase the level of security of supply in these areas as compared to the level in 2013, especially in the case of major disturbances. Security-of-supply requirements were set separately for conurbations, sparsely populated areas as well as islands and exceptionally sparsely populated areas.

148. According to section 51 of the Electricity Market Act of 2013, a distribution system must be designed, constructed and maintained so that the failure of the network as a result of storms or snow loads does not result in a power outage for more than six hours in city or town plan areas and in a power outage of more than thirty-six hours in other areas. In exceptionally sparsely populated areas and islands with no bridges, a distribution system operator may deviate from the described level in accordance with local conditions. A distribution system operator must meet the requirements within its area of responsibility within fifteen years, i.e., by the end of 2028 at the latest. In exceptional cases, the EA may grant an extension of a maximum period of eight years.

149. For transmission systems and high-voltage distribution systems, it is required that width of the wire passages shall be wide enough so that trees cannot fall over the wires.[39]

150. The technical solutions required for reaching the level of security of supply are determined by the system operators. System operators can use the most cost-effective technology solutions to meet the design criteria. Therefore, there is no forced cabling. However, meeting this objective in practice required a substantial increase in the degree of underground cabling for medium voltage and low voltage lines in the distribution networks of rural areas.

39. *See* ss 40 and 50 of the Electricity Market Act.

§4. Pricing Principles in System Operation

I. General Principles for Setting Tariffs for Transmission, Distribution and Connections

A. General

151. According to the Government Bill for the Electricity Market Act of 2013,[40] the Finnish legislation governing the electricity market aims at prohibiting monopoly pricing, encouraging system operators to be efficient in their business operations and facilitating an efficiently functioning electricity market. The general pricing principles for system operation have been set out in Chapter 4 of the Electricity Market Act of 2013. Basically, these principles are applied to all system operators. In addition, Regulation (EC) No. 714/2009 and Commission Regulation (EU) No. 838/2010 on laying down guidelines relating to the inter-TSO compensation mechanism and a common regulatory approach to transmission charging are applied to the transmission system. The general pricing principles for system operation are also applied to connection services, although there are important differences between the pricing principles for connections and for transmission and distribution services.

152. The most important conditions for tariffs in system operation are that they must be cost reflective and non-discriminatory. Additionally, transmission and distribution tariffs must not be distance-related. Any unfounded terms or restrictions obviously limiting competition within the electricity trade and special charges for customer switching are also forbidden.

153. According to the Finnish regulatory system, the EA confirms *ex ante* the methods for tariff calculation to be used by each system operator. However, the system operators have an independent right to decide on their tariffs within the framework of the EA's confirmation decision. The tariffs should also reflect the cost structure of each system operator. Thus, there is a large variation in the tariffs of different operators.

B. Cost Correlation and Impartiality in Pricing

154. According to the obligation to transmit in section 21 of the Electricity Market Act of 2013, the system operator must sell electricity transmission and distribution services for reasonable compensation to those that need them within the limits of its system transmission capacity. Section 24(2) orders that the pricing of system services must be reasonable as a whole.

40. *See* Government Bill HE 20/2013 vp.

155. The obligation to establish reasonable pricing means that tariffs must reflect those system operation costs that are caused by the customers. In addition to this, the rate of return must reflect an appropriate risk level for such a monopoly. This interpretation of the concept of 'reasonableness' can be derived from the law drafting material for the Electricity Market Act of 2013 as well as from the praxis of the Supreme Administrative Court.

156. The Government Bill for the Electricity Market Act of 2013[41] states that the monopoly power of a system operator calls for reasonableness in pricing. Principally, this means that pricing should reflect those costs that have been generated in system operation. Additionally, pricing should ensure that the funds generated from operations are adequate to put the system operator in a sound financial position. The system operator's pricing can cover the reasonable costs of maintaining, using and developing the electricity system as well as providing a rate of return that can be regarded as reasonable. The charges collected by system operators must also reflect the costs of maintaining the electricity systems. In addition to this, system operators have a right to expect income that will be adequate for the development of the system. After covering the obligatory costs for maintaining, using and developing the system, the income remaining must give the system operator a reasonable rate of return. The Government Bill also states that the low-risk level, low financing costs and long useful life for the equipment should be taken into consideration when assessing the reasonableness of the rate of return.

157. According to section 24(1) of the Electricity Market Act of 2013, the charges and terms of the system services and the criteria according to which they are determined must be equitable and non-discriminatory for all system users. Exceptions to these requirements may be made only on special grounds. This means that generally services should be supplied to customers on the same terms. The pricing should also be equal for similar customers. However, the amount of electricity consumed, or the type of electricity consumption can justify differences in charges. Also, exceptional types of service, when ordered by a customer, justify variation from the operator's common charges.

158. The cost reflective pricing methodology is applied at the company level, not with respect to the supply of system services to individual customers. If a system operator's tariff system leads to equitable and non-discriminatory treatment of customers, it is acceptable that the tariffs are only cost reflective on average regarding individual customers.

159. In 2017, the Electricity Market Act of 2013 was amended with a provision which sets a ceiling on transmission and distribution tariff increases. According to section 26a, a system operator may increase the transmission and distribution

41. *See* Government Bill HE 20/2013 vp.

charges up to 15% as compared to the transmission and distribution charges collected twelve months prior to the increase. This ceiling also covers the upgrades to be charged within the next twelve months.[42]

C. Ban on Distance-Related Charges

160. As described earlier, the spot pricing principle is one of the key elements when creating a liberalized electricity market. It aims at making competition possible in the electricity market by its requirement for customers to get access to the entire electricity system from their connection points by entering into a contract with a single system operator. According to the spot pricing principle, the price for system services is determined on the basis of the types of services the customer needs.

161. The ban on distance-related charges in transmission and distribution is another precondition for creating a well-functioning, liberalized electricity market. If the pricing of transmission were based on distance, it would be necessary to ascertain where each electricity lot was produced and consumed. This would lead to a much more complex system for the settlement of electricity deliveries. Additionally, longer transmission distances and higher transmission costs would restrict the generators' ability to offer their electricity in the market and the end users' ability to get tenders from the market. The ban on distance-related charges in transmission is a complement to the spot pricing principle: both principles are necessary preconditions for a liberalized electricity market. Further, the spot pricing principle cannot function well without non-distance-related transmission tariffs.

162. Distance-related transmission charges are banned in Article 14(1) of the Regulation (EC) No. 714/2009. A corresponding ban on distance-related distribution charges is included in section 55 of the Electricity Market Act of 2013. According to this section, the price of system services within a distribution system must not depend on where the customer is located geographically within the system operator's area of responsibility. However, where parts of the system operator's area of responsibility are geographically separated, the transmission prices of each area shall apply. In individual cases, the EA may grant an exemption for the application of separate prices for transmission services if the cost levels and pricing criteria for the parts of the distribution system operator's area of responsibility do not differ much from each other.

D. Ban on Terms Hampering the Electricity Trade

163. The pricing principles for system services in the Electricity Market Act of 2013 include a ban on terms hampering the electricity trade. Section 24(3) orders

42. *See* SäädK 590/2017.

that the pricing of system services must not present any unfounded terms or restrictions obviously limiting competition within the electricity trade. However, the pricing must take account of any terms needed for the reliable and efficient operation of the electricity system as well as the costs and benefits that arise from the connection of an electricity generation installation to a system. Thus, a system operator has a right to set conditions that are justified for the secure use of the system even though these conditions may restrict customers' ability to use the system.

164. The ban on terms hampering the electricity trade includes special provisions for supplier switching in section 26 of the Electricity Market Act of 2013. According to this section, the system operator may not collect a separate fee for its services related to supplier switching.

II. Provisions on Charges for Transmission

165. The provisions on charges for transmission have been issued in Article 14 of Regulation (EC) No. 714/2009. According to paragraph 1, transmission charges shall be transparent, take into account the need for system security, and reflect actual costs incurred insofar as they correspond to those of an efficient and structurally comparable system operator and are applied in a non-discriminatory manner. Those charges must not be distance related.

166. According to paragraph 2, producers and consumers ('load') may be charged for access to networks. The proportion of the total amount of the network charges borne by producers will, subject to the need to provide appropriate and efficient locational signals, be lower than the proportion borne by consumers. Where appropriate, the level of the tariffs applied to producers and/or consumers will provide locational signals at European level and take into account the amount of network losses and congestion caused and the investment costs for infrastructure.

167. Paragraph 3 orders that payments and receipts resulting from the inter-TSO compensation mechanism and actual payments made and received as well as payments expected for future periods of time, estimated on the basis of past periods, are to be taken into account when setting the charges for system access.

168. Paragraph 4 orders that setting the charges for network access under this Article shall be without prejudice to charges on declared exports and declared imports resulting from congestion management referred to in Article 16 of the Regulation.

169. Paragraph 5 bans charges on individual transactions for declared transits of electricity.

170. Article 18 of the Regulation gives the European Commission the power to issue guidelines on the inter-TSO compensation mechanism. Currently, the applied compensation mechanism is based on the Commission Regulation (EU) No. 838/

2010 on laying down guidelines relating to the inter-TSO compensation mechanism and a common regulatory approach to transmission charging.

III. Provisions on Distribution Charges for Generation

171. The Electricity Market Act of 2013 includes special provisions on system service charges for generation in distribution systems. Section 56 aims at facilitating an increase of small-scale decentralized generation in distribution systems. As in Article 14(2) in Regulation (EC) No. 714/2009, the new provisions mandate that the proportion of the total amount of the network charges borne by generators in distribution systems is to be lower than the proportion borne by consumers. Section 56 also gives the government the power to issue decrees on distribution charges for generation in distribution systems. Currently, the government has set a price cap for distribution charges directed to generation.[43] According to the provisions, distribution charges for generation must be based only on the amount of energy. In addition, the annual distribution charge for an individual generator must not exceed Euro (EUR) cents 0.07 per kilowatt-hour (kWh) on average.

IV. Provisions on Charges for Connection Service

172. The provisions on charges for connection services in the Electricity Market Act of 2013 are based on the common principles for the pricing of system service – that is, reasonableness and cost reflectivity.

173. The main rule is included in the provision of obligation to connect in section 20. It orders that, on request and for reasonable compensation, the system operator must connect to its system all electricity consumption sites and power-generating installations that meet the required technical specifications within its area of operation. The connection conditions and technical requirements must be impartial and non-discriminatory, and they must take note of the conditions of the reliability and efficiency of the electricity system. At the request of the subscriber, the system operator must give it a comprehensive and sufficiently detailed estimate of the subscription costs. The system operator has the right to charge a reasonable fee to cover the costs of connection and operation of the system. Because of their obligations under the Electricity Market Act for the overall development of the transmission and distribution systems, system operators pay for reinforcements of their electricity systems made necessary by new connections. In addition, it has been necessary to underline the provisions on the division of system development costs in distribution systems by ordering that charges for connecting small-scale generation to distribution systems must not include costs that result from the reinforcement of the system capacity.

---

43. *See* s. 5 of the Decree on the Electricity Market (Valtioneuvoston asetus sähkömarkkinoista; SäädK 65/2009).

174. The cost reflectivity of charges for connection services is examined at the regional or even the individual level rather than at the company level. In this respect, the pricing of connection services differs from the pricing of transmission and distribution services.

175. The EA confirms *ex ante* the methods for calculating connection charges to be used by each system operator.

§5. Systems Obligations for the Transmission and Distribution Operators and Other Parties

I. General

176. Trade in electricity differs from trade in material commodities because supplies of electricity are always bound to an electricity system that links together generators and consumers and because it is a physical fact that electricity cannot be stored in large-scale. Electricity flows in electricity systems in compliance with the physical principles, and it is not possible to speak about electricity flow from certain generators to certain consumers in common electricity systems. Physically, there is only the common total production, which is the sum of electricity generated by all generators, and the common total consumption, which is the sum of electricity consumed by all consumers. Because it is not possible to store electricity in large-scale, there must be a constant balance between produced and consumed electricity in the power system. Thus, the power system and the individual electricity systems form an integrated hierarchic system, which provides for cooperation among the system operators as well as generators, electricity retailers and consumers participating in the electricity market. It is necessary to have common rules for this cooperation in order to secure an open and non-discriminatory, liberalized market for electricity.

177. Systems obligations include the systems responsibility for the national power system: the balance responsibility, the responsibility for balance determination and settlement of electricity deliveries and the secrecy obligation related to systems obligations.

178. The rules for systems obligations have been issued in Chapters 5 and 11 of the Electricity Market Act of 2013, in the Government Decree on Measuring and Settlement of Electricity Deliveries (Valtioneuvoston asetus sähköntoimitusten mittauksesta ja selvityksestä; SäädK 66/2009), which sets out detailed rules for the measurement and settling of electricity deliveries, and in the Decree of the Ministry of Economic Affairs and Employment on Communication for Trade in Electricity and Settlement of Electricity Deliveries (Työ-ja elinkeinoministeriön asetus sähkökaupassa ja sähköntoimitusten selvityksessä noudatettavasta tiedonvaihdosta; SäädK 273/2016), which sets detailed rules for the form and the schedule for communication for trade in electricity and settlement of electricity deliveries.

II. Systems Responsibility

179. The systems responsibility for the national power system is the most important systems obligation when assessing the functioning of the electricity market. The systems responsibility is composed of the duties and services that, in practice, can be taken care of in each control area by a single system operator. In Finland, the systems responsibility for the national power system is a legal monopoly granted to the national TSO, Fingrid Oyj.

180. The duties of the TSO with the systems responsibility include four key sectors: (1) responsibility for the technical operability and reliability of the national power system, (2) national balance responsibility, (3) responsibility for national balance settlement and (4) responsibility for the maintenance and development of that operator's activities and services in order to ensure the existence of the prerequisites for an efficiently functioning electricity market.

181. According to section 45 of the Electricity Market Act of 2013, the EA orders one TSO to be responsible for the technical operability and reliability of Finland's electricity system and to take care of the duties involved in national balance responsibility and responsibility for national balance settlement in an appropriate manner that is equitable and non-discriminatory for all electricity market participants (*systems responsibility*). National balance responsibility means the responsibility for maintenance of the balance between electricity generation and use in the whole country during each hour. The TSO with the systems responsibility must maintain and develop its activities and services within the systems responsibility and maintain, operate and develop its electricity system and other equipment needed for fulfilling the systems responsibility and the connection to other systems so that the prerequisites for an efficiently functioning national and regional electricity market as well as for the internal market in electricity can be ensured.

182. According to section 4 of the Decree of the Ministry of Economic Affairs and Employment on the Systems Responsibility of the TSO (Työ- ja elinkeinoministeriön asetus kantaverkonhaltijan järjestelmävastuusta; SäädK 635/2013,) the systems responsibility includes: (1) maintenance of operational reliability and control of transmission, (2) maintenance of voltage, (3) duties for national balance responsibility including maintenance of frequency and (4) duties for responsibility for national balance settlement. Since Fingrid is allowed to own only part of the reserves necessary for the system services, the maintenance of reserves is partly arranged as a service purchased from reserve holders. System services are offered in accordance with the power system operation agreement signed with the other Nordic TSOs.[44]

183. The TSO with systems responsibility may impose conditions on the use of the electricity transmission system, as well as on the use of the power stations and

44. *See* www.fingrid.fi.

loads connected to the electricity transmission system, in order to meet its responsibilities. The conditions, after being authorized by the EA, are applicable to individual cases. The authorized conditions may be applied despite an appeal unless the Court of Appeal provides otherwise.

184. According to section 46 of the Electricity Market Act of 2013, the terms of acquisition for electricity needed for maintaining national balance responsibility and the terms of trade for balancing electricity must be equitable and non-discriminatory for all electricity market participants, and they must not contain any conditions or limitations that would be unfounded or that would obviously restrict competition within the electricity trade. However, these terms will take account of the conditions needed to ensure the reliability and efficiency of the electricity system. The terms shall also provide for appropriate signals for system users to balance their inputs and outputs of electricity in the national power system. This means, for example, that the pricing principles for balancing power should steer the trade with it so that end users will not use the trade for balancing power as a substitute for actual supply of their electricity. In addition, the pricing of balancing power must be reasonable, which means that it must be cost reflective. Arbitrary margins of profit are banned; in other words, the profits from balancing services should be reasonable. The TSO with the systems responsibility should aim for cost efficiency in its balancing activities.

185. The EA shall confirm by its decision *ex ante* the terms of the services under the systems responsibility and the methods used to determine the fees charged for the services. The TSO must publish the terms applied to the sale and acquisition of services associated with the systems responsibility, including the grounds for determining these terms, and the sale and acquisition prices, including the grounds for determining these prices, as well as the conditions on the use of the electricity transmission system and on the use of the power stations and loads.

186. The TSO with the systems responsibility has duties to all parties in the electricity market, and its position is considered a public administrative task delegated to a body other than a public authority.[45] Thus, it is considered that in these cases, the TSO has the position and duties of a public authority.

III. Balance Responsibility

187. Each party operating in the electricity market must take continuous care of its power balance; that is, the party must maintain a continuous power balance between its electricity production and procurement as well as its consumption and sales. This obligation is called the balance responsibility. The legal basis for the balance responsibility is enacted in section 73 of the Electricity Market Act of 2013.

45. *See* the opinion of the Constitutional Law Committee of the Parliament of 24 Mar. 2000 (PeVL 4/2000 vp).

Further provisions on the contents of balance responsibility are included in Chapter 2 of the Government Decree on Measuring and Settlement of Electricity Deliveries.

188. In practice, the balance responsibility means that each party operating in the market must have an open supplier that balances the power balance of the party. A party whose open supplier is the TSO with systems responsibility is called a balance provider. Parties operating in the market take care of their balance responsibility through so-called *open supply contracts*, which guarantee a balancing supply of electricity to the party concerned. The parties operating at the transmission system level may also use contracts for fixed amounts of electricity. However, it is not technically possible to have a fixed supply for a party connected to a distribution system. The power balance in the national power system is secured with the help of chains of open supply contracts that extend from the TSO with the systems responsibility via balance providers to each end user connected to the national power system.

189. Section 75 of the Electricity Market Act of 2013 obliges parties operating in the electricity market to provide measurement data and other information on the electricity generation, use and supply needed to fulfil their balance responsibility. Further provisions on the notification procedure of this data have been issued in the Decree of the Ministry of Economic Affairs and Employment on Communication for Trade in Electricity and Settlement of Electricity Deliveries.

IV. Responsibility for Balance Determination and Settlement of Electricity Deliveries

190. The organization and methodology of balance determination and settlement of electricity deliveries are based on the provisions of section 74 of the Electricity Market Act of 2013. Further provisions on the contents of balance determination have been issued in Chapters 4 and 5 of the Government Decree on Measuring and Settlement of Electricity Deliveries.

191. According to these provisions, system operators and balance providers are responsible for balance determination. Balance determination is organized in a hierarchic system in which the distribution system operators take care of balance determination in their distribution systems and the balance providers take care of balance determination for those customers operating at the transmission system level for whom they are the open suppliers. At the top of the organization, the TSO with the systems responsibility takes care of balance determination for the balance providers.

192. Balance determination is based on electricity metering or a combination of metering and type-load curves and on supply reports. Finland adopted a smart metering policy in 2009 that aims to have electricity consumption measured hourly also in distribution systems. According to this policy, balance determination is primarily based on hourly measurement of electricity consumption in the entire national power system. Currently, the rollout level of smart meters and hourly settled consumption sites is about 99.6%.

193. Balance determination is one of the statutory duties of electricity system operators. Thus, the general obligations for system operation and the pricing principles for system services also apply to balance determination. Because electricity suppliers are also involved as balance providers in the organization for balance determination, it has been ordered in section 74 that, in addition to the provisions on system services in Chapter 4, balance determination services must be offered on equitable and non-discriminatory terms to the electricity market participants. The balance determination services offered may not include any conditions or limitations that would be unfounded or that would obviously restrict competition.

194. Section 75 of the Electricity Market Act of 2013 obliges parties operating in the electricity market to provide the measurement data and other information on electricity generation, use and supply needed for balance determination. Further provisions on the notification procedure of this data have been issued in the Decree of the Ministry of Economic Affairs and Employment on Communication for Trade in Electricity and Settlement of Electricity Deliveries.

V. Secrecy Obligation Related to Systems Obligations

195. While taking care of their statutory duties, the electricity system operators and other parties involved in the organization for balance determination have to process information from other parties that might have the nature of a business secret or be delicate with regard to personal privacy. The new metering technology, in particular, increases the amount of this kind of information. Because of this, those operators tending to services of system operators or duties referred to in Chapter 11 of the Electricity Market Act of 2013 or in regulatory provisions laid down by virtue of it are bound by a secrecy obligation related to systems obligations. According to section 76 of the Electricity Market Act, sections 22 and 23, as well as subparagraph 20 of section 24(1), of the Act on the Openness of Government Activities (621/1999) apply to the secrecy obligation regarding documents received or drawn up and the information included in them, to the pledge of secrecy, to the ban on exploitation of this information and to the breach of the secrecy obligation. The secrecy obligation for operators in section 76 parallels a corresponding obligation for public authorities.

Chapter 3. Generation

§1. Overall View of the Electricity Generation Market

196. The generation of electricity has been opened up to competition by the Electricity Market Act. The Finnish government does not set any legally binding generation capacity targets for the electricity generating companies but uses policy guidance instead by adopting long-term energy and climate strategies. The Council of State adopted its latest energy and climate strategy for 2030 in 2016. It includes targets for future energy production in Finland and introduces means and actions aiming to reach these targets. The permanent standing committees of the Finnish Parliament have considered the strategy and heard experts on it. Finally, the Parliament has given its reply[46] to the strategy. The treatment by the Parliament of government strategies adds democratic elements to them and enhances their overall legitimacy. In 2014, Parliamentary Energy and Climate Committee adopted a memorandum on energy roadmap for 2050. Both the energy roadmap for 2050 and the Energy and Climate Strategy for 2030 aim at diminishing CO_2 emissions by 80%–95% as compared to the level that existed in 1990. The main means to reach the ambitious target is to move towards carbon-neutral society, for example, by abandoning the use of coal in the energy production.

197. The Council of State may decide to organize a public tender on the construction of new electricity generation capacity or, on the demand side, management measures to secure the sufficiency of electricity in the national market. This decision can be made should the supply of electricity not meet the electricity demand, whilst taking into account the electricity generation plants planned or under construction and transmission connections as well as demand side management measures. It is also required that there are no other means to secure the supply of electricity.[47]

198. According to the Electricity Market Act, the operator of a power plant is required to notify the EA of the construction, commissioning and decommissioning of a power plant.[48] Such notification enables the EA to monitor the national electricity generation capacity and thus to fulfil its responsibility for monitoring the balance between supply and demand of electricity in the electricity market.[49] Operators of power plants with a capacity of at least 100 MVA are required to give prior notification to the EA of service cuts that are to take place between 1 December and 28 February. The EA has the power to require power plant operators to postpone their planned service cuts if this does not cause any danger with regard to the technical operation or the safety of the power plant. The EA has the power to impose conditional fines for failure to postpone service cuts.[50]

---

46. *See* EK 19/2009 vp.
47. *See* s. 63 of the Electricity Market Act.
48. *See* s. 64 of the Electricity Market Act.
49. *See* s. 65 of the Electricity Market Act.
50. *See* s. 65 of the Electricity Market Act.

199. Collaboration among the Nordic electricity systems preceded the EU's internal electricity market project, which was launched at the beginning of the 1990s. NORDEL, an organization intended to facilitate cooperation among the Nordic TSOs, had already been established in 1963.[51] Electricity systems in Finland, Sweden, Norway and Denmark form part of the overall Nordic electricity network. The electricity systems that make up the Nordic network are synchronously balanced; that is, network frequency is the same all around the network, and there is always a momentary balance between the production and the consumption of electricity. These Nordic countries have also formed an integrated wholesale electricity market that has been operating since the late 1990s. However, the retail electricity markets of the Nordic countries have remained national.[52] The Nordic electricity market has gradually integrated with the Baltic and continental European electricity markets.

200. Currently, Finland is physically interconnected to the Swedish, Norwegian, Russian and Estonian transmission networks. Between Finland and Sweden, there is a transmission network with 400 kV and 220 kV AC (AC) interconnectors and the Fenno-Skan 1 (400 MW) and Fenno-Skan 2 (800 MW) direct current (DC) lines. The transmission capacity from Finland to Sweden is 1,650 MW and from Sweden to Finland 2,050 MW. Finland is connected to the Norwegian transmission network with a 220 kV AC interconnector. The transmission capacity from Finland to Norway and vice versa is 100 MW. Finland is physically interconnected to Russia with a DC station and one 400 kV and two 110 kV interconnectors, the interconnection capacity of these being 1,300 MW. The import capacity of the Estlink 1 DC cable between Finland and Estonia is 350 MW and Estlink 2 DC cable is 650 MW.

201. Notwithstanding the lengthy history of Nordic collaboration, the ways electricity is actually generated in Finland, Sweden, Norway and Denmark do not follow the same pattern. In Norway, electricity is mainly produced by hydropower. In Sweden, hydropower and nuclear power each account for approximately 45% of Sweden's electricity production. In Denmark, condensing power and CHP make up approximately 90% of its electricity production. The share of wind power in Denmark is continuously increasing. In Finland, nuclear power currently accounts for approximately one third of its electricity production. The share of condensing power and CHP is considerable (approximately 55%), whereas in Sweden the share of condensing power is moderate (approximately 6%).

202. The decision as to which electric power plants are to be exploited in electricity generation – that is, the dispatching – in the Nordic electricity market is not made centrally; rather, each individual electricity producer chooses the electricity power plant it deems to be the cheapest when its variable costs at a given point in time are calculated. In the Nordic market, electricity can thus be produced by a power plant that has the cheapest production costs. The ability to vary the fuels

51. On 1 Jul. 2009, the ETSO for Electricity took over all operational tasks of the six existing TSO associations in Europe, including NORDEL.
52. *See*, e.g., the European Commission's Decision 2006/422/EC, para 3.

relied on for electricity generation brings economic gains when compared with a situation where each country would need to provide individually for its own electricity production. Due to the almost complete dependence on hydropower in Norway's electricity generation and the large share of hydropower in Sweden's electricity generation, the price of electricity in the Nordic electricity market is heavily dependent on weather conditions – the more it rains, the lower the price of electricity is, and inversely the less it rains, the higher the price of electricity is.

203. The share of net electricity imports of all electricity consumed in Finland varies annually depending heavily on weather conditions – the amount of rainfall in the Nordic electricity market and whether there is a mild or cold winter. Generally, net electricity imports account for more than 10%.

§2. Generation Capacity

204. The total available generation capacity is roughly 13,300 MW, the total installed generation capacity being around 17 gigawatts (GW). The gross consumption of varies annually.

205. Because indigenous energy resources are scarce in Finland, multiple fuel types are used in the generation of power. Finland has hydropower of its own. It also has its own biomass as well as peat resources. Nuclear power accounts for approximately one-third (33.7% in 2016) of the electricity generated, hydropower for approximately 20% (23.6% in 2016), natural gas approximately 5% (5.3% in 2016) and biomass for approximately 15% (16.3% in 2016), coal for approximately 10% (10.4% in 2016), peat for approximately 4% (4.4% in 2016), oil for approximately 1% and wind approximately 5% (4.6% in 2016).[53] Of the total electricity produced, 45% was based on renewable energy sources, 78% carbon-neutral and 50% indigenous.

§3. Peak Load Power Reserve System

206. Electricity consumption in Finland has increased considerably during the past few years without any major electricity generation plants being commissioned. The construction of the fifth nuclear power plant has been delayed, and its commissioning is currently foreseen in 2019. Simultaneously, the use of condensing power has diminished due to the high price of such electricity generation in the Nordic electricity market. To tackle the situation, Act on Peak Load Power Reserves (Laki sähköntuotannon eräiden tehoreservien käytettävyyden varmistamisesta (1086/2006)) was adopted in 2006. The Act entered into force in December 2006 and remained in force until 2011 which was originally thought to be the time when the fifth nuclear power plant would be commissioned. The Act was subsequently

53. Energiateollisuuden verkkosivusto saatavilla, https://energia.fi/perustietoa/energiantuotanto/sähköntuotanto.

repealed by the Act on Peak Load Power Reserves Securing the Balance between Electricity Consumption and Production (117/2011).

207. The EA has the duty to define the volume of peak load power reserve each four years. Public procurement procedure is followed whilst selecting the peak load power reserve. The EA acts as the contracting authority carrying out the public procurement procedure. Condensing power plant operators may offer their power plants to be used in the system. They guarantee that these power plants are part of the system and that their use will be conducted according to the principles the plant operators have agreed upon with the TSO. These power plants are to be in a state of preparedness for at least twelve hours during the period between 1 December and 28 February and for at least one month during the rest of the year. The TSO compensates the power plant operators participating in the peak load power reserve system. The peak load reserve system obligations are defined as public service obligations.[54]

208. The purchase of the peak load power reserve is based on an open and non-discriminatory procedure. The offer of the power plant operator may be refused if the offered power plant does not meet with the requirements of the system, if the compensation for the power plant operator exceeds acceptable costs for a public service obligation or if the offer does not otherwise correspond to the conditions of the tender.[55]

209. When the power plant operator's offer is acceptable, the TSO concludes an agreement with the operator on the use of the power plant in the peak load power reserve system. The operator is obliged to carry out its task in accordance with the conditions stipulated in the Act on Peak Load Power Reserves Securing the Balance between Electricity Consumption and Production. The TSO defines the rules to be followed when the peak load power reserves are to be offered to the electricity market. The compensation paid to the operator may not exceed the level that is necessary to cover the costs incurred in the fulfilment of the operator's obligations.[56]

210. The peak load reserve system is financed by payments that the TSO collects from the users of the transmission services.[57]

211. It is submitted that in the strongly competition-based Finnish/Nordic electricity market, structured with determination during some fifteen years, the adoption of the system on peak load power reserve marks a noteworthy move towards a system based on public service. The Act has, in fact, introduced the notion of public service obligations in the modern Finnish electricity market. By applying the peak

54. *See* ss 1, 4, and 5 of the Act on Peak Load Power Reserves Securing the Balance between Electricity Consumption and Production.
55. *See* s. 7 of the Act on Peak Load Power Reserves Securing the Balance between Electricity Consumption and Production.
56. *See* ss 5–7 of the Act on Peak Load Power Reserves.
57. *See* s. 12 of the Act on Peak Load Power Reserves Securing the Balance between Electricity Consumption and Production.

load power reserve system, the State interferes artificially in the functioning of an electricity market that has been opened up to competition. The need to adopt the Act indicates that the competitive electricity market itself has not been capable of giving adequate investment signals to the electricity generators and therefore in extreme situations there is not enough electricity generation capacity available and the electricity market is malfunctioning.[58]

§4. Renewable Energy Sources

212. The share of renewable energy in the electricity production of Finland is some 45%.

213. For the time being, the government supports the generation of electricity from renewable energy sources by giving investment subsidies to energy investments aiming to increase the use of renewable energy sources in Finland's electricity generation. Such subsidies may be allocated to private firms, municipalities or other public bodies investing in projects to increase the use of renewable energy, energy saving and energy efficiency and projects to decrease the environmental damage related to the production and use of energy. The legal basis of such support schemes is stipulated in the Government Decree on the General Conditions of Granting Energy Aid (Valtioneuvoston asetus energiatuen myöntämisen yleisistä ehdoista (1063/2012)). Electricity generated from renewable energy sources is also supported by subsidies based on the Act regarding the Tax on Electric Energy and Fuels (Laki sähkön ja eräiden polttoaineiden valmisteverosta (1260/1996)).

214. The Act on the Subsidy for the Generation of Electricity from Renewable Energy Sources (laki uusiutuvilla energialähteillä tuotetun sähkön tuotantotuesta, 1396/2010) was entered into force in 2011. The aim of the Act is to enhance the generation of electricity from renewable energy sources and to strengthen the competitiveness of these sources as well as to diversify electricity generation. The aim is also to improve self-sufficiency in electricity production. The Act applies to state subsidy by means of feed-in tariff to electricity produced from wind power, biogas or firewood. The system is based on a market-based guaranteed price system. It concerns plants using forest converted chips, wind power, biogas or firewood in their electricity production. Wind power plants are accepted to the system for as long as the overall generation capacity of such plants exceeds 2,500 megavolt-ampere, for biogas plants the maximum capacity is 19 megavolt-ampere and for firewood power plants 150 megavolt-ampere.

58. Alice Guimaraes-Purokoski, *Vertikaalinen toimivallanjako EU-oikeudessa. Tutkimus yhteisön toimivallan kehittymisestä energia-alalla sekä julkisen palvelun velvoitteiden ja yleispalvelun sääntelystä sähkön sisämarkkinoilla. A-sarja N:o 290* (Helsinki: Suomalainen Lakimiesyhdistys, 2009). (Jyväskylä: Gummerus Kirjapaino Oy, 2009), 310.

215. The feed-in tariff system is reserved for power plants situated on the Finnish mainland or in Finnish territorial waters and that has been connected to the electricity network. The power plant shall need to have the functional and economic means to carry out electricity production.[59] Regarding wind power plants, biogas plants and firewood plants, the system is applicable only to new plants.[60]

216. Electricity producers willing to join the feed-in tariff system shall first need to make a preliminary announcement to the EA of its intention to join. It shall subsequently need to make an application to join the system to the EA. The application shall need to be made prior to the putting into operation of the new power plant.

217. The target price for the feed-in tariff is EUR 83.5/MWh for other power plants than such that are using forest converted chips in their electricity production. For power plants using forest converted chips, the target price is variable and interconnected with the price of peat.[61] The feed-in tariff would cover the difference between the market price of electricity and the feed-in tariff.[62] Producers accepted in the system are actors in the electricity market, but the application of the scheme eliminates the price risk associated with electricity generation from renewable energy sources as defined in the Act.

218. The EA pays the feed-in tariff for electricity producers after the expiry of each tariff period.

§5. Legislation on the Construction and Operation of Electricity Generation Plants

I. Environmental Law

219. Several pieces of environmental law apply to the planning, construction, operation or modification of electricity generation plants. According to the Environmental Protection Act (Ympäristönsuojelulaki (86/2000)), an environmental permit is required for activities causing the risk of pollution.[63] The Environmental Protection Decree (Ympäristönsuojeluasetus; 169/2000) specifies energy production to be among such activities. Energy production is described to include nuclear power stations and power stations, boiler plants or other facilities using oil, coal, wood, peat, gas or other combustible substances that have a maximum fuel power of over 5 MW or that use fuel with an annual energy value of at least 54 TJ. An environmental permit is also required for peat production and related drainage works if the production

59. Section 7 of the Act on the Subsidy for the Generation of Electricity from Renewable Energy Sources.
60. Sections 9, 10 and 11 of the Act on the Subsidy for the Generation of Electricity from Renewable Energy Sources.
61. Section 23 of the Act on the Subsidy for the Generation of Electricity from Renewable Energy Sources.
62. *Ibid.*, 8–9, 45.
63. *See* ss 3.1 and 28.1 of the Environmental Protection Act.

area exceeds 10 hectares.[64] The Environmental Permit Authority is responsible for issuing environmental permits relating to the above-mentioned energy production activities.[65]

220. All power plants will need to comply with the requirements set up in the Land Use and Building Act (Maankäyttö- ja rakennuslaki (132/1999)). A more detailed examination of this law is presented in Part IV, Chapter 5, 'Land Use and Expropriation'.

221. While studying the objectives of the Environmental Protection Act and the Land Use and Building Act, one observes a certain interaction between environmental law and energy law. According to the Land Use and Building Act, regional land use planning aims to promote, for example, economical utilization of natural resources,[66] whereas the Environmental Protection Act aims, for example, to enhance the rational utilization of natural resources, to prevent climate change and to support sustainable development.[67] It is, however, to be noted that there is no coherent set of energy laws stipulating the energy-specific objectives that should be followed while planning or constructing electricity generation plants. Apart from government energy strategies that are approved by the Council of State and subsequently dealt with by the Finnish Parliament, a special regime obliging the involvement of the Finnish government and the Finnish Parliament is applicable solely to new nuclear power plants and new hydropower plants. There is also the Act on Feed-In Tariff of Electricity Produced from Fuel Peat in Condensing Power Plants (Laki polttoturpeesta lauhdutusvoimalaitoksissa tuotetun sähkön syöttötariffista (322/2007)). These regimes will be dealt with further in the later sections on nuclear power, hydropower and peat.

II. The Impact of EU Energy Law on the Choice of Fuels

222. The impact of EU energy law on the fuels to be used in an EU Member State's electricity generation and on the decision-making concerning the construction of new electricity generation plants is rather restricted. Each EU Member State has the right to choose the palette of fuels that are used in its electricity generation, and there are no direct EU legal obligations as to which energy resources should or should not be used in a Member State's electricity generation. While this leaves the Member States a large area in which to manoeuvre, EU law does oblige Member States to follow the EIA procedure prior to constructing a new electricity generation plant or upgrading the capacity of an existing plant and does create obligations regarding large combustion plants (LCPs) and incineration of waste. For more details on the EIA procedure, *see* Part IV, Chapter 2, 'Decision-Making and Public

64. *See* s. 1, items 3.a and b and 7.d of the Environmental Protection Decree.
65. *See* s. 5, items 3.a and b and 5.c of the Environmental Protection Decree.
66. *See* s. 5.1 of the Land Use and Building Act.
67. *See* s. 1, items 6 and 7 of Environmental Protection Act.

Participation'. For further information on LCP requirements and waste incineration, *see* Part IV, Chapter 4, 'Environmental Protection and Waste Management', section 6.

223. It is submitted that Directive 2001/77/EC of the European Parliament and Council on the promotion of electricity produced from renewable energy sources in the internal electricity market[68] as amended and its replacement, Directive 2009/28/EC of the European Parliament and Council on the promotion of energy produced from renewable energy sources,[69] have had an indirect effect on Member States' choices among different energy sources used in their electricity generation. Energy produced from renewable energy sources is defined in Article 2a of Directive 2009/28/EC. Renewable energy is produced from energy sources other than fossil fuels – that is, from wind or solar power, air thermal power, geothermal energy, hydrothermal energy and ocean power, hydropower, biomass, gas and biogas from dumping areas and sewage treatment plants. Directive 2001/77/EC set non-obligatory targets for the share of renewable energy sources in the Member States' electricity generation. The non-obligatory target set for Finland in the Annex of the Renewable energy sources directive is currently 33%. Directive 2009/28/EC sets obligatory targets for the share of renewable energy sources in the Member States' total energy consumption by 2020.[70] The obligatory target for Finland is 38%. The Member States must implement Directive 2009/28/EC through their national legislation by 5 December 2010 at the latest. Although neither Directive 2001/77/EC nor Directive 2009/28/EC obliges the Member States to choose a specific renewable energy source to be used in their electricity generation, the directives do move Member States towards increasing the utilization of renewable energy resources in their electricity production and thus diminish indirectly the utilization of other than renewable energy sources in Member States' electricity generation.

III. EU Public Procurement Provisions Applying to Entities Operating in the Energy Services Sector

224. According to Article 3.1 of Directive 2004/17/EC coordinating the procurement procedures of entities operating in the water, energy, transport and postal services sectors,[71] the Directive shall apply to the following activities in the electricity sector:

68. Directive 2001/77/EC of the European Parliament and of the Council of 27 Sep. 2001 on the promotion of electricity produced from renewable energy sources in the internal electricity market, OJ No. L 283, 27 Oct. 2001, 33.
69. Directive 2009/28/EC of the European Parliament and of the Council of 23 Apr. 2009 on the promotion of energy produced from renewable energy sources, OJ No. L 140, 5 Jun. 2009, 16.
70. *See* Arts 1, 3.1, 3.2 and 3.3 and Annex I.A.
71. Directive 2004/17/EC of the European Parliament and of the Council of 31 Mar. 2004 coordinating the procurement procedures of entities operating in the water, energy, transport and postal services sectors, OJ No. L 134, 30 Apr. 2004, 1–113.

(a) the provision or operation of fixed networks intended to provide a service to the public in connection with the production, transport or distribution of electricity; or
(b) the supply of electricity to such networks.

225. Article 30.1 of Directive 2004/17/EC provides that contracts intended to enable, for example, the above-mentioned activities in the electricity sector to be carried out will not be subject to the Directive if, in the Member State in which it is performed, the activity is directly exposed to competition in markets to which access is not restricted. According to Article 30.2 of Directive 2004/17/EC, the question of whether an activity is directly exposed to competition is decided on the basis of criteria that are in conformity with the treaty provision on competition, such as the characteristics of the goods or services concerned, the existence of alternative goods or services, the prices and the actual or potential presence of more than one supplier of the goods or services in question.

226. Finland submitted a request in accordance with Article 30.4 of Directive 2004/17/EC on 20 February 2006. The request concerned production, including cogeneration, as well as the sale (wholesale and retail) of electricity.

227. The European Commission rendered its Decision on the Finnish request on 19 June 2006.[72] As to the electricity generation activities, the Commission referred in its Decision to its earlier Communication,[73] noting that with respect to electricity generation, one indicator of the degree of competition on national markets is the total market share of the biggest three producers. It concluded that during significant parts of the year, there is a competitive pressure derived from the potential to obtain electricity from outside Finnish territory, the more so as no transmission fee is charged between the Nordic countries. The Commission stated this to indicate a direct exposure to competition. The Commission also considered the workings of the balancing markets as an indicator with respect to electricity production.

228. The Commission concluded that the condition of direct exposure to competition laid down in Article 30.1 of Directive 2004/17/EC should be considered to be met with respect to the production and sale of electricity in Finland, excluding the Åland Islands. The further condition of free access to the activity was deemed to be met in the Finnish electricity market.

72. Commission Decision of 19 Jun. 2006 establishing that Art. 30(1) of Directive 2004/17/EC of the European Parliament and of the Council coordinating the procurement procedures of entities operating in the water, energy, transport and postal services sectors applies to the production and sale of electricity in Finland, excluding the Åland Islands (2006/422/EC), OJ No. L 168, 21 Jun. 2006, 33–36.

73. Communication from the Commission to the Council and the European Parliament, 'Report on Progress in Creating the Internal Gas and Electricity Market', COM(2005) 568 final of 15 Nov. 2005.

229. Thus, Article 1 of the Commission's Decision provides that Directive 2004/17/EC does not apply to contracts awarded by contracting entities and intended to enable them to carry out electricity generation or the sale of electricity in Finland, excluding the Åland Islands.

230. It is to be noted that the Commission does not make any distinction in its Decision as to the fuel to be used in electricity generation. Its Decision is therefore applicable to all means of electricity generation.

IV. Electricity Security

231. According to the Electricity Security Act (Sähköturvallisuuslaki (410/1996)), each appliance and installation generating electricity will need to be planned, constructed, produced, fixed, overhauled and used in a way that does not cause danger to anyone's life, health or property. These appliances and installations must not cause excessive electrical or electromagnetic disturbance, and their functioning must not be easily disturbed electrically or electromagnetically. These requirements will need to be fulfilled prior to putting these appliances and installations into operation. It is the responsibility of the constructor of the appliance or installation to make sure that these requirements are fulfilled. Should the constructor neglect to carry out or be prevented from carrying out these responsibilities, the possessor of the appliance or installation becomes responsible for it.[74]

232. The national authority responsible for ensuring that appliances and installations generating electricity fulfil the requirements prescribed in the Electricity Security Act is the Safety Technology Authority (*Turvatekniikan keskus* or TUKES).

V. Nuclear Power

233. There are currently four nuclear power units in operation in Finland: two pressurized water reactors (PWRs) owned and operated by Fortum PLC are sited at Loviisa, and two boiling water reactors (BWRs) owned and operated by Teollisuuden Voima Oyj (TVO) are sited at Olkiluoto. The first unit at Loviisa was commissioned in 1977 and the second in 1980. The installed capacity of both these units is 488 MW. The first unit at Olkiluoto was commissioned in 1978 and the second in 1980. The installed capacity of both these plants is 860 MW.

234. There is no domestic production of nuclear fuel in Finland, and, thus, all the nuclear fuel used in Finland for electricity generation are purchased from abroad.

74. *See* ss 1, 4, 5, 16, 17, 19 of Electricity Security Act.

235. A special regime enacted by the Nuclear Energy Act (Ydinenergialaki (990/1987)) applies to the construction of new nuclear power plants. The overall objective of the Nuclear Energy Act is to maintain the utilization of nuclear energy in accordance with the general interest of the society and in particular to make sure that the utilization of nuclear energy is safe from the point of view of the people and the environment and does not promote the proliferation of nuclear weapons. The general principles of the Nuclear Energy Act are thus that the utilization of nuclear energy should be both in the general interest of the society and safe by not harming the people, environment or property.[75]

236. The utilization of nuclear energy requires a licence; minor research and development activities are exempted from the licence requirement.[76] The licensing procedure applied to the construction of a new nuclear power plant is divided into three phases: (1) decision-in-principle by the Council of State, (2) construction licence and (3) licence to operate. These phases are further explained below.

A. *Decision-in-Principle by the Council of State*

237. First, the construction of a new nuclear power plant, having a notable general significance, requires a decision-in-principle by the Council of State. The purpose of the decision-in-principle is to verify that the construction of the nuclear power plant is in accordance with the general interest of the society. All nuclear power plants aiming to generate nuclear energy with a thermal capacity exceeding 50 MW are deemed to have a notable general significance, and, thus, the requirement of the decision-in-principle by the Council of State applies.[77]

238. The application for a decision-in-principle is addressed to the Council of State. The Ministry of Employment and the Economy is the authority that prepares the decision-in-principle. The Ministry is first required to seek a preliminary prognosis of the security of the planned nuclear power plant from the Radiation and Nuclear Safety Authority (*Säteilyturvakeskus*). It must also ask for opinions on the planned nuclear power plant from the Ministry of the Environment, from the municipal council of the municipality where the nuclear power plant is to be sited and from the neighbouring municipalities.[78] It is to be noted that, in addition to preparing the decision-in-principle, the Ministry of Employment and the Economy applies the EIA procedure relating to the construction of new nuclear power plants.[79] This choice of the authority to carry out these tasks may illustrate the pertinence of energy policy-specific aspects of the licensing procedure as it relates to the construction of new nuclear power plants.

75. *See* ss 1, 5, 6 of the Nuclear Energy Act.
76. *See* s. 8 of the Nuclear Energy Act.
77. *See* s. 11 of the Nuclear Energy Act.
78. *See* s. 12 of the Nuclear Energy Act.
79. *See* s. 6.3 of the Environmental Impact Assessment Act.

239. Prior to the Council of State's decision-in-principle, the applicant is required to make public a general explanation regarding the planned nuclear power plant, its estimated environmental impact and its security. The Ministry of Employment and the Economy must ensure that the inhabitants of the immediate surroundings of the planned nuclear power plant and the affected municipalities and local authorities have the opportunity to express their opinions on the planned nuclear power plant in written form. The Ministry must also organize a public hearing on the site of the planned nuclear power plant. All opinions expressed during these preparatory phases are forwarded to the Council of State.[80]

240. A prerequisite for the decision-in-principle is that the municipality where the planned nuclear power plant is to be sited has given its approval for its construction and that, conditions sufficient to ensure, in particular, the security of the planned nuclear power plant exist. If these prerequisites are met, the Council of State will consider the decision-in-principle on the basis of the general interest of the society. It will, in its consideration, take into account the benefits and disadvantages of the nuclear power plant and pay a particular attention to: (1) the importance of the planned nuclear power plant to the security of the electricity supply of the State, (2) the suitability of the municipality where the nuclear power plant is to be sited and the environmental impact of that plant and (3) the arrangements relating to nuclear fuel management and nuclear waste management.[81]

241. The decision-in-principle is by its very nature political, and it cannot be appealed.[82] Notwithstanding the fact that the conditions to be applied by the Council of State in its decision-making are transparently stipulated in the Nuclear Energy Act, some of these requirements do leave the Council a rather large area in which to manoeuvre in its consideration of the application for the decision-in-principle. This is apparent vis-à-vis the Council of State's consideration of the existence of the general interest of the society and of the importance of the planned nuclear power plant to the security of the electricity supply of the State. The context of the Council of State's consideration is thus manifestly nationwide, not EU-wide. The interrelationship of the decision-in-principle to the EU Treaty provisions on the freedom of establishment and the free movement of capital might be of some further academic interest.

242. There are, at the moment, three applications for decisions-in-principle on the construction of new nuclear power plants pending before the Ministry of Employment and the Economy. The applicants are TVO, Fortum and Fennovoima. The installed capacities of the planned nuclear power plants of TVO and of Fortum would be 1,000 to 1,800 MW. The planned nuclear power plant of TVO would be sited at Olkiluoto and that of Fortum at Loviisa. Fennovoima has applied for the construction of either one nuclear power plant with an installed capacity of some 1,800 MW or two smaller units with an installed capacity of 1,000 to 1,200 MW

80. *See* s. 13 of the Nuclear Energy Act.
81. *See* s. 14 of the Nuclear Energy Act.
82. *See* s. 75 of the Nuclear Energy Act.

each. The planned nuclear power unit(s) of Fennovoima would be sited at Simo, Pyhäjoki or Ruotsinpyhtää. All the municipalities where the new nuclear power plants are to be sited – that is, Olkiluoto, Loviisa, Simo, Pyhäjoki and Ruotsinpyhtää – have already given their approval to the siting. The approvals of Loviisa and Ruotsinpyhtää have been appealed by an *actio popularis* to the administrative court. The estimated timetable for submitting the applications to the Council of State for consideration is at the turn of the year 2009/2010.

243. The decision-in-principle then needs to be scrutinized and approved in the Parliament by a majority of the votes cast. The Parliament has the power either to repeal or to give its approval to the decision-in-principle as it stands; the Parliament cannot change its contents. There are no means to appeal the approval or repeal the decision-in-principle by the Parliament.[83]

244. The Parliament has once repealed a decision-in-principle of the Council of State on the construction of a new nuclear power plant. This took place in 1993. The nuclear power plant planned by IVO was to be sited in Loviisa. There were 107 votes cast against the decision-in-principle and 90 votes for it.

245. The applicant is not allowed to take any measures that might, by their economic importance, impede the ability of the Council of State or the Parliament to use their discretion when deciding the issue.[84]

B. Construction Licence

246. After the decision-in-principle is approved, the proposed nuclear power plant requires a construction licence issued by the Council of State. The construction licence may be issued only to a natural person, a legal person or an authority coming under the jurisdiction of an EU Member State.[85] The conditions relating to the granting of the construction licence are stipulated in the Nuclear Energy Act (section 18) and include, for example, the applicant's safety plans, siting of the nuclear power plant, conservation of the environment, nuclear waste management and final disposal of high-level radioactive waste. There needs to be an area reserved for the construction of the nuclear power plant in the local detailed plan based on the Land Use and Building Act, and it is necessary that the applicant have it in its possession for the operation of the nuclear power plant. The applicant is also required to have sufficient economic means to carry out the plan and to operate the nuclear power plant.[86]

247. The Council of State's decision to issue the construction licence can be appealed to the Supreme Administrative Court. The appeal can be grounded on the

83. *See* s. 15.1 of the Nuclear Energy Act.
84. *See* s. 15.2 of the Nuclear Energy Act.
85. *See* s. 17 of the Nuclear Energy Act.
86. *See* ss 16 and 18 of the Nuclear Energy Act.

legality of the licence but not on its expediency, which is deemed to be within the political discretion of the Council of State.

248. TVO applied for a licence to construct a new nuclear power unit at Olkiluoto in 2001 (Olkiluoto 3). The decision-in-principle of the Council of State was made in 2002. The Parliament gave its approval to the decision-in-principle in April/May 2002. The Council of State granted the construction licence on 17 February 2005. The new plant is a third-generation European pressurized water reactor (EPW) with a technical operating lifetime of sixty years. The installed capacity of the new plant is 1,600 MW. The commercial operation of the new plant is currently expected to begin in 2012 – some four years later than initially planned. The delay has caused legal proceedings between the subscriber and the vendor consortium of Areva and Siemens.

C. Operating Licence

249. Finally, a new nuclear power plant requires an operating licence, which is also issued by the Council of State. The Ministry of Employment and the Economy is responsible for the preparation of the operating licence. The operating licence may be issued if the nuclear power plant and its operation fulfil the safety requirements of the Nuclear Energy Act and if the safety of the employees and of the population is duly taken into account. The applicant is also required to have sufficient and adequate means of organizing the nuclear waste management, the final disposal of nuclear waste and the decommissioning of the nuclear power plant. The applicant must also have sufficient expertise and must meet the requirements necessary to operate the nuclear power plant in a safe way and in accordance with the international treaty obligations binding Finland.[87]

250. The operating licence may be issued only to a natural person, a legal person or an authority coming under the jurisdiction of an EU Member State.[88] EEA Member State residents and residents of third countries are thus not allowed to operate a nuclear power plant in Finland.

251. A nuclear power plant cannot be operated until the Radiation and Nuclear Safety Authority has approved the safety requirements and the Ministry of Employment and the Economy has verified that the applicant is prepared to pay the costs of nuclear waste management.[89]

252. The Council of State's decision to issue the construction licence can be appealed to the Supreme Administrative Court. The appeal can be grounded on the legality of the licence but not on its expediency, which is deemed to be within the political discretion of the Council of State.

87. *See* s. 20.1 of the Nuclear Energy Act.
88. *See* s. 17 of the Nuclear Energy Act.
89. *See* s. 20.2 of the Nuclear Energy Act.

253. The operating licence is issued for a fixed period of time. The operating licence may expire if the operation of the nuclear power plant does not commence within a fixed period counted from the date of issue of the licence.[90]

254. The conditions of the operating licence may be modified in order to comply with the general principles of the Nuclear Energy Act as well as the requirements of the operating licence.[91] The modification of the conditions of the operating licence may prove to be necessary to ensure the safe utilization of nuclear energy, to secure nuclear waste management, to fulfil security or preparedness requirements, to meet the obligations of international nuclear energy treaties or to prevent the proliferation of nuclear weapons.

255. The operating licence may be cancelled if there is a significant departure from the general principles of the Nuclear Energy Act applicable to the operation of nuclear energy. This may be the case where the operator breaches the conditions of the licence or neglects the requirement to prepare for the costs of nuclear waste management.[92]

VI. Hydropower

256. The first Finnish hydropower plant that was utilized for nationwide electricity production was sited at Imatrankoski in the southeastern part of Finland in the 1920s. Since then, the biggest rivers in the northern part of Finland – that is, the Kemijoki and the Oulujoki, both of which empty into the northern part of the Gulf of Bothnia – have been exploited for hydropower generation. The most important rivers in the Gulf of Bothnia have also been harnessed for hydropower generation.

257. Hydropower generation currently accounts for approximately 20% of Finland's total electricity generation,[93] corresponding to 13.2 TWh[94] on average annually. It is not possible to substantially exploit new hydropower because most waterfalls that can be exploited for hydropower generation are already harnessed. Most waterfalls that could – based on their energy potential – be exploited for hydropower generation are protected by law due to their natural values. The Act on the Protection of Falls (Koskiensuojelulaki (35/1987)) forbids the construction of hydropower plants on specific water systems or parts of water systems listed in the Act. There are altogether fifty-two water systems or parts of water systems where construction of a hydropower plant is forbidden.[95] The Act on the Special Protection of Ounasjoki (Laki Ounasjoen erityissuojelusta (703/1983)) and the Act on the

90. *See* s. 24 of the Nuclear Energy Act.
91. *See* s. 25 of the Nuclear Energy Act.
92. *See* s. 26 of the Nuclear Energy Act.
93. *See* International Energy Agency, 'Energy Policies of IEA Countries, Finland 2007 Review', 63, 85.
94. Pitkän aikavälin ilmasto- ja energiastrategia. Valtioneuvoston selonteko eduskunnalle 6. päivänä marraskuuta 2008, s. 40.
95. *See* s. 1 of the Act on the Protection of Falls.

Special Protection of Kyrönjoki (Laki Kyrönjoen erityissuojelusta (1139/1991)) forbid the construction of hydropower plants on these specific water systems.

258. The exploitation of hydropower is specifically regulated by Chapter 3 of the Water Act (Vesilaki (264/1961)), but certain general provisions of Chapter 2 of the Water Act on the construction of the water system are also of utmost pertinence when permission to construct a new hydropower plant is sought. It is to be noted that the Water Act and not the Environmental Protection Act applies to, for example, a water power plant project requiring the building of a reservoir/artificial lake, which may have water contamination effects.[96] The national authority with jurisdiction to issue water licences based on the Water Act is the Environmental Permit Authority. Its decisions may be appealed to the Vaasa Administrative Court and further to the Supreme Administrative Court.

259. The proprietor of the water system also possesses the hydropower of this system. The status of hydropower ownership is considered to be comparable to that of real estate ownership.[97]

260. According to section 5 of Chapter 2 of the Water Act, a construction licence cannot be issued if the construction would imperil public health, cause considerable harmful changes in the relations of the natural environment or in the water nature or its function or cause living or economic conditions of the region to seriously deteriorate. If none of these absolute conditions is fulfilled, section 6 of Chapter 2 becomes applicable. According to this provision, the licence may be issued if the construction does not significantly offend private or public interest and if the plan for the power plant is, due to its profitable or protective nature, necessary for the rational utilization of the water area or for the use of property situated around it for another profitable economic activity. This provision stipulates an interest comparison. Should the disadvantages of the plan exceed its advantages, the licence may not be issued.

261. The construction of a water power plant also requires a construction licence based on section 125 of the Land Use and Building Act. The applicant is required to take into consideration the prescriptions of the city plan, but the fact that the planned hydropower plant is included into the city plan does not exempt the applicant from the requirement to apply for a construction licence based on the Land Use and Building Act.[98] According to section 130 of the Land Use and Building Act, the authority with jurisdiction to issue construction licences is the municipal authority responsible for building surveillance. The decision of the municipal authority responsible for building surveillance may be appealed to the appropriate administrative court, which is determined on the basis of section 12 of the Act on Administrative Proceedings (Hallintolainkäyttölaki (586/1996)).

---

96. Kari Kuusiniemi (ed.), *Uusi ympäristönsuojelulainsäädäntö* (Helsinki: Edita, 2001), 423.
97. *Ibid.*, 435, 444.
98. *Ibid.*, 427.

262. In addition to these licensing requirements, the Natural Conservation Act may apply to the construction of a new hydropower plant. This is the case, for example, where the construction of the planned hydropower plant would probably considerably degrade the natural values of an area included in the Natura 2000 network, based on Council Directive 92/43/EEC of 21 May 1992 on the conservation of natural habitats and of wild fauna and flora. The same applies where the planned hydropower plant would be constructed outside the Natura 2000 network, but would probably cause considerable deterioration of an area included in the Natura 2000 network.[99] In these cases, the developer is required to assess the impact of the plan on the areas concerned. The licensing authority must verify that the developer has completed the Natura 2000 assessment and then seek an opinion on the plan from the appropriate Regional Environment Centre and from those who have the area affected in their possession. Should it be determined that the completion of the plan would considerably degrade the natural values of the area concerned, the licensing authority is not allowed to issue the licence. The plan may be approved notwithstanding its negative impact on the natural values if the Council of State decides that a very important public interest makes completion of the plan imperative and there is no alternate solution. If there are certain habitats or species listed in Annex I or II of Council Directive 92/43/EEC in the area concerned, the approval of the Council of State presupposes that, in addition to the requirements noted above, there are imperative reasons related to the health of people, the public security or the environment that would have very important profitable effects elsewhere, thus requiring the approval of the plan. In the latter mentioned case, the Council of State consults the European Commission.[100]

263. It is submitted that 'imperative reasons based on a very important public interest' are by definition reasons of expediency and may be related to, for example, the security of the energy supply, notwithstanding the absence of energy-specific notions in the pertinent provision of the Natural Conservation Act. The inspiration for this submission may be drawn from the case law of the Court of Justice of the European Communities (EC) relating to the EC Treaty provisions on the free movement of goods (Article 28 EC) and exceptions to this (Article 30 EC). The European Court of Justice concluded in its famous judgment in case 72/83, *Campus Oil*, that the notion of public security in Article 30 EC includes security of the energy supply.[101]

264. The decision of the Council of State may be appealed to the Supreme Administrative Court. As explained earlier in the context of the regime applicable to the construction of new nuclear power plants, an appeal of the decision of the Council of State can be grounded on the legality of the licence, but not on its expediency.

---

99. *See* s. 65.1 of the Natural Conservation Act.
100. *See* s. 66 of the Natural Conservation Act.
101. Case 72/83, *Campus Oil*, judgment 10 Jul. 1984, ECR, 1984, 2727, paras 27, 33–35, 37, 39, 44, 45, 47 and 51. *See also* case C-398/98, *Commission v. Greece*, judgment of 25 Oct. 2001, ECR, 2001, I-7915, confirming the conclusions of the earlier *Campus Oil* case.

265. The EIA may be completed simultaneously with the impact assessment stipulated in the Natural Conservation Act.

266. The most notable hydropower construction plan of the immediate past was the plan to construct the Vuotos reservoir and hydropower plant in the Kemijoki water area in the northern part of Finland. The Supreme Administrative Court, by its decision of 18 December 2002 (KHO: 2002:86, deposit copy no. 3339, Diary No. 2405/3/01), annulled an earlier decision of the Water Court (*vesioikeus*) of 29 February 2000 to allow a construction permit to be issued to Kemijoki Oy. The Supreme Administrative Court thus confirmed the decision of the appellate Vaasa Administrative Court of 14 July 2001 annulling the decision of the Water Court. The Supreme Administrative Court based its decision on the application of section 5 of Chapter 2 of the Water Act as it stood at the point in time when the application was first initiated. As noted earlier, each of the three conditions listed in that provision forms an absolute obstacle to the construction in the water system. This was the first time that an application for a construction licence for a new hydropower plant was refused on the basis of that provision. The Supreme Administrative Court stated that the application of that provision is by its very nature a legal consideration and not one based on the expediency of the plan. Consideration based on expediency is generally deemed to belong to the executive power – that is, the government – and not to the judiciary.

267. Both the Vaasa Administrative Court and the Supreme Administrative Court concluded that the plan did not imperil public health or gravely damage living or economic conditions of the region. Thus, two of the three conditions of the provision were not fulfilled. However, both courts concluded that the plan would cause considerable and far-reaching harmful changes in the relations of the natural environment or in the water nature or its function. During the time when the application was introduced, the last-mentioned condition was somewhat stricter than it currently is. According to the provision applicable at the time, not only was it required that the plan would cause considerable and harmful changes in the relations of the natural environment or in the water nature or its function, but also it was required that these changes would be far-reaching. The Supreme Administrative Court noted that some of the expressions in the provision are by their very nature flexible, mentioning among others *harmful change*, *far-reaching* and, in particular, 'considerable'. When interpreting this provision in the context of the planned Vuotos reservoir, the Supreme Administrative Court drew inspiration from, among other things, the particular importance the legislature had given to the natural values during the time the provision was approved.[102] The Supreme Administrative Court considered, among other factors, that the Vuotos region was precious by its nature and the planned reservoir would largely destroy the natural flora and

102. An individual factor proving the particular importance of the natural values mentioned in the Decision was the need expressed by the Parliament to amend the expertise in natural economy in the Supreme Administrative Court. It is to be noted that this Decision of the Supreme Administrative Court was not unanimous and that the dissenting opinion was expressed by the environmental counsel of the Supreme Administrative Court.

fauna of the region. This reasoning of the Supreme Administrative Court is seen by some commentators as reflecting the changing values in the interpretation of environmental legislation.[103]

268. The Council of State stated in its most recent long-term climate and energy strategy, issued at the end of 2008, that the government in power may not during its term of office put forward a government proposal aiming to amend the Water Act in order to enable the construction of the Vuotos reservoir.[104] The current legislative period terminates in the spring of 2011. It has been common for some time now that the government sits throughout the whole legislative period. Thus, until the spring of 2011, no Council of State construction licences are foreseen for the Vuotos reservoir.

VII. Peat

269. Peat is an indigenous energy resource in Finland. Of all the EU Member States, Ireland, Estonia and Sweden utilize peat in their energy production. Some 80,000 hectares of the total 10 million hectares of Finnish peatland/swamp are used for peat production.[105] Peat is utilized to strengthen the security of the national energy supply under both normal and exceptional conditions. Peat may be utilized as a substitute for imported fuels used for energy production – coal and natural gas, in particular – thus diversifying the supply of energy resources. The significance of peat production in northern, eastern and central Finland is considerable when estimated from an employment and regional policy perspective.[106] Peat makes up some 7%–8% of the fuel used to generate electricity in Finland if calculated by TWh/a.[107]

270. The most important negative aspect of the utilization of peat in energy production is its large CO_2 content, which is calculated on the basis of the amount of CO_2 emissions resulting from burning peat. The CO_2 content of peat is greater than that of coal, thus diminishing the ability to utilize peat in future energy production as the CO_2 allowances set forth by the emissions trading regimes are becoming smaller.[108] For further information on emissions trading regimes, *see* Part IV.

---

103. Kari Kuusiniemi, 'Arvojen muutos ja ympäristölakien tulkinta teoksessa Oikeuden tavoitteet ja menettelyt, Muistokirja Hannu Tapani Klamille', in *Turun yliopiston oikeustieteellisen tiedekunnan julkaisuja A. juhlajulkaisut N:o 12*, ed. Ari-Matti Nuutila (Helsinki: Edita, 2003), 63–79.
104. Pitkän aikavälin ilmasto- ja energiastrategia. Valtioneuvoston selonteko eduskunnalle 6. päivänä marraskuuta 2008, 40.
105. *Ibid.*, 43.
106. *Ibid.*, 42.
107. Annual Report 2009 – Energy Market Authority, Finland, 62. Figures date back to 2008.
108. Pitkän aikavälin ilmasto- ja energiastrategia. Valtioneuvoston selonteko eduskunnalle 6. päivänä marraskuuta 2008, 42.

271. The construction of a peat production reserve requires an environmental permit issued by the Environmental Permit Authority on the basis of the Environmental Protection Act. The Natural Conservation Act may also apply if the area concerned is situated in the Natura 2000 network.[109]

272. The Act on Feed-In Tariff of Electricity Produced from Fuel Peat in Condensing Power Plants (Laki polttoturpeesta lauhdutusvoimalaitoksissa tuotetun sähkön syöttötariffista (322/2007)) was adopted on 30 March 2007. The purpose of this fixed-term act, which expired on 31 December 2010, is to enhance the security of the electricity supply in Finland. To do this, the Act provides that, in the Finnish electricity system, primacy among the electricity generation plants is given to condensing power plants burning domestic peat instead of such plants burning coal, natural gas or oil. The feed-in tariff is paid for electricity generated by burning domestic peat that is then fed into the network. The transmission network operator pays to the electricity generator the feed-in tariff, which is calculated on the basis of a detailed formula using MWh of electricity generated by burning peat. The formula is defined in section 4 of the Act. The feed-in tariff system is financed by a specific feed-in tariff charge collected by the transmission network operator from the electricity consumers. The EA supervises the application of the Act and is responsible for recovering feed-in tariff pay that is paid erroneously, is too much or is clearly unfounded.

273. According to the government bill,[110] the Act was meant to promote the security of supply of domestic peat fuel and the competitiveness of domestic peat fuel in the condensing power plants. The system, which was established for a fixed period of time, expires at the end of 2010 because it was estimated that by then the fifth nuclear power station would be commissioned. Due to its high price as a result of its high CO_2 content, the competitiveness of domestic peat – as well as other fuels such as coal and heavy fuel oil used in condensing power plants – is rather weak vis-à-vis other fuels used for electricity generation. Often condensing power plants burning peat – or coal and heavy fuel oil – are used for a very limited period of time per year.

274. According to the government bill, the feed-in tariff was not to be regarded as state aid, and, therefore, the requirement based on Article 88.3 EC to notify the European Commission of it was not considered to apply. This conclusion was drawn from the case law of the European Court of Justice. The Court, in case C-379/98, *PreussenElektra*, determined that a German feed-in tariff system aiming to enhance the utilization of electricity produced from renewable energy resources generated in Germany was in accordance with the EC state aid rules.

---

109. As an example of a case where the requirements of Directive 92/43/EEC on the Conservation of Natural Habitats and of Wild Fauna, as implemented in the Natural Conservation Act, were not fulfilled, *see* the judgment of the Supreme Administrative Court of 7 Oct. 2008, KHO: 2008:72.

110. Hallituksen esitys Eduskunnalle polttoturpeen ja sillä tuotetun sähkön toimitusvarmuuden turvaamista koskevaksi lainsäädännöksi, HE 100/2006 vp.

275. A potentially pertinent difference between the Finnish feed-in tariff system and the German regime based on *Stormeinspeisungsgesetz*, which was scrutinized in the *PreussenElektra* case, is that, while the German system applied only to electricity generated domestically, the Finnish system aims also to enhance the competitiveness of domestic peat fuel, consequently weakening the competitiveness of other non-domestic (and domestic) fuels used in the electricity generation. Thus, the Finnish system protects both domestic fuel and domestic electricity generation. It is also to be noted that, contrary to what is stated in the government bill, the Court of Justice did not find that the German system was in accordance with Article 28 EC. Rather, the Court of Justice found on good grounds that the German system breached Article 28 EC but deemed that the system was justified, despite this infringement of EC law. The justifying grounds were twofold. First, the Court of Justice convoked Article 30 EC, and, second, the Court considered that justification grounds applied and there the ground based on environmental protection although the system directly discriminated against electricity produced from renewable energy resources in other EU Member States. It is to be noted, however, that according to Article 11.4 of Directive 2003/54/EC, which was in force during the time when the national law was adopted, a Member State may, for reasons of security of supply, direct that priority be given to the dispatch of generating installations using indigenous primary energy fuel sources, to an extent not exceeding in any calendar year, 15% of the overall primary energy necessary to produce the electricity consumed in the Member State concerned. A similar provision was included in Article 15.4 of Directive 2009/72/EC. These provisions would seem to be applicable to the feed-in tariff applied to indigenous fuel peat.

276. During the parliamentary scrutiny of the government bill, the Parliamentary Standing Committee on Environment considered that the acceptability of the Act on Feed-In Tariff of Electricity Produced from Fuel Peat in Condensing Power Plants from the environmental point of view was based on the fact that, due to the feed-in tariff system, domestic peat fuel would become a more profitable fuel option than coal.[111] One is left rather perplexed as to find where the environmental thinking is, behind this statement. The Parliamentary Standing Committee on Economic Affairs noted that the impact of the feed-in tariff system in terms of increasing CO_2 emissions would be rather limited.[112]

§6. Ownership of Electricity Generation Plants

277. There are some 120 companies generating electricity and approximately 550 electricity generation plants. Of the total installed capacity of some 16,900 MW, the share of fossil fuels is approximately 50% (8,417 MW), hydropower less than 20% (3,031 MW), renewable energy sources some 17% (2,801 MW) and nuclear

111. *See* Ympäristövaliokunnan lausunto 35/2006 vp – Hallituksen esitys polttoturpeen ja sillä tuotetun sähkön toimitusvarmuuden turvaamista koskevaksi lainsäädännöksi.
112. *See* Talousvaliokunnan mietintö 23/2006 vp – Hallituksen esitys polttoturpeen ja sillä tuotetun sähkön toimitusvarmuuden turvaamista koskevaksi lainsäädännöksi.

power more than 15% (2,651 MW).[113] The major electricity generating companies in Finland are Fortum Power and Heat Oy and Pohjolan Voima Oy (PVO).

113. Annual Report 2008 – Energy Market Authority, Finland, 38. MW figures date back to 2007.

Chapter 4. Trade and Supply

278. No licences are required for entities supplying or trading electricity in Finland. As noted above, the EA is required to collect information on the level of electricity supply and demand in Finland.

279. In Finland, supply and trade in electricity have been opened up for competition since 1995 when the Electricity Market Act entered into force. As noted above, the opening up of the electricity market for competition first applied to the major industrial consumers and only since 1998, as load-curving metering was introduced to the minor consumers, has the electricity market been opened up for all customers. The requirement for full electricity retail market opening was introduced at the EU level only on 1 July 2007 by Directive 2003/54/EC concerning common rules for the internal market in electricity. It is to be noted that as the right of the major industrial consumers to choose freely their electricity supplier was introduced, the major Finnish electricity-consuming industrial company Outokumpu chose to purchase electricity from Sweden. The Court of Justice of the European Community was asked to give its judgment in a request for a preliminary ruling in case C-213/96, *Outokumpu*, on the compatibility of the then applied Finnish electricity excise taxation legislation with Article 90 EC. The Court of Justice deemed the Finnish legislation to breach Article 90 EC, since it caused imported electricity to be, in certain occasions, more severely taxed than electricity supplied by the national electricity generators.[114]

280. There are approximately 3.1 million electricity customers and approximately seventy retail suppliers in Finland. Prior to the opening up of the electricity market for competition, most of the vertically integrated electricity utilities[115] supplied electricity only in the same area where their distribution networks existed. The rate of electricity consumers changing their supplier has remained lower than in neighbouring countries since less than 7% of electricity consumers per year change their supplier. While the rate has lately increased significantly,[116] it is to be noted that some two-thirds of retail suppliers do not supply outside their traditional supply area.[117]

281. According to section 67 of the Electricity Market Act, an electricity retailer in a major market position within the area of responsibility of a distribution system operator must deliver electricity at reasonable prices to consumers and other users of electricity whose place of electricity use is equipped with main fuses of 3 × 63 amperes at maximum or receives no more than 100,000 kWh of electricity annually. Should no such electricity retailers exist, the obligations of an electricity

114. Case C-213/96, *Outokumpu*, judgment of 2 Apr. 1998, ECR, 1998, I-1777.
115. That is, the same electricity utility performed the activities of generation, distribution, supply and trade of electricity.
116. Energy Market Authority Press Release, issued 15 Oct. 2009.
117. Annual Report 2008 – Energy Market Authority, Finland, 10.

retailer in a major market position are applied to an electricity retailer whose market share is the highest in the area of responsibility concerned. In response to Directive 2003/54/EC, Finland has notified the European Commission that this so-called *obligation to deliver* is one of the Finnish public service obligations. No derogation from the Directive was necessary in order to continue with the mentioned obligation to deliver.

282. According to section 68 of the Electricity Market Act, an electricity retailer in a major market position must deliver the terms of retail sale and prices and the criteria underlying these to the EA prior to their introduction.

283. The electricity vendor is obliged on the basis of section 86 to give its customer an itemized account of how the price of electricity is determined. The retailers are to also supply the general public with information concerning the average electricity price level applied.

284. During the parliamentary preparations of the initial Electricity Market Act of 1995, the Commerce Committee of the Parliament drew the attention of the government to the importance of consumer protection in the electricity market.[118] The Parliament thus asked the government to give it a new bill that introduced provisions on consumer protection in the Electricity Market Act without any further delay. Chapter 6a of the old Electricity Market Act and Chapter 13 of the current Electricity Market Act contained provisions concerning electricity market contracts. According to section 85, no exceptions to the provisions of this chapter may be made by agreement to the detriment of the consumer. The Consumer Ombudsman supervises the legality of the terms of the consumer contracts referred to in the Chapter 6a.

285. According to sections 91–92, a retailer may not terminate an electricity sale contract when the user of electricity encompassed by the obligation to deliver is a consumer. A retailer may terminate some other electricity sale contract encompassed by the obligation to deliver only if a legislative amendment or an essential change in the circumstances makes it unreasonable for it to keep the contract in force. The notice period for terminating an electricity sale contract is two weeks for the user of electricity and three months for the retailer. The notice period for terminating a contract outside the obligation to deliver is two weeks for the retailer. If a fixed-term electricity sale contract has been concluded outside the obligation to deliver with a consumer for a period exceeding two years, the consumer may terminate the contract after the period of two years in the same way he may terminate a contract that is valid indefinitely.

286. Section 93 stipulates the conditions under which the retailer may change the prices and other terms of an ongoing electricity sale contract. Such an opportunity must be included in the contract itself, or it must be based on legislative

118. *See* TaVM 56/1994.

amendments or on a decision made by the authorities, or there must be an essential change in the circumstances. Minor changes not affecting the principal content of the contract are, however, allowed.

287. The connecting party and the user of electricity are, on the basis of section 96, entitled to receive compensation for damage suffered because of delay unless this delay is caused by an obstacle that is beyond its control.

288. Furthermore, according to section 100, the user of electricity is entitled to standard compensation for continuous interruption of system service. The amount of standard compensation for the annual system service fee is gradual, increasing with the length of the interruption time to a maximum amount of EUR 700.

289. According to section 102, the distribution system operator may not interrupt the electricity supply for a reason attributable to the retailer until the distribution system operator has notified the user of electricity of the interruption of the electricity supply and of the reason for this. The consumer needs to be supplied with electricity for at least three weeks after the dispatch of the notification.

290. Based on section 103, the supply of electricity can be interrupted if the user of electricity has materially defaulted on the payments to the retailer or to the distributor. Before interrupting the supply of electricity, the user of electricity must be sent a written notification. The supply of electricity may not be cut between the beginning of October and the end of April in an electrically heated building that is used as a permanent residence.

Chapter 5. Separation of Activities

§1. General

291. Separation of business activities – in other words, unbundling – means separation of business activities of different types that are carried on in diverse markets from each other in vertically integrated companies. Usually, unbundling requirements aim at increasing transparency and neutrality in vertically integrated companies by preventing cross-subsidies and market abuse. Unbundling regimes also aim at making the functioning of the market in question more efficient as well as making the regulatory work easier in that market. In the electricity market, the objective of the unbundling of business activities is to separate the transmission and distribution activities that are carried on as a natural monopoly from the electricity generation and supply activities that are carried on under competition.

292. In the electricity market, four different types of unbundling can be seen: (1) unbundling of accounts, (2) legal unbundling, (3) operative unbundling and (4) unbundling of ownership – in other words, effective unbundling. Currently, all these options are applied in the Finnish electricity market legislation. Thus, the legislation aims at implementing the provisions of the third Electricity Directive (2009/72/EC).

293. The rules for ownership unbundling of TSOs were adopted in the Finnish legislation by the Electricity Market Act of 2013. With the new law, Finland set the ownership unbundling according to Article 9 of the Directive 2009/72/EC as the only option for the TSOs. Additionally, general rules for unbundling in accounts are set out in Chapter 12 of the Electricity Market Act of 2013 and in the Decree of the Ministry of Trade and Industry on Unbundling of Electricity Operations (Kauppa-ja teollisuusministeriön asetus sähköliiketoimintojen eriyttämisestä; SäädK 79/2005), which sets rules on unbundling in accounts of electricity undertakings. Finally, the Decree of the Ministry of Trade and Industry on Operative Unbundling Requirements for the Electricity Distribution System Operators (Kauppa-ja teollisuusministeriön asetus sähkönjakeluverkonhaltijan toiminnallisista eriyttämisvaatimuksista; SäädK 922/2006) includes provisions on operative unbundling requirements for distribution operators having at least 50,000 customers. The legislation sets up different requirements for unbundling in the TSOs and in distribution system operators. These requirements are explained below.

§2. Unbundling in the TSO

294. Before the Electricity Market Act of 2013, the regulatory framework in Finland with regard to the unbundling of the TSO was based on an individual model created in 1996 when the separate state-owned and industry-owned transmission systems were merged. As a result of this history, the Finnish TSO operator, Fingrid Oyj, had a specific ownership structure when compared, for example, to other TSOs in Europe. First, two generator companies (Fortum Oyj and PVO) were minority shareholders in Fingrid. However, the Finnish TSO model aimed at avoiding the negative consequences of vertical integration with a balanced ownership structure that combined the two generators, the State and a group of institutional investors. Thus, the company structure was based on a three-part balance according to which neither the State block nor the private block nor the generators together can dominate the TSO.

295. The entry into force of the third Electricity Directive 2009/72/EC[119] caused a need for a major reassessment in the Finnish unbundling regime for transmission system operation because the ownership and company structures of Fingrid at that time did not fulfil the unbundling requirements of the Directive. The requirements of effective unbundling in Article 9 of the Directive 2009/72/EC were implemented in Fingrid in series of transactions during 2011–2013. The most important transaction was the acquisition of the shares of Fortum Oyj and PVO by the State of Finland and Ilmarinen Mutual Pension Insurance Company. In 2013, the provisions for effective unbundling were then introduced in the Electricity Market Act of 2013. In March 2014, the EA certified Fingrid Oyj as a TSO according to the principles of effective unbundling.[120]

296. Nowadays Fingrid Oyj is owned by the State (including the National Emergency Supply Agency, NESA) and some financial and insurance institutions (the State 28.24%, National Emergency Supply Agency 24.90% and institutional investors 46.83%, with corresponding voting rights for the State of 37.66%, NESA 33.20% and institutional investors 29.13%). Rights to sell TSO shares to outsiders are restricted by the articles of association and the shareholder agreements.

297. The following table shows the current ownership structure of Fingrid:[121]

Shareholders	*Number of Shares*	*Percentage of Shares*	*Percentage of Votes*
Republic of Finland	939	28.24	37.66
National Emergency Supply Agency	828	24.90	33.20
Ilmarinen Mutual Pension Insurance Company	661	19.88	17.15
The State Pension Fun	1	0.03	0.01
Aino Holdingyhtiö Ky	878	26.41	11.74
Elo Mutual Pension Insurance Company	1	0.03	0.01

119. *See* Art. 9 of the Directive 2009/72/EC of the European Parliament and of the Council concerning common rules for the internal market in electricity and repealing Directive 2003/54/EC.
120. *See* Commission opinion on 17 Jan. 2014 C(2014) 329 final and EA decision on 14 Mar. 2014.
121. *See* https://www.fingrid.fi/en/pages/investors/shares-and-shareholders/.

Shareholders	*Number of Shares*	*Percentage of Shares*	*Percentage of Votes*
Imatran Seudun Sähkö Oy	10	0.30	0.13
Fennia Life Insurance	6	0.18	0.08
Pohjola Insurance	1	0.03	0.01
Total	**3,325**	**100.00**	**100.00**

298. The provisions of unbundling of TSOs have been set in sections 32–39 of the Electricity Market Act of 2013. Section 32 lays down the requirements for independence of a TSO while the other provisions regulate the procedures for verification of independence and decision-making powers of the national authorities. Simultaneously, the certification procedure in Article 3 of the Regulation (EC) 714/2009 plays a central role in the procedure for verification of independence of TSOs.

299. According to section 32(1) of the Electricity Market Act of 2013, a TSO has to ensure that in its organization and decision-making: (1) the same person or persons are entitled neither: (a) directly or indirectly to exercise control over an undertaking performing any of the functions of generation or supply, and directly or indirectly to exercise control or exercise any right over a TSO or over a transmission system; nor (b) directly or indirectly to exercise control over a TSO or over a transmission system, and directly or indirectly to exercise control or exercise any right over an undertaking performing any of the functions of generation or supply, (2) the same person or persons are not entitled to appoint members of the supervisory board, the administrative board or bodies legally representing the undertaking, of a TSO or a transmission system, and directly or indirectly to exercise control or exercise any right over an undertaking performing any of the functions of generation or supply, and (3) the same person is not entitled to be a member of the supervisory board, the administrative board or bodies legally representing the undertaking, of both an undertaking performing any of the functions of generation or supply and a TSO or a transmission system. The rights referred to in points 1) and 2) of paragraph 1 of the section 32 of the Electricity Market Act of 2013 shall include: 1) the power to exercise voting rights; 2) the power to appoint members of the supervisory board, the administrative board or bodies legally representing the undertaking; or 3) the holding of a majority share. According to paragraph 3, where the person referred to in paragraph 1 is the State or another public body, two separate public bodies exercising control over a TSO or over a transmission system on the one hand, and over an undertaking performing any of the functions of generation or supply on the other, shall be deemed not to be the same person or persons. Paragraph 4 allows also end users that produce economically low amounts of electricity to be shareholders in a TSO.

300. The State of Finland owns shares both in the TSO Fingrid and in several electricity generation and natural gas supply companies. Due to this, there are separate ministries that exercise ownership steering authority for Fingrid and for other state-owned energy companies.

301. Section 33 of the Electricity Market Act of 2013 lays down the provisions for the verification of TSOs independence. The EA makes the decision on the verification. Before the final decision by the EA, it shall, in each case, notify the European Commission of its opinion. In its final decision, the EA shall take into account, that opinion. The EA shall open a certification procedure to ensure such compliance: (1) upon notification by a TSO; (2) on its own initiative where it has knowledge that a planned change in rights or influence over transmission system owners or TSOs may lead to an infringement of section 32, or where it has reason to believe that such an infringement may have occurred; or (3) upon a reasoned request from the Commission.

302. Sections 34–36 regulate situations where persons from third countries, i.e., countries that are not members of the EU or the EEA take control in a TSO. In this situation, the verification and certification procedures will be supplemented with opinions by the Commission and the Ministry of Economic Affairs and Employment regarding impacts on security of supply in Finland and in the EU. In its final decision, the EA shall comply with the assessment by the Ministry, if the Ministry considers that the control of persons from third countries in a TSO will endanger security of supply in Finland or in the EU.

303. According to section 37, a TSO or involved parties shall not engage in any intended transaction which opens verification and certification procedures, before the procedures have been completed. The Market Court may, on the proposal of the EA, order a transaction to be cancelled, if the verification on it has been refused.

304. Section 30 of the Electricity Market Act of 2013 includes the rules for situations where TSOs and legally unbundled system operators are entitled to purchase and supply electricity. According to this section, a TSO may purchase and supply electricity if the purpose of the operation is to:

(1) purchase the loss energy for the transmission system;
(2) tend to the duties under the systems responsibility;
(3) manage congestion;
(4) operate movable reserve power machinery for the construction, operation and maintenance of the transmission system and supply electricity generated by this machinery for the transmission system; and
(5) purchase electricity for internal consumption in the premises, transformer stations, link stations or other corresponding objects of the TSO.

305. In addition to this, section 77 of the Electricity Market Act of 2013 obliges a TSO to unbundle transmission and distribution operations in its accounts if it performs both of these business operations.

§3. Separation of Activities in Distribution System Operators

306. The requirements for separation of activities in distribution system operators form a complex system in the Finnish electricity market legislation. This is because there are many operators and they are very different in size. As a starting point, there are no requirements for ownership unbundling for distribution system operators. With regard to large and medium-size system operators, legal and operative unbundling is required. With regard to small system operators, unbundling in accounts is satisfactory. However, there are three different categories of requirements based on the size of a system operator. Legal and operative unbundling requirements cover the vast majority of system operators based on the amount of energy transmitted. Requirements also extend to much smaller system operators than Directive 2009/72/EC requires.

307. The following figure illustrates the unbundling requirements for distribution system operators (DSOs) in Finland:

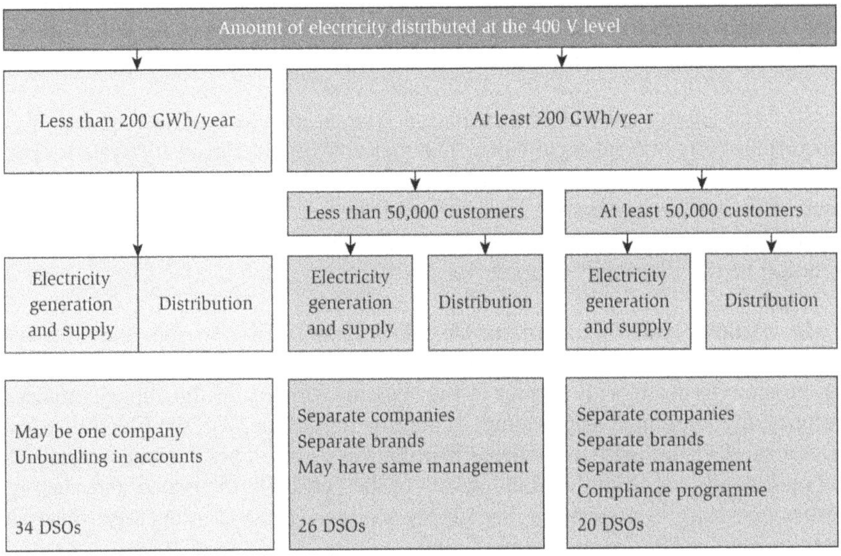

308. The legal unbundling of system operation from electricity supply and generation activities is required for distribution system operators that have distributed at least 200 gigawatt-hours (GWh) annually through their 400-V distribution network for the last three calendar years. At the end of 2015, a total of forty-six distribution system operators of eighty operators were legally unbundled in Finland.[122] When looking at the number of customers, the threshold value of 200 GWh corresponds to about 20,000 customers.[123]

309. According to section 60 of the Electricity Market Act of 2013, a distribution system operator that has distributed at least 200 GWh annually through its 400-V distribution network for the last three calendar years must be independent in terms of its legal form, organization and decision-making from the electricity generation and electricity supply operators of the utility or group of utilities if that system operator functions as part of a utility engaged in electricity generation or electricity supply or of a group of utilities under the same party's control (*legally unbundled electricity system operation*). Here, *control* means rights, contracts or other means that either separately or together allow the party to exercise decisive control in the utility and in its bodies, taking the relevant real and legal conditions into account. A change in the corporate structure concerning legally unbundled electricity system operation shall be implemented within two years of the end of the calendar year during which the threshold value was reached.

310. The legally unbundled distribution system operators are not required to be structured in any special legal form. The majority of the electricity system operators own their assets, but they are also allowed to operate with leased network assets. However, every system operator needs to fulfil the common technical, economic and organizational preconditions for the electricity system licence set out in section 6 of the Electricity Market Act of 2013.

311. Article 26(3) of Electricity Directive 2009/72/EC provides that vertically integrated distribution system operators cannot, in their communication and branding, create confusion with respect to the separate identity of the supply branch of the vertically integrated undertaking. According to section 60 of the Electricity Market Act of 2013, a legally unbundled distribution system operator must ensure that its brand stands out from the brand names of the vertically integrated undertaking´s entities operating in generation and supply sectors. The system operator must also communicate in his own name and brand.

312. Section 30 of the Electricity Market Act of 2013 includes important demarcating rules for situations where legally unbundled distribution system operators are entitled to purchase and supply electricity. According to this section, a legally unbundled distribution system operator may purchase and supply electricity if the purpose of the operation is:

122. *See* Energy Authority, National Report 2016 to the Agency for the Cooperation of Energy Regulators and to the European Commission, Ref. 1518/601/2016.

123. *See* Energy Market Authority, 'Annual Report to the European Commission', 15 Jul. 2009, Ref. 412/601/2009, 35.

(1) to purchase the loss energy for the distribution system;
(2) to operate movable reserve power machinery for the construction, operation and maintenance of the distribution system and to supply electricity generated by this machinery to the distribution system;
(3) to purchase electricity for internal consumption on the premises or in transformer stations, link stations or other corresponding objects of the distribution system operator; or
(4) by virtue of its responsibility under the Electricity Market Act, to deliver electricity to end users in a situation where the delivery of a retail supplier has been interrupted for a reason attributable to the supplier.

313. The operative unbundling requirements for large and medium-sized distribution system operators are set out in sections 60 and 61 of the Electricity Market Act of 2013 and in the Decree of the Ministry of Trade and Industry on Operative Unbundling Requirements for the Electricity Distribution System Operators (SäädK 922/2006). There is a threshold of 50,000 customers that set up additional operative unbundling requirements for system operators.

314. Section 61 of the Electricity Market Act of 2013 provides that a person managing a system operator engaged in legally unbundled electricity system operation with 50,000 customers or more may not act as the managing director of a utility in charge of electricity generation or electricity supplier or as a member of its board of directors or a corresponding organ if the system operator and the utility are under the control of the same party. This requirement covers twenty distribution system operators in Finland.[124]

315. The requirements set out in the Decree of the Ministry of Trade and Industry on Operative Unbundling Requirements for the Electricity Distribution System Operators and paragraph 3 of section 60 of the Electricity Market Act of 2013 include the operative unbundling requirements for professional interests of the persons managing the system operator and compliance programmes for the largest distribution system operators. These requirements are limited to legally unbundled electricity system operators with 50,000 customers or more and currently cover twenty distribution system operators in Finland.[125]

316. With regard to the operative unbundling requirements in the Finnish electricity market legislation, it is important to note that the requirement for effective decision-making rights for resources needed for the operation, maintenance and development of an electricity system in Article 26(2)(c) in Directive 2009/72/EC is applied to all distribution system operators. This provision is included in section 6 of the Electricity Market Act of 2013, which regulates the preconditions for electricity system licences.

124. *See* Energy Authority, National Report 2016 to the Agency for the Cooperation of Energy Regulators and to the European Commission, Ref. 1518/601/2016.
125. *Ibid.*

317. Unbundling in accounts applies to all electricity system operators that are not required to be legally unbundled. Currently, there are about thirty-six distribution system operators that have to comply only with this obligation. However, their distribution activities cover only about 10% of electricity consumed in Finland. Additionally, unbundling in accounts is required in the legally unbundled companies that have other activities besides system operation activities if these activities are not relatively small.

318. Rules for unbundling in accounts are included in Chapter 12 of the Electricity Market Act of 2013. In addition to this, the Decree of the Ministry of Trade and Industry on Unbundling of Electricity Operations (SäädK 79/2005) applies to all electricity undertakings.

319. According to section 77 of the Electricity Market Act of 2013, a utility operating in the electricity market must unbundle the accounts of any electricity system operations from those of other electricity trade operations and the accounts of any electricity trade operations from those of other trade operations. The system operator must unbundle the following electricity system sub-operations from each other: (1) transmission system operations and distribution system operations and (2) distribution system operations carried out in parts of the area of responsibility that are geographically separate from each other if separate prices for distribution services are applied in these parts. Electricity trade operations need not, however, be unbundled from each other or from other trade operations if the trade operations are of minor significance in terms of volume or the other trade operations carried out by the utility. Business activities whose annual revenue is less than EUR 500,000 and less than 10% of the company's total revenue have been considered activities of minor significance by law.

320. In the Electricity Market Act of 2013, unbundling in accounts means that an income statement and a balance sheet must be drawn up for any electricity trade operation to be unbundled for each financial period. The income statement and the balance sheet, which must be derivable from the utilities' accounts, are to be drawn up, *mutatis mutandis*, in accordance with the provisions of the Accounting Act (SäädK 1336/1997). The electricity trade accounting of a municipal establishment engaged in electricity trade operations must be unbundled from the municipality's other accounting and from the accounting of the municipality's other establishments for each financial period. A separate income statement and balance sheet must be drawn up for such municipal establishment.

321. Section 80 of the Electricity Market Act of 2013 sets out the rules for drawing up the unbundled financial statements. Transactions and balance sheet items are to be entered in income statements and balance sheets according to the matching principle. Joint income and expenditures are to be numerically entered when drawing up the financial statements for different functions in such a way that the matching principle is followed as far as possible. In unbundled financial statements, depreciation is based on purchase expenditures. Upon drawing up unbundled financial statements for the first time, purchase expenditures are to be reduced by depreciation according to plan. The unbundling procedure chosen must be continuously followed unless there is justification for changing it. An account must be made of any changes made in the financial statements.

322. The unbundled income statements, balance sheets and any supplementary information of unbundled operations are audited as part of the statutory auditing. These documents are used by the EA when it assesses whether system operators have complied with the tariff regulation during the regulatory period in question.

323. Finnish energy market legislation also aims at wide disclosure for the unbundled financial statements. According to section 82 of the Electricity Market Act of 2013, the unbundled financial statements of electricity trade operations must be made public. The unbundled financial statements also must be attached to the official financial statements, the published annual report or corresponding public documents made available to the stakeholders of a utility. At the same time, certain additional economic indicators depicting the system operator's operations must also be published.

Chapter 6. Consumption

324. The electricity consumption of Finland was 85.5 TWh in 2017. The level of consumption has been quite stable since 2012.[126]

325. There are some 3.5 million electricity customers in Finland. The industrial and construction sectors account for 47% of the total consumption of electricity. The residential and agriculture sectors account for 28%, and the services and public sectors account for approximately 22% of the total consumption of electricity. Within the industrial sector, the forest industry is the most significant customer (20 TWh/year in 2017), followed by the metal industry (9 TWh/year), chemical industry (7 TWh/year) and construction and other industries (5 TWh/year). As for other consumption, housing and agriculture account for the largest share (24 TWh/year in 2017), followed by services and public sectors (19 TWh/year) and the share of losses being some 3 TWh/year.[127]

326. The highest peak load of Finland reached 15,100 MW on January 2016.[128] Until to the late 2000s, the consumption of electricity in Finland increased some 2% per year, and the amount of peak load electricity consumption increased some 300 MW per year. However, during the 2010s the volume of consumption and peak electricity seem to have been on a fairly stable level. The volume of electricity consumption is not steady though since the electricity consumption level depends on the severity and duration of the winter period.[129]

327. CHP generation accounts for approximately 25% of electricity consumption, nuclear power for approximately 25%, hydropower for approximately 17%, wind power for approximately 6% and conventional condensing power for approximately 4%. The share of net electricity imports varies from year to year, mainly due to weather conditions and market prices in the Nordic power market. During the last decade, it has accounted for more than 20% per year several times.[130] Import of electricity from Sweden and Norway rises due to wet weather conditions, whereas cold and dry weather conditions increase the need to import electricity from Russia and Estonia.

---

126. Tilastokeskus. Suomen virallinen tilasto. Energian hankinta ja kulutus. 2017, 4. neljännes.
127. Tilastokeskus. Suomen virallinen tilasto. Energian hankinta ja kulutus. 2017, 4. neljännes.
128. Fingrid Oyj. Annual Review and Financial Statements. 1 Jan. 2016 31 Dec. 2016.
129. Hallituksen esitys Eduskunnalle laiksi sähköntuotannon eräiden tehoreservien käytettävyyden varmistamiseksi (HE 228/2006) and, https://energia.fi/ajankohtaista_ja_materiaalipankki/materiaalipankki/energiavuosi_2017_-_sahko.html#material-view.
130. https://energia.fi/ajankohtaista_ja_materiaalipankki/materiaalipankki/energiavuosi_2017_-_sahko.html#material-view.

Chapter 7. Supervision and Penalties

328. There are several national authorities responsible for the coordination, surveillance and regulation of the electricity market in Finland. The denser the regulation of the electricity market becomes, the wider the powers and responsibilities of these authorities grow.

329. At the government level, the Ministry of Economic Affairs and Employment is responsible for the general supervision of the implementation of the Electricity Market Act of 2013. The Ministry is also responsible for the general supervision of the implementation of the Act on Peak Load Power Reserves.

330. The Ministry of the Environment is responsible for the general supervision and implementation of environmental legislation.

331. The role of the EA has substantially grown in importance during its existence. It was first established in the mid-1990s during the time of the opening up of the national electricity market to competition as a compact unit responsible for the *ex post* surveillance of tariffs of the electricity network operation. It had fewer than ten employees. Currently, there are some eighty employees, and its responsibilities extend, in addition to electricity markets, to natural gas markets and other energy policy areas as well as emissions trading.

332. The provisions for regulatory powers of the EA and penalties are currently enacted in the Law on Supervision of Electricity and Natural Gas Markets (Laki sähkö- ja maakaasumarkkinoiden valvonnasta; SäädK 590/2013). The Law on Supervision of Electricity and Natural Gas Market is applied to all the duties the EA has as a national regulatory authority based on the national and the EU electricity market legislation. Thus, it defines the regulatory of the EA while the substantive law is defined in the Regulation (EC) 714/2009 of the European Parliament and the Council on conditions for access to the network for cross-border exchanges in electricity and repealing Regulation (EC) No. 1228/2003 and the Regulation (EU) No. 1227/2011 of the European Parliament and of the Council on wholesale energy market integrity and transparency. As the national regulatory authority for electricity market, the EA's powers can be divided into *ex ante* regulatory powers, *ex post* supervisory powers and powers to propose penalties.

333. The EA decides *ex ante* on the conditions of service and the methods of service pricing to be applied by the transmission and distribution network operators. It is empowered to require network operators to decrease the level of network payments by the amount they have exceeded the reasonable profit level or to increase the level of network payments by the amount they are below the reasonable profit level. Should the reasonable profit level be exceeded by more than 5%, the EA is empowered to require extra compensation.[131]

---

131. *See* ss 10–15 of the Law on Supervision of Electricity and Natural Gas Markets.

334. Second, the EA has a general *ex post* supervisory power regarding compliance with the Electricity Market Act and the EU regulations on the internal market in electricity. According to its general supervisory power, the EA has the power to require transmission and distribution network operators and retail suppliers to correct their errors or omissions. It may also order how these errors or omissions are to be corrected. The EA has the power to order a refund to a customer of a fee for which he has been incorrectly charged. It may set conditional fines for network operators and suppliers.[132] The EA's *ex post* supervisory powers also cover the rules for concessions and construction of power lines in the Electricity Market Act.[133]

335. Another form of the EA's *ex post* supervisory powers have been enacted in section 20(a) and 20(b) of the Law on Supervision of Electricity and Natural Gas Markets. According to them, the EA has a power to set penalty payments and public cautions for minor offences against the Regulation (EU) No. 1227/2011 of the European Parliament and of the Council on wholesale energy market integrity and transparency. The amount of the penalty payment is based on an overall assessment. When assessing the amount of the penalty payment, the quality, scope and duration of the offence must be taken into account. The penalty payment to be charged to a legal person is at least EUR 5,000 and a maximum of EUR 100,000. The penalty payment for a natural person shall be at least EUR 500 and a maximum of EUR 10,000.

336. Third, the EA has a power to propose penalties for breaches of the Electricity Market Act, the Regulation (EC) 714/2009 of the European Parliament and the Council on conditions for access to the network for cross-border exchanges in electricity and repealing Regulation (EC) No. 1228/2003 and the Regulation (EU) No. 1227/2011 of the European Parliament and of the Council on wholesale energy market integrity and transparency. The possibility of imposing a penalty payment on the breach of the Electricity Market Act and the regulations on the internal market for electricity on a system operator or a generator covers the essential obligations of the law and the regulations.[134] A penalty payment is determined by the Market Court (*markkinaoikeus*) on the proposal of the EA. Determination of the amount of the penalty payment should be based on an overall assessment which must take account of the nature and extent of the offence or omission, the degree of the complacency and the duration. The penalty payment may not exceed 10% of the legal person's turnover for the last year for which the offence or omission exceeds and up to 10% for a natural person of his last income in taxation, up to a maximum of EUR 100,000.[135]

337. Most of the decisions of the EA based on the Electricity Market Act or the Law on Supervision of Electricity and Natural Gas Markets can be appealed to the Market Court. This concerns especially the decisions the EA has adopted as a

132. *See* s. 9 of the Law on Supervision of Electricity and Natural Gas Markets.
133. *See* Ch. 5 of the Law on Supervision of Electricity and Natural Gas Markets.
134. *See* paras 1 and 3 of s. 16 of the Law on Supervision of Electricity and Natural Gas Markets.
135. *See* ss 17 and 18 of the Law on Supervision of Electricity and Natural Gas Markets.

national regulatory authority. However, its decisions regarding concessions and supervision of concessions can be appealed to the appropriate administrative court. The judgments of the administrative court and the Market Court can be appealed to the Supreme Administrative Court. A precondition for appeal to a judgement by an administrative court is a leave to appeal by the Supreme Administrative Court.[136]

338. The EA also supervises the application of the Act on Peak Load Power Reserves Securing the Balance between Electricity Consumption and Production of 2011. It confirms the rules relating to the maintenance of the peak load power reserve plants, the operation of these plants and the supply to the electricity market of the peak load power reserves. It also confirms the grounds for payments of the system. Should the obligations stipulated in the Act on Peak Load Power Reserves Securing the Balance between Electricity Consumption and Production be breached, the EA has the power to require reparation. It also has the power to set conditional fines. The EA has the power to order an agreement on the use of the peak load power reserve to be rescinded if the operator breaches the public service obligations of the agreement. It also has the power to recover compensation erroneously paid and to inspect the premises of the peak load power reserve plants.[137]

339. The EA is also the supervisory authority for the feed-in tariff for electricity generated from renewable energy sources.[138]

340. The EU legislation on the internal electricity market is primarily supervised by the national regulatory authorities. However, there is also a regulatory agency of the EU, namely the ACER. The ACER has also some regulatory and supervisory powers regarding the EU electricity market legislation, especially in situations in which the competent national regulatory authorities fail to make unanimous regulatory decisions for interconnectors.[139]

341. The Radiation and Nuclear Safety Authority is responsible for the supervision of the application of the Nuclear Energy Act.

342. Motiva Oy has the task of promoting energy saving and energy efficiency in the national plan.

136. *See* s. 114 of the Electricity Market Act and ss 36 and 37 of the Law on Supervision of Electricity and Natural Gas Markets.
137. *See* Ch. 3 of the Act on Peak Load Power Reserves Securing the Balance between Electricity Consumption and Production.
138. *See* s. 4 and Ch. 6 of the Act on the Subsidy for the Generation of Electricity from Renewable Energy Sources.
139. *See* the Regulation (EC) 713/2009 of the European Parliament and the Council on an Agency for the Cooperation of Energy Regulators, especially Art. 8.

Part II. Natural Gas

Chapter 1. Introduction

343. The building of the first natural gas pipeline in Finland begun at the start of the 1970s, and the first deliveries took place in January 1974. The natural gas markets in Finland are very different from the natural gas markets in most of the other EU Member States. Finland is the last remaining natural gas island in Europe. The objective of this chapter is to examine these differences and their effect on the regulatory framework of the Finnish natural gas markets. As with most of the EU Member States, the Finnish laws governing the energy markets for both electricity and natural gas are derived from the EU regulation. In line with the EU energy acquis, the regulatory approaches to the electricity and natural gas markets are very similar. The framework for regulating the electricity markets has been examined in detail in Part I. This chapter will not repeat the matters discussed previously and will not cover issues that are similarly regulated in both natural gas and electricity markets. Instead, this chapter will focus on the details of the Finnish natural gas markets.

344. The Finnish natural gas pipeline network is limited to the southeasternmost part of the country. In continental Europe, in general, the natural gas pipeline network covers the entire area, similarly to the electricity network. Most European countries have some competing gas suppliers or at least significant potential for some level of competition. Great Britain, the Netherlands, Denmark and Norway, among others, have their own gas reserves.

345. Natural gas covers approximately 8% of Finland's total energy requirements,[140] while the average within the EU area is over twice that amount.[141] In Finland, nearly 70% of natural gas is used in industry-related processes and energy production. CHP generation accounts for approximately 36% of total natural gas consumed.[142] Industries use natural gas, for example, in various heating and drying processes as well as in steam production. Natural gas is also used in the forest and chemical industries. In smaller power plants, natural gas is utilized as an efficient

140. www.gasum.fi. (https://www.gasum.com/kaasusta/maakaasu/maakaasu/).
141. 22% in 2015 (http://ec.europa.eu/eurostat/statistics-explained/index.php/Consumption_of_energy).
142. www.kaasuyhdistys.fi *Natural gas consumption in Finland* (www.kaasuyhdistys.fi/sisalto/statistics).

source of heat and power. While the most common form of natural gas usage in Finland is CHP production, other important uses include the production of condensing power and district heating as well as various industrial processes.

346. Currently, Finland is still dependent on Russian natural gas imports and receives all of its pipeline gas supplies through a single pipeline from Russia. There is no interconnection to any other network in Europe. Thus, Finland is an isolated market for natural gas as regulated in Article 28(1) of the Second Gas Directive (as defined *infra*).[143] This situation will change in 2020 when the construction of the Balticconnector-pipeline from Finland to Estonia is completed. In August 2016, the European Commission decided to grant the Balticconnector-pipeline EUR 187.5 million from the Connecting Europe Facility which is 75% of the total construction costs of the pipeline. In addition, the Finnish state has invested EUR 30 million to the project.

347. Due to geological factors, Finland does not have indigenous gas production and does not possess any natural storage areas for natural gas. With the abovementioned Balticconnector-project, there are plans to connect the Finnish natural gas networks with the Baltic natural gas network to allow the use of the underground storage areas in Lithuania. The entire natural gas supply chain is controlled by very few companies. OAO Gazprom (Gazprom) owns the Russian natural gas source from which all Finland's natural gas comes and transfers pipeline gas to the Finnish border.[144] In Finland, there is only one importer and wholesaler of pipeline gas, Gasum Ltd (Gasum), which, in turn, transfers the natural gas from the Russian border into Finland. Gasum is owned by the Finnish government. Currently, the Finnish natural gas pipeline network consists of one transmission pipeline from Russia to the eastern border of Finland (the receiving station of Räikkölä in Imatra) and one transmission pipeline bringing the gas further to southern Finland.

348. Currently, the length of the Finnish transmission pipeline is 1,288 kilometre (km), and the length of the distribution pipeline is 1,955 km.

349. In 2016, the use of natural gas in Finland decreased by 6.7% over that in 2015.[145] In 2016, Gasum's annual natural gas sales amounted to 23.8 TWh.[146] The usage of natural gas in the future is uncertain and will be affected by several factors, e.g., taxation as well as the opening of the markets with the Balticconnector-pipeline.

350. On 4 February 2005, Gasum and Gazprom entered into an agreement in which the companies agreed on continuing delivery of natural gas from Russia to

143. A regulation concerning isolated natural gas markets is also included in Art. 49(1) of the Third Gas Directive (as defined *infra*). However, Finland currently has [] off-grid LNG-terminals which are mainly build to serve local natural gas needs.
144. The transfer of title takes place at the border.
145. Eurostat (http://ec.europa.eu/eurostat/statistics-explained/index.php/Natural_gas_consumption_statistics#Consumption_trends).
146. Gasum Ltd Annual Report 2016, 32.

Finland until 2025. Because its natural gas network is not connected to the natural gas network of any other EU country, Finland does not have to comply with all of the regulations of the First Gas Directive (defined *infra*). This situation will change with the completion of the construction of the Balticconnector-project.

Chapter 2. Regulatory Basis of the Natural Gas Pipeline Industry in Finland

351. Natural gas pipelines, with their transportation and the distribution systems, can be characterized as having a natural monopoly character.

352. The Natural Gas Market Act and the supervision of natural gas markets in Finland resemble the regime under the Electricity Market Act.

353. The Ministry of Economic Affairs and Employment set up a working group in 2014 in order to prepare a proposal for reformation of the Natural Gas Market Act (508/2000, as amended) and for opening the Finnish natural gas market. A government proposal was published on 10 March 2017 and the new Natural Gas Market Act (587/2017) (New Natural Gas Market Act) entered into force on 1 January 2018. The new Natural Gas Market Act completed the implementation of the First Gas Directive.

354. In 1998, the European Council issued Directive 98/30/EC of the European Parliament and of the Council of 22 June 1998 concerning common rules for the internal market in natural gas (the First Gas Directive). The First Gas Directive, which entered into force on 10 August 1998, set common rules for the transfer, distribution, delivery and storage of natural gas. The goal of the First Gas Directive was to open the natural gas markets for competition. As the opening of natural gas markets was not feasible, Finland enjoyed an exemption from many of the provisions of the First Gas Directive. Under this First Gas Directive, these exemptions will remain applicable until there is another pipeline connection to Finland. During this transition period, the Finnish natural gas markets needed to be adapted to the European markets. This adaptation began with the enactment of a duty of the existing gas pipeline owners to sell gas transportation services to qualified wholesale buyers. These qualified buyers were the users of natural gas and retailers who used or sold at least 5 million m^3 of natural gas a year and whose usage of gas was measured with remote meter reading devices.[147] Among other innovations of the First Gas Directive was the creation of the Finnish Energy Market Authority (EA). In Finland, the EA supervises compliance with the Natural Gas Market Act and promotes the operation of a competitive natural gas market.

355. In 2003, the European Council issued Directive 2003/55/EC of the European Parliament and of the Council of 26 June 2003 concerning common rules for the internal market in natural gas and repealing Directive 98/30/EC (the Second Gas Directive). This Second Gas Directive entered into force on 4 August 2003. The Member States needed to bring into force the laws, regulations and administrative provisions necessary to comply with this Second Gas Directive no later than 1 July 2004.[148]

---

147. *Ibid.*, 10.

148. Article 33 of the Second Gas Directive.

356. In 2009, the European Council issued Directive 2009/73/EC of the European Parliament and of the Council of 13 July 2009 concerning common rules for the internal market in natural gas and repealing Directive 2003/55/EC (the Third Gas Directive). The exemptions granted to Finland under the First and Second Gas Directives will continue to apply under the Third Gas Directive until the factual conditions justifying the exemption for an isolated natural gas market are removed with the completion of the construction of the Balticconnector-project. The Third Gas Directive also expanded the scope of this exemption by specifying that the exemption covering Estonia, Latvia and Finland would remain valid until any of those Member States is directly connected to the interconnected system of any Member State other than Estonia, Latvia, Lithuania and Finland.[149]

357. One of the main changes in the New Natural Gas Market Act is the opening of the natural gas wholesale and retail markets for competition in accordance with the national energy and climate strategy as Finland renounces application of the derogation. The main reason for the need to develop the legal framework for the Finnish natural gas market was the weakened competitiveness status of natural gas in the energy markets. Especially in the Finnish energy production, currently, natural gas competes with other fuels on inequitable terms.

358. Unbundling obligation of the TSO will become effective on 1 January 2020. The objective of ownership unbundling of the transmission network from the sale of natural gas is creating independence for the transmission, as required by Internal Market rules. The unbundling model required in the New Natural Gas Market Act is full ownership unbundling (OU). Appointing an OU requires the natural gas suppliers to abandon all other rights related to ownership of the transmission network other than right to the dividend. As full unbundling is mandatory, no supply or production company is allowed to hold a majority share or interfere in the work of a TSO. Owning of the transmission network independently is possible in current form.

359. The unbundling will apply to TSO Gasum (not DSOs), which owns and controls the natural gas transmission system in Finland. The organizational responsibility will, in practice, be unbundled and transferred to a company fully owned by Gasum. Separately, the transmission system for natural gas and the ownership of the transmission network could be in the same company.

360. Accounting unbundling applies to all natural gas system operators. The Third Natural Gas Directive enables derogation from applying judicial and functional unbundling if the transmission network has less than 100,000 customers. All Finnish gas distribution system operators fall below the limit set by the Directive. Thus, there are no requirements for judicial or functional unbundling of natural gas transmission and distribution system operators, whereas the derogation can still be applied.

149. Article 49 of the Third Gas Directive.

361. In the beginning of 2020, the TSO's transfer duty will be expanded to cover all customers that meet the conditions defined in the Directive. Customers eligible for access are customers that are part of a contactless measuring system, in which any customer may be included. The only way to accomplish full third party access is to give network users the freedom to book entry and exit capacity independently, which will be guaranteed based on a public tariff system. Transfer duty will also be expanded to Liquefied Natural Gas (LNG) any on-grid terminals.

362. Interconnectors, LNG-terminals and biogas facilities constitute entry points of the transmissions system and usage points form exit points, where the transmissions fees based on the entry-exit system are collected. When preparing renunciation of the exception for isolated markets, Finland shall ensure that the access to transfer- and transmission networks is put into practice based on a tariff system, which can and will be applied to customers that meet the conditions defined in the Directive. Access based on the tariff system will be performed impartially and in a non-discriminatory manner.

363. The new Natural Gas Market Act contains definitions on a customer who meets the conditions according to the Natural Gas Market Directive, and rules that guarantee customers that meet the conditions a possibility to get natural gas deliveries from businesses in the natural gas industry per a differentiated line.

364. The New Natural Gas Markets Act applies also to off-grid LNG-terminals. TPA and regulated tariffs will also apply to off grid terminals, and the obligation to transfer also concerns LNG-terminals, in addition to biogas facilities.

365. The national energy authority will confirm tariffs and terms of use. Pricing principles and capacity need to be made public and TPA must be granted within the limits of capacity, although in a non-discriminatory manner. Capacity cannot be booked for own use, and all capacity should be equally divided using the same principles and procedures.

366. It is notable that not all regulations applicable to on-grid LNG-terminals apply, and that special features of the off-grid terminals are taken into account in the New Natural Gas Market Act.

367. In connection with the opening of the Finnish gas market and thereby the end of applying the exemptions granted to Finland under the EU Gas Directive, the Regulation (EC) No. 715/2009 of the European Parliament and of the Council of 13 July 2009 on conditions for access to the natural gas transmission networks and repealing Regulation (EC) No. 1775/2005 (the EU Gas Regulation) will become directly applicable on the Finnish market as of 1 January 2020. The EU Gas Regulation sets out rules for operation in the natural gas transmission network, including on third-party access services to the natural gas transmission systems as well as storage and LNG facilities, tariff principles, capacity allocation, congestion management, transparency, balancing rules and imbalance charges, as well as capacity trading. The national authority in Finland ensuring that the market operators fulfil their obligations is the EA. In addition, certain guidelines, of which are annexed to the EU Gas Regulation, provide for the minimum harmonization degree required.

368. The general guidelines for setting tariffs for network users are set out in Article 13 of the EU Gas Regulation. The tariffs shall be transparent, reflect actual costs incurred by the TSO, enabling, however, an appropriate return on investment. Further, the tariffs must be non-discriminatory and be set separately for each entry or exit point into our out of the transmission system, as well as be approved by the EA.

369. Articles 16 and 17 of the EU Gas Regulation set out the principles for capacity allocation mechanisms as well as congestion management procedures, on the one hand, for TSOs and, on the other, for storage and LNG facilities. TSOs as well as LNG and storage system operators shall, under Articles 18 and 19, also make public the information concerning the services they offer, conditions applying to such services, technical information needed to gain network or facility access, information on their capacities and information on the bases for their tariffs.

370. Further, every transmission, storage and LNG system operator shall allow for free trading of capacity rights market under Article 22 of the EU Gas Regulation, as well as develop contracts and procedures on the primary market in order to facilitate secondary trade of capacity.

371. According to the EU Gas Regulation, the tasks of ENTSO-G include, *inter alia*, preparing networks codes as prioritized by the European Commission. As of March 2018, the following gas network codes have been adopted by the European Commission and therefore apply as such to cross-border gas market transactions on markets where the EU Gas Regulation applies:[150]

- the Network Code on Interoperability and Data Exchange Rules;
- the Network Code on Gas Balancing of Transmission Networks;
- the Network Code on Capacity Allocation Mechanisms in Gas Transmission Systems;
- the European Commission's rules on congestion management procedures; and
- the network code on harmonized transmission tariff structures for gas.

372. All the areas for which network codes should be set are listed in Article 8(6) of the EU Gas Regulation. For 2018, the Commission's proposal was that priority should lie on the implementation of the above-mentioned codes and rules.[151]

150. The European Commission: Gas network codes, https://ec.europa.eu/energy/en/topics/markets-and-consumers/wholesale-market/gas-network-codes (visited on 23 Mar. 2018), 2.

151. The European Commission: Public Consultation Paper – Establishment of the annual priority lists for the development of network codes and guidelines for 2018 and beyond, https://ec.europa.eu/info/sites/info/files/public_consultation_paper_on_priorities_for_network_codes2017_en.pdf (visited on 23 Mar. 2018).

373. Regulation (EU) No. 1227/2011 of the European Parliament and of the Council on the wholesale energy market integrity and transparency (REMIT) sets out market rules for the energy market in order to prohibit market abuse and use of insider information (REMIT Article 1). REMIT applies to the gas wholesale markets and place obligations on all energy market participants, including TSOs, entering into transaction in wholesale energy markets in the EU. *Inside information* under Article 2(1) of REMIT includes information relating to the capacity and use of facilities for production, storage, consumption or transmission of natural gas or related to the capacity and use of LNG facilities, including planned or unplanned unavailability of these facilities. In short, REMIT prohibits persons possessing insider information from using it while acting on the energy wholesale market but also obliges such a person to disclose insider information. The national regulatory authorities monitor the enforcement of REMIT, while the ACER functions as a coordinating body ensuring a consistent application of REMIT.[152]

152. ACER: Questions & Answers on REMIT, 21st ed., https://documents.acer-remit.eu/wp-content/uploads/REMIT_21st_edition_QA_v1.0.pdf (visited on 23 Mar. 2018), 8.

Chapter 3. Network Licence and the Project Permit

374. The two material permits needed by the gas TSOs in Finland are the network licence[153] and the project permission. The network licence is the basic permit required to operate a pipeline, and the project permit concerns the building of certain types of pipelines.[154]

375. The natural gas network licence is granted by the EA. The licence is granted until further notice or, for a special reason, for a specified period of time. The licence can be granted to a corporation or a utility. In an individual case, the EA may exempt the network operator from the licence requirement for a specified period or until further notice if the network operator's natural gas network is of a minor significance in terms of natural gas transmission. Gasum has been granted a natural gas network licence for the operation of a natural gas transmission network in Finland.

376. According to Chapter 2, section 5 of the New Natural Gas Market Act, the licence is granted if the applicant has the technical, economic and organizational prerequisites to operate a natural gas network in the manner provided for by the legislation on the natural gas markets. The applicant must meet the following prerequisites (Chapter 2, section 6):

(1) The applicant is a company or as regards, a DNO or a municipal facility.
(2) The applicant's organization must be appropriate to the scope and nature of its network operation.
(3) The applicant must employ a sufficient number of personnel which corresponds to the size and character of the business of the applicant.
(4) The applicant must employ a person who has been appointed as the supervisor of operations and who has the qualifications laid down by the Act on the safe handling of dangerous chemicals and exposions (390/2005) and the ability to supervise the use of the pipeline.
(5) The applicant must have the economic prerequisites for the operation of a profitable natural gas network.

377. Conditions considered necessary for the operation of the pipeline can be included in the licence. The licence cannot be assigned to another utility or corporation. The operation of a natural gas distribution network also calls for a licence, which is granted by the EA.[155] The EA had granted twenty-four natural gas distribution licences by September 2017.[156]

378. According to the Natural Gas Market Act, when the EA grants a natural gas network licence, it orders one transmission network operator to be responsible for

153. Chapter 2, s. 4 of Maakaasumarkkinalaki (New Natural Gas Market Act) (587/2017).
154. Chapter 2 ss 4 and 12.
155. Chapter 2, s. 5 of the New Natural Gas Market Act.
156. www.energiamarkkinavirasto.fi, 8 Nov. 2009.

the technical operability and reliability of the transmission system and to discharge the duties involved in the balance responsibility for the transmission system in a manner that is equitable and non-discriminatory for the parties to the natural gas market (the systems responsibility).[157]

379. Similar to the electricity market, the operation of the natural gas market, as defined in the Natural Gas Market Act, requires a TSO that has certain tasks and obligations. The TSO is responsible for the technical operability of the transmission system, including the duties involved in the balance responsibility for the transmission system. The duties of the TSO also encompass the balance clearing duties that will become necessary as the natural gas market is deregulated. The EA ordered Gasum to act as TSO as of 1 March 2001.

157. Chapter 2, s. 7 of the New Natural Gas Market Act.

Chapter 4. Sales and Obligation to Supply

380. The sale of natural gas is not subject to a licence. The vendor of natural gas must, however, meet certain special requirements and fulfil certain obligations. The unbundling of natural gas sales from network activities was required as of 1 January 2001, and a profit and loss account and a balance sheet must be drawn up in the same manner as in the natural gas network operations. However, it is not required that insignificant sales of goods and services be separated from the sale of natural gas. An operation is considered to be of minor significance if its turnover does not exceed 10% of the turnover of natural gas sales.[158]

381. According to the obligation to supply, the wholesale vendor who has significant market power in a natural gas transmission network must supply natural gas it has acquired from Russia through the transmission network to be delivered to retail customers in distribution networks.[159] A retail vendor who has significant market power in a natural gas distribution network must supply natural gas for a reasonable price to customers who use natural gas mainly for heating purposes or customers whose connection capacity for the consumption site is at most 250 kW. In case there are no vendors who have significant market power with the distribution network, the obligation to supply lies with the vendor whose share of delivered natural gas within the area that has customers under the obligation to supply is the largest.[160]

382. Vendors of natural gas must publish the terms of sale and selling prices of natural gas.[161] A natural gas vendor in a dominant market position in a distribution network may not apply unreasonable pricing.[162] The vendor must specify the price used and terms of sale whose connection capacity for the consumption site is at most 250 kW and inform the EA of these conditions.[163] The EA can publish other requirements concerning the format in which a vendor needs to publish and submit the terms of sale and the prices of services.[164] EA also publishes these terms on its website.[165]

158. Chapter 13, s. 60 of the New Natural Gas Market Act.
159. Chapter 4, ss 42 and 44 of the New Natural Gas Market Act.
160. Chapter 8, s. 44.
161. Chapter 4, s. 26, whole seller Ch. 8, s. 42, retailer in a dominant position Ch. 8, s. 44.
162. Chapter 8 s. 44.
163. Chapter 4, s. 26 and Ch. 6, s. 38.
164. Chapter 8, s. 45.
165. www.energiamarkkinavirasto.fi, 14 Oct. 2017.

§1. Pricing of Natural Gas

383. A supplier of natural gas who is in a dominant position must deliver natural gas to users for a reasonable fee.[166] In Finland, the price of natural gas has to be reasonable, but it does not have to be approved by any authority before trading may commence.

384. The price of natural gas is tied to an index basket; that is, the price fluctuates with the price development of competing fuels (heavy fuel oil and coal) as well as the development of the Finnish bank price index for domestic supply.

385. The natural gas companies are allowed to set their tariffs and other conditions by themselves within the limits set forth by the requirement of reasonable profits. The EA can intervene and require adjustments to ensure compliance with the natural gas market legislation.[167]

386. The EA does not give natural gas companies any strict rules concerning pricing methodology or revenue level. The network companies have an obligation to inform the EA about the new public tariffs. The regulator subsequently monitors the tariffs (to determine whether the rate of return is at a reasonable level and whether the tariffs are cost reflective) on a case by case basis (*ex post* regulation). A uniform and public pricing system has been followed in the natural gas trade in Finland since 1991.[168]

387. Gasum's public natural gas wholesale pricing system is called M2017.[169] The M2017 pricing system for natural gas is applied to Gasum's delivery contracts for natural gas in Finland entered into and/or coming into effect following the coming into effect of M2017. According to the M2017 pricing system, the total price of natural gas in the deregulated natural gas market consists of the transmission price and the supply price of natural gas. Using different weightings, the price of natural gas is bound to the price of crude oil (Platts Dated Brent) and coal (API2) as well as to the sub-index E35 of the domestic base price index.

388. The general terms of sale and selling prices of the network services provided by the network operator must be public, equitable and reasonable while ensuring sufficient cash-flow financing and a reasonable return for the network operator. The network operator has an obligation to calculate the key figures describing the price level of its network services and the efficiency and quality of its operations and to deliver them to the EA.[170]

---

166. Chapter 8, ss 42 and 44.
167. www.energiamarkkinavirasto.fi, 14 Oct. 2017.
168. *Ibid.*
169. www.gasum.fi, 15 Nov. 2017.
170. www.energiamarkkinavirasto.fi, 15 Nov. 2017.

389. In accordance with the above, balance clearing in the natural gas trade is included in the systems responsibility and falls under the duties of Gasum. The network operator is responsible for the metering of natural gas and the clearing of natural gas transactions.[171]

390. In accordance with the above, balance clearing in the natural gas trade is included in the systems responsibility and falls under the duties of Gasum.

171. Chapter 4, s. 17 of the New Natural Gas Market Act.

Chapter 5. Unbundling

391. In Finland, the supply of gas and the transportation services need to be separate businesses according to the Natural Gas Market Act. The operations are known as natural gas distribution and retail. In a corresponding manner, the transmission and wholesale of natural gas must be unbundled by Gasum. Moreover, the businesses not belonging to the natural gas branch must be unbundled into separate businesses. Full ownership unbundling was introduced by the New Natural Gas Market Act.

392. According to Chapter 13, section 60 of the New Natural Gas Market Act, 'A natural gas undertaking shall separate the natural gas network operation, sale and storage as well as the operation of LNG terminal from each other and from any other business operations not belonging to the natural gas sector.' As mentioned above, if the non-gas business operations are of minor significance, such sales of goods or services of minor significance need not be separated from natural gas sales.

393. Legally, the term unbundling means that, for any natural gas business operations to be separated, a profit and loss account and a balance sheet must be generated for each financial period, referred to as unbundling of accounts. The profit and loss account and the balance sheet, which must be derivable from the undertaking's accounts, must be drawn up, *mutatis mutandis*, in compliance with the Finnish Accounting Act (1336/1997, as amended). Thus, Finland has adopted a derogation based on Article 9 of the Third Gas Directive for further unbundling obligations.

394. There will be a separate act concerning the obligation to unbundle the natural gas transmission services. This act will enter into force on 1 January 2020 when the construction of the Balticconnector-pipeline is completed.

Chapter 6. Transmission

395. The Second Gas Directive recognized that the First Gas Directive had made significant contributions towards the creation of an internal market for gas and that in order to complete the internal gas market, non-discriminatory access to the network of the transmission and the distribution system operators was of paramount importance.[172] However, even with this regulatory history, the Third Gas Directive states that at present, there are obstacles to the sale of gas on equal terms and without discrimination or disadvantages in the EC. In particular, non-discriminatory network access and an equally effective level of regulatory supervision do not yet exist in each Member State.[173]

396. The key role of free cross-border trade in the EU energy acquis relates to the internal market objective of the EU. Because of this, it is hardly a surprise that the regulation of transit predates the more general gas market regulation. This regulation was carried out through Directive 91/296/EEC concerning the transfer of natural gas (the Transit Directive). One prerequisite for the applicability of the regulations of the Transit Directive was that the pipeline must cross at least one border between two EU countries. The Transit Directive was to be implemented by the Finnish Natural Gas Market Act, but since all Finland's natural gas comes from Russia, this prerequisite was not fulfilled, and, thus, the regulations of the Transit Directive were not applied to Finland.[174] The Second Gas Directive repealed the Transit Directive.

397. The network operator is under an obligation to provide transmission services for reasonable compensation to those customers who meet the requirements. The obligation to transmit entered into force on 1 March 2001 on the basis of a government resolution.[175] The obligation to transmit concerns the network operators whose customers are users or retailers of natural gas. The obligation to develop imposed on the network operator means, among other things, that capacity shortages, bottlenecks and shortages of free capacity may be only a temporary impediment to the provision of transmission services.[176] According to Chapter 4, section 16 of the Natural Gas Market Act, the network operator must sell transmission services for reasonable compensation within the limits of its network transmission capacity to customers. The precondition for the obligation to transmit is that the customer uses a remote gas meter reading for both its usage of natural gas and input of natural gas into the network.

398. Gas pipeline owners have a duty to offer gas transportation services for a fee to everyone, and the pricing of the services must follow the principles set forth

172. Recital 3 of the Second Gas Directive (L 176/57).
173. Recital 4 of the Third Gas Directive (L 211/9).
174. Hallituksen esitys maakaasumarkkinalaiksi [Government Proposal for Natural Gas Market Act] (134/1999), 6.
175. Valtioneuvoston asetus Maakaasumarkkinoista (622/2000).
176. Chapter 4, s. 14 of the Natural Gas Market Act.

in the Natural Gas Market Act. Currently, the purchasing of natural gas is dependent on one pipeline and one gas producer.

399. The EA has published guidelines according to which reasonable prices regarding network services must be calculated.[177] There are two sets of guidelines, one for services in the transmission pipeline network and another for services in the distribution pipeline network. Therefore, the monitoring of the pricing of network services is partly *ex post* monitoring.[178]

§1. Obligation to Connect

400. The network operators have an obligation to connect; that is, upon request, the network operator must connect to the network, the consumption and other sites, that have been specified in the New Natural Gas Market Act and meet the technical requirements. Chapter 4, section 15 of the New Natural Gas Market Act states: 'On request and against reasonable compensation, the network operator shall connect to his network the natural gas consumption and storage sites as well as LNG facilities,[179] biogas production facilities as well as separate lines meeting the required technical specifications (obligation to connect).' The costs caused by connection – for example, by location – may be collected from the customer. The Finnish Natural Gas Association has designed a model for a connection contract including terms of connection for the distribution network operators.[180]

§2. Rates for Transfer

401. In Finland, the tariffs for the transmission services are set by the natural gas companies themselves. However, the pricing principles are regulated *ex ante* on the basis of the Natural Gas Market Act.

402. Chapter 4, section 20 of the Natural Gas Market Act sets forth the pricing principles for the transportation services. It states that services must be offered to all customers with the same, common preconditions. The transportation price is not dependent on whose natural gas is being transported. The pricing principles should be impartial and non-discriminatory. The pricing should be reasonable, taken as a whole. The pricing should reflect the costs of operations and the costs of the network holder and guarantee sufficient cash-flow financing and solvency for the system operator. The revenues may cover the pipeline's maintenance, use, development and reasonable construction costs and, in addition, provide a reasonable profit onto invested capital. Reasonable costs should reflect the level of financial risk that is

177. Maakaasun jakeluverkkotoiminnan hinnoittelun kohtuullisuuden arvioinnin suuntaviivat vuosille 2016–2023.
178. *See* the decision of the Finnish Market Court (Drno 307/08/E2).
179. Currently, Finland does not have any on-grid connected LNG facilities.
180. www.energiamarkkinavirasto.fi, 15 Oct. 2017.

directed to the invested equity to the network assets of the network holder, the low investment costs of debt as well as the long-term usage of the facilities. The reasonable costs should also enable the long-term development of the network. Network holder should be able to carry out profitable network business which may at some point require capital increases.[181]

403. Chapter 4, section 16 of the Natural Gas Market Act states that the buyers of natural gas pay for their right to use the pipeline and the transportation service to the owner of the pipeline to which they have been connected. A natural gas pipeline customer may buy transportation services directly from the owner of the pipeline or from the supplier of natural gas who has an agreement concerning this arrangement with the owner of the pipeline. Chapter 14, section 72 of the Natural Gas Market Act states that a consumer has an option to enter into only one agreement, which includes both the supply of natural gas and its transportation.

181. Hallituksen esitys maakaasumarkkinalaiksi [Government Proposal for Natural Gas Market Act] (50/2017), 79–80.

Chapter 7. Development of Secondary Markets for Natural Gas in Finland

404. There has been a growing need in Finland to develop natural gas markets. Dealing in natural gas in the secondary market began on 1 March 2001. Gasum had developed the secondary market trading of natural gas in Finland by establishing a separate company, Kaasupörssi Ltd, in 2001 to handle the trading markets. With regard to efficient competition in the market, it is crucial that the rules of the game are equitable and promote both volume of supply and competition. The main issue in the development of the secondary market, and the branch as a whole, will be to further develop the tariff structures of the transmission network operator so that these structures will comply with the principles of market legislation and the definition of the functions and responsibilities included in the system responsibility as well as the confirmation of the related terms.

405. In the secondary market, the users of natural gas may trade among themselves natural gas that they have purchased from the wholesale market. In practice this means that the system does not trade with gas contracts because Gasum owns all the gas that is being transferred. Kaasupörssi accepts offers to sell and buy unused delivery capacity of natural gas.

406. So far, the so-called *secondary market* in natural gas has been deregulated only for parties that meet certain requirements. The users or retailers of natural gas who purchase over 5 million m^3 of natural gas annually, whose metering takes place via remote reading and whose pricing has been agreed upon since the Natural Gas Market Act entered into force can participate in the operation of the secondary market. After the transition period, the right to receive transmission services will be extended. The transition period will end when the Finnish natural gas network has been connected to the interconnected system of some other Member State of the European Union[182] or when Finland has two external gas suppliers, neither one of which has a share that exceeds 75%. This will happen with the completion of the contemplated construction of the Balticconnector-pipeline project.

407. The transportation contracts for natural gas in the wholesale market are currently based on the delivery capacity of the customers. The annual basic capacity agreed to by a customer is standard for the whole year. The customer pays for the basic capacity regardless of whether it uses the whole capacity or not. The price of the reserved capacity is 15%–25% of the total price of the natural gas.

182. In case of a connection to Estonia or Latvia, the exemption for Estonia, Latvia and Finland will remain valid until any of those Member States is directly connected to the interconnected system of any Member State other than Estonia, Latvia, Lithuania and Finland. *See* Art. 49 of the Third Gas Directive.

408. The following figure illustrates the daily routines in the trading of natural gas in the secondary market by Kaasupörssi:[183]

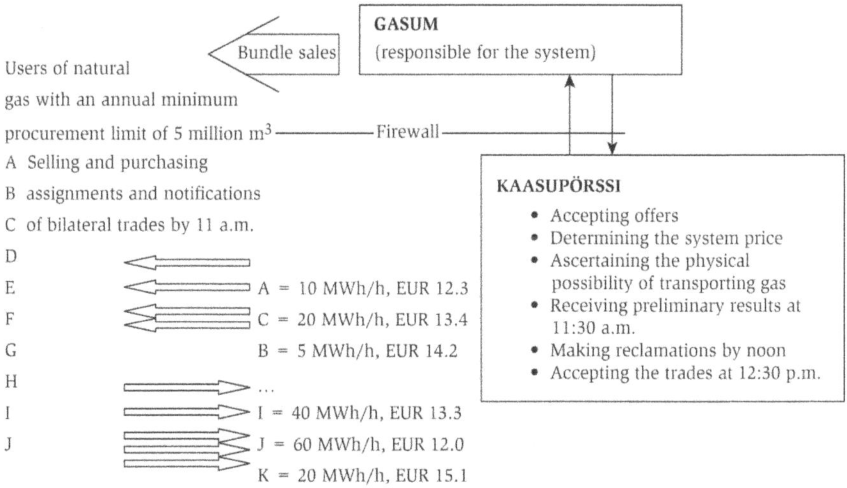

409. The parties announce their bilateral trades to Kaasupörssi for two reasons: first, so that the capacity can be checked, and second, in order to make a balance clearance. In 2016, Kaasupörssi's Gas Physical Forward was 1,353 GWh compared to 992 GWh in 2015. The parties to the trade should themselves agree what happens if the transportation of the gas is not possible. The fact that this secondary market does not bring any competition to the Finnish gas markets lessens its economic significance.[184]

183. *Energiayhtiöt* magazine (2001), 40.
184. This has also been reflected in the recent decision from the Finnish Market Court (Drno 307/08/E2).

Chapter 8. Provisions for and Actions in a Potential Disturbance in the Natural Gas Supply

410. In November 2001, the Ministry of Trade and Industry[185] confirmed contingency instructions for the natural gas supply in exceptional circumstances. Since the Act on the Openness of Government Activities (621/1999) stipulates that the contingency instructions be classified, the Ministry's Oil Supplier Pool and Natural Gas Section were assigned the task of quickly replacing natural gas with alternative forms of energy or of using alternative fuels in cases where the supply of natural gas is, for some reason, interrupted for an indefinite period. Alternative actions in such situations include adjusting and interrupting production.[186]

411. If the interruption in the availability or supply of natural gas, or any other exceptional circumstances does not fulfil the criteria for emergency conditions as stipulated in the Emergency Powers Act (1552/2011, as amended), the powers under this Act cannot be used and the contingency plans cannot be based on the Emergency Powers Act. In such a situation, the law providing the only guidance for such a situation is the Natural Gas Market Act, which is intended to provide the conditions for well-functioning natural gas markets where the availability of reasonably priced natural gas of sufficiently good quality can be secured. Gasum has overall systems responsibility (the decision of the EA on the Grid License of Gasum, Diary No. 59/71 1/2001, 21 August 2001) and is, for its part, responsible for securing the adequate operation of the natural gas transfer grid and the necessary connections abroad. In cases of supply problems, Gasum must, in conjunction with other participants in the natural gas markets, direct the supply of natural gas in such a way that the damages caused by the disturbances in supply are minimized. During emergency conditions, the distribution of natural gas can be rationed by authorities. If natural gas cannot be imported, but the import of oil continues without any problems, official rationing may not have to be imposed. If oil is available in normal commercial markets, it may also not be necessary to use all of the obligatory emergency reserves held for the eventuality of interruptions in the natural gas supply. According to the Act Governing the Obligatory Emergency Reserves of Imported Fuels (1070/1994, as amended), the use of the obligatory emergency reserves can be started when the National Emergency Supply Agency decides that the disturbance in the supply of the subject commodity threatens to halt the production or commercial operations of the operator responsible for maintaining the emergency reserve.[187] The authorization to use the obligatory emergency reserves is given without delay in cases where the supply of natural gas is interrupted for an indefinite period (for reasons other than a technical problem). The stipulations and powers of the Emergency Powers Act may have to be imposed in cases where there are problems in using emergency fuel systems or oil transport cannot be secured through commercial means. During a severe problem regarding imported fuels (emergency

185. Currently, the Ministry of Economic Affairs and Employment of Finland.
186. National Board of Economic Defence Oil Suppliers Pool, Provisions for and Actions in a Potential Disturbance in the Natural Gas Supply, 1.
187. Chapter 5, s. 16 of the Act Governing the Obligatory Emergency Reserves of Imported Fuels.

conditions), an Oil and Gas Distribution Centre can be established in conjunction with the Finnish Oil Federation, if so required. The duties of such a Distribution Centre include directing the emergency fuel supply of users of natural gas – that is, the procurement and transport of alternative fuels. During emergency conditions, the rationed supplies of fuel and production control must be matched with the general rationing and control systems for energy and the control system for industrial production. The plants using natural gas as their principal fuel cannot therefore be considered in isolation; instead, a model as uniform as possible must be applied to all plants. During emergency conditions, the authorities will issue more detailed instructions and regulations regarding the operation of the Oil and Gas Distribution Centre.[188]

412. The customers are warned of reduced imports of natural gas. An attempt to restrict the use of gas is made by increasing the additional transfer price. At the same time, the voluntary or contractual preparedness of customers to start using alternative fuels is established. During a disturbance, the operator that has overall systems responsibility controls the gas grid, as required by its technical operability. When there is not enough gas to meet the total demand of all users, the operator that has overall systems responsibility will endeavour to shave off the excess consumption by increasing the price for excess gas. The next step involves interrupting the supply to users that have agreed to this contractually in advance.[189]

413. If the availability of gas is further diminished, the contractual capacities will also have to be reduced. Gasum does not possess any quick means of limiting the natural gas consumption of its customers. The restriction on use must be based on an order that Gasum issues to its customers, lowering their contractual capacity until such time that the imports of natural gas are restored to a level that meets demand. The order is made more effective by multiplying the price of natural gas. For the sake of treating all bulk customers of natural gas equally, Gasum will reduce the contractual capacities of all its customers pro rata based on their respective contractual capacities. However, the customers who have reserved the option of getting gas from the importer's propane-air plant will continue to receive at least the equivalent amount of natural gas during the restrictions.[190]

414. In November 2014, Finland and Estonia have agreed on a joint plan to develop the regional natural gas market and improve gas-based energy security as part of the EU's Connecting Europe Facility (CEF) programme.

---

188. National Board of Economic Defense Oil Suppliers Pool, 'Provisions for and Actions in a Potential Disturbance in the Natural Gas Supply', 2.
189. *Ibid.*, 2–3.
190. *Ibid.*, 3.

Chapter 9. Development of Natural Gas Markets

415. Further development of Finland's natural gas markets requires extension of the natural gas network. Increasing the use of natural gas is vital in order both to meet the objectives set for climate policy and to ensure the profitability of natural gas import connections. A key project in increasing the security of supply of natural gas to Finland is the Balticconnector-pipeline project.

416. The Baltic connector is one of the key projects also in the Baltic Energy Market Interconnection Plan (BEMIP) in the eastern Baltic Sea region. The BEMIP was launched at the initiative of European Commission President Barroso at the autumn 2008 meeting of the European Council. The two main goals of the BEMIP initiative, within the context of the EU's 20/20/20 objectives, are the full integration of the three Baltic states into the European energy market and the strengthening of interconnections with their neighbouring EU countries. On 17 June 2009, eight Baltic Sea EU Member States signed a Memorandum of Understanding on the BEMIP with the European Commission.[191] Initially, the Balticconnector-project was developed by Gasum together with Elering AS (Elering) from Estonia. In the autumn of 2015, a decision was made by Gasum to give up the implementation of the Balticconnector -project. On the basis of studies conducted, the project would not have been commercially viable for Gasum and there would not be sufficient demand for it in the Finnish market.[192] After Gasum decided not to pursue the project, the Finnish Government established Baltic Connector Oy (Baltic Connector) on 8 October 2015 to implement the Finnish part of the Balticconnector-project between Finland and Estonia. The Balticconnector-pipeline project will play a major role in the energy strategies of both Finland and the EU. The project will: (1) improve regional security of supply by diversifying gas sources, (2) create a framework for market opening and growth and enable the use of alternative sources, such as LNG and biogas, (3) enable the interconnection of the Finnish and Baltic gas markets and their integration with the EU's common energy market. The total cost of the project is EUR 250 million. The project would not be viable without considerable support from the EU. In 2016, the European Commission (CEF) granted funding of EUR 187.5 million to the project for Baltic Connector and Elering.

417. Nord Stream is a gas pipeline consisting of two parallel pipelines. It runs from Vyborg, Russia to Lubmin, Germany. The twin pipelines have a combined capacity of transporting 55 billion m^3 of gas per annum. The pipeline consists of two 1,224 km offshore pipelines in addition to which there is an onshore pipeline connecting the pipeline to the Russian transmission system.

418. In 2000, the project to build a pipeline through the Baltic Sea was declared as part of the TEN-E guidelines by the EU and, in 2005, a letter of intent for building a pipeline was signed by the three companies that would later establish the North European Gas Pipeline Company. Nowadays, the Swiss-based company is

191. ec.europa.eu/energy/infrastructure/bemip_en.htm.
192. Gasum Financial Statements 2015, 2.

called Nord Stream AG and has five shareholders. The company was responsible for the building of the pipeline and now operates it. Nord Stream AG is a consortium, the shareholders of which are OAO Gazprom with a 51% stake, Wintershall Holding Gmbh (a subsidiary of BASF) and PEGI/E.ON with a 15.5% stake each and N.V. Nederlandse Gasunie and ENGIE with a 9% stake each.[193]

419. The construction of the first pipeline began in April 2010 and was completed in June 2011. The construction of the second line began in May 2011 and was completed in April 2012. Total investment in the pipeline was EUR 7.4 billion of which approximately 30% was financed by Nord Stream's shareholders in equity contributions.[194] In 2016, the pipeline operated at approximately 80% of its total delivery capacity.[195]

420. In 2012, North Stream conducted a study to examine the possibility and demand for building another pipeline across the Baltic Sea. After initial consultations with the concerned countries, a company called North Stream 2 AG was established. North Stream 2 is wholly owned by Gazprom but its investment consortium includes ENGIE, OMV, Shell, Uniper and Wintershall. Nord Stream 2 AG is responsible for the planning, construction and subsequent operation of the planned pipeline. The twin pipelines are planned to be completed in 2019.

421. The pipe laying is scheduled to begin in 2018. When completed the offshore pipeline would be over 1,200 km in length and have the same capacity of 55 billion m^3 per annum as its predecessor. The pipeline will follow largely the route of the first Nord Stream pipeline and travel through territorial waters and/or exclusive economic zones (EEZs) of Russia, Finland, Sweden, Denmark and Germany, so, permits for the project must be obtained from each of these countries. Additional consultations are needed under the Espoo convention from Poland, Lithuania, Latvia and Estonia. In addition, several EIAs of the project are required under the national legislation of the countries concerned.

422. In Finland, the EIA procedure was completed in July 2017 and the two required permit applications (one for the exploitation of the Finnish EEZ and one for constructing and operating of the pipeline) have been submitted. In Denmark, the application for construction, EIA and the Espoo report were submitted in April 2017. In Germany, the permitting process is at the public hearing phase. In Russia, Nord Stream 2 has completed public consultations on the draft EIA. The Swedish permit application was sent for public referral in April 2017.[196]

193. Secure Energy for Europe, 21–22.
194. https://www.nord-stream.com/about-us/.
195. Press release by Nord Stream 2, dated 10 Jan. 2017.
196. https://www.nord-stream2.com/environment-permitting/permitting-overview/.

423. The pipeline has brought on strong opposition in certain countries, especially Denmark, Poland and Ukraine. There is a legislation process pending in the parliament of Denmark that would prevent the route of Nord Stream 2 from passing through Denmark's territorial waters.

424. In the spring of 2017, the European Commission announced that it will seek a mandate from the Member States to negotiate with Russia about the terms of delivery for gas but this mandate was refused. In November 2017, the European Commission proposed to amend the EU Gas Directive so that the core principles of EU energy legislation would apply to all gas pipelines to and from third countries. This would mean that for example, the provisions of third-party access, transparency and tariff regulation would be applicable to all existing and future pipelines equally, however, according to the Commission, Member States will be able to grant derogations for existing pipelines. Therefore, if the legislation enters into force before Nord Stream 2 is completed, it will have to comply fully with the demands of the directive. In connection with the proposition, the Commission announced that it will continue to seek the mandate for negotiations to reach a solution for the conflict of laws with Russia.[197]

425. The Baltic Pipe (also called the Northern Gate) is a planned pipeline through the Baltic Sea that would connect the Danish and Polish gas transmission systems. The project is led by Polish gas transmission operator GAZ-systems S.A. and Danish gas transmission operator Energinet. The aim is to connect the Norwegian gas deposits with the Danish and Polish markets and at the same time enable the supply of gas from Poland to the Danish and Swedish markets as well as to their neighbouring countries' markets.[198] A final investment decision in the project is expected in 2018 and the Baltic Pipe is planned to be operational by the end of 2022.[199] The EU has listed the Baltic Pipe as one of its project of common interest (PCI) projects. The length and other measurements of the Baltic Pipe are still unclear since the final route is yet to be determined.

426. In 2016, a feasibility study was conducted by the two entities organizing the project. The feasibility study was also co-financed by the European Commission under the CEF programme. Based on the study, the planned capacity is estimated at approximately ten-billion m^3 per year to Poland and up to three-billion m^3 per year to Denmark and Sweden.[200]

---

197. Commissions Press Release 8 Nov. 2017.
198. http://www.baltic-pipe.eu/the-project/north-sea-offshore/ (visited on 27 Nov. 2017).
199. https://en.energinet.dk/Infrastructure-Projects/Projektliste/BalticPipe (visited on 22 Nov. 2017).
200. http://en.gaz-system.pl/our-investments/integration-with-european-gas-tramsmission-system/baltic-pipe/ (visited on 22 Nov. 2017).

427. The project is now in the Open Season procedure phase. Phase one of the Open Season was concluded in July 2017 and in phase two, participants interested in the capacity of the planned pipeline should submit their bids by 31 October 2017. After that, the bids will be evaluated and the capacity allocated.[201]

201. http://en.gaz-system.pl/our-investments/integration-with-european-gas-tramsmission-system/baltic-pipe/ (visited on 22 Nov. 2017).

Part III. Regulatory Framework Concerning Oil and Coal

Chapter 1. General

428. The purpose of Part III is to examine the key elements of the Finnish oil market from different regulatory perspectives, taking into account the development of the market structure. In addition to oil, this part will deal with the key elements relating to coal in Finland. However, as the coal market in Finland is mainly competing in the power plants with alternative energy sources and imported electricity, the focus of this part is on the oil markets and oil market regulation.

429. The free movement of goods and investments plays an important part in the Finnish oil market. The Finnish market is competing for products and investments in markets with more dense populations. The geographical situation of Finland, which borders on Russia, the Baltic Sea, Sweden and Norway provides various alternatives for oil trading in Finland. On the demand side, suppliers of oil are intensively competing with other sources of energy – in particular, nuclear power and renewable sources of energy. The global changes supporting environment friendly fuel products have provided[202] possibilities for Finnish refinery industry to increase export of renewable fuel products worldwide.

430. The European Commission's energy and climate change policy agreed by the European Council[203] includes ambitious targets for the oil and coal industries in the EU. The targets to reduce greenhouse gas emissions by 20%, to have a 20% renewable energy share in the energy mix and to have a 20% energy efficiency improvement by 2020 have already had major effects in the Finnish oil market. Finland and ten other Member States achieved their 2020 targets already in 2016.[204] In November 2016, the Commission published its proposal for a revised renewable energy directive to ensure that the target of at least 27% renewables in the final energy consumption in the EU by 2030 is met. The long-term energy vision for Europe – covering the functioning of the energy market, security of the energy supply, a long-term commitment to CO_2 reduction, the EU emission trading schemes, energy efficiency and targets for renewable energy and biofuels – are challenging

202. World Energy Outlook OECD 2017.
203. EU Climate and Energy package 12.2008.
204. Eurostat News release 17 (2018).

the current position of the oil sector in all EU countries, including Finland. The national renewable energy targets range from 10% to 49%. Renewable sources of energy are expected to meet 40% of the increase in primary demand. Although the rate of global oil demand is expected to grow at a steadily decreasing pace up to 2040, the oil industry has faced the situation where not only renewable fuel products will change the markets but major challenge comes from the demand for electric car fleets instead of conventional cars that run with gasoline or diesel. Global coal demand is decreasing and coal´s share in the global energy mix is anticipated to still decline despite the availability of coal reserves. The surge in renewables and energy efficiency improvements has set a dent in coal demand and consumption. Increasing coal use in India and other Asian countries has not been able to offset the decline in other parts of the world.[205]

431. Finland's energy mix is highly diverse. Globally, oil, natural gas and coal provide about 80% of world energy. Oil amounts to approximately one-quarter of total Finnish energy consumption, being approximately 7.7 million tonnes per year. The volume of oil consumed has decreased, and its share of the total energy volume has come down significantly since its peak at the beginning of the 1980s.[206] The volume of coal consumed amounted to approximately 3.2 million tonnes in 2016, which was approximately 10% of total energy consumption. The amount of coal imports have been correlated with the annual rainfall, as the use of hydropower has been supplemented with coal during years of less rain. Almost all coal imported to Finland in 2016 came from Russia.[207] Other coal-exporting countries are Poland, Australia and the United States. Coal is used for electricity production and district heating and plays a key role as an alternative energy source for natural gas in safeguarding the security of the energy supply. However, climate change and the need to reduce greenhouse gas emissions are creating strong pressure to decrease the use of coal – particularly because there are alternative energy sources for electricity and heating – whereas the situation is less demanding for oil, and especially for traffic fuels.

432. This chapter will examine the regulatory framework of the operators in the Finnish oil market and describe the different roles of the business operators while taking into account the opportunities and challenges in the market. Although an attempt is made to provide a practical and solid description of the Finnish oil market, this chapter cannot provide a comprehensive review of the market. Its chapters cover the supply market, distribution and consumption, quality issues, transport matters and security-of-supply matters. Base oil, lubricants, bitumen and speciality chemical products are not covered in this part.

205. International Energy Authority Report 2017.
206. Energy review 2009.
207. Statistics Finland 2017.

Chapter 2. Supply Market

433. The Act on Economic Zone describes[208] the area of Finland's economic zone and authorizes the government to grant permits to search for and use natural resources in the economic zone. Any drilling for or use of oil, coal or gas reserves or other related activity in the Finnish water zone or economic zone is subject to an environmental permit.[209] However, Finland has no known oil or coal reserves on its territory. The Baltic Sea is not known for oil or coal reserves, and Finland has no access to the oil sources in the Arctic region. However, Finland is a member of the Arctic Council, and during its chairmanship in the Council for 2017–2019, Finland will strengthen the Arctic cooperation and its continuity at the highest political level.[210] Regarding oil and coal, the Finnish market is totally dependent on their import but the growing demand for renewable energy in the energy mix is providing alternatives for the Finnish energy industry. There are long traditions in the importation of oil into the Finnish markets. The first import contracts with oil producers from Baku and Azerbaijan, were already established about a hundred years ago. And as in other industrialized countries, coal used to be an important energy source for industry, particularly for the steel industry. In the 1960s, coal started to be replaced partly by oil and, due to the climate change, the use of coal is now further declining.

434. A fundamental change in the Finnish oil market was caused by deregulation at the beginning of the 1990s, opening Finland to imported oil and thus forcing the state-owned company Neste to face intense competition in its home market. However, initially, the local refinery capacity and the increasing demand continued to provide secure business for the Finnish oil company. The current status is now different, as the Finnish oil market is subject to strong international competition and to the volatile and open global oil commodity market. The changes in the global energy market have also brought opportunities for local Finnish business to benefit from the change by entering into the local energy market. The legal framework of the Finnish oil market includes the zoning, building and environmental protection legislation on fuel terminals, service stations and unmanned sites. As for the transport of oil, the legislation on the transport of dangerous products is applicable. The impact on oil depends partially on the legislation on quality issues. All these items will be separately covered in this chapter. The fundamental driving force in the energy section is the need to reduce CO_2 emissions. The report on future climate and energy policy by the Council of State[211] states that the aim of the policy is to reduce Finnish climate emissions by at least 80% from 1990 levels by 2050 as part of an international cooperative effort. Finland has continued on the systematic approach to reduce greenhouse gas emissions by 2050 for achieving even 80%–95%

208. Act on Economic Zone of Finland. The Supreme Administrative Court gave its decision on environmental permit for the Nord Stream pipeline on 22 Jun. 2011 (KHO 3424/1/10). Currently, there is a pending application for Nord Stream 2 by New European Pipeline AG.
209. Act on Environmental Protection.
210. Ministry for Foreign Affairs for Finland.
211. The Council of State Review on the Future Climate and Energy Policy, 15 Oct. 2009.

reduction in the emissions. As part of the National Energy and Climate Strategy for 2030, the share of transport biofuels will be increased to 30%, and an obligation to blend light fuel oil used in machinery and heating with 10% of bioliquids will be introduced. The share of renewable energy in the end consumption will increase to approximately 50% and the self-sufficiency in energy to 55%.[212]

435. Oil imports typically include crude oil and oil products. Finland imported a total of 11.3 million tonnes of crude oil in 2016, in comparison to approximately 11.9 million tonnes of crude oil in 2008. During the previous decade, the imports of crude oil to Finland varied roughly between 9.1 million tonnes and 12.2 million tonnes. Approximately 88% of the crude oil imports in 2016 came from Russia, while minor shares came from Norway, the EU and other countries. The total value of the crude oil imported to Finland amounted to approximately EUR 3.6 billion in 2015 showing a major decline of costs in comparison, e.g., to EUR 5.6 billion in 2008.[213]

436. In addition to crude oil, other oil products are being imported to Finland in significant volume. Finland imported a total of 6.8 million tonnes of oil products in 2016. Middle distillates from Russia accounted for a major part, being about 2 million tonnes of the imports, while other main exports came from Russia, the EU and other countries. The government is targeting to halve the import of oil for domestic purposes during the 2020 decennial.[214] The total value of the oil products imported to Finland amounted to approximately EUR 2.2 billion in 2015 being on the same level as in 2008 when the total value was approximately EUR 2.3 billion.[215]

437. There are two oil refineries in Finland, both owned by Neste Oil Oyj (Neste Oil), a Finnish listed company having the State of Finland as its majority shareholder. Neste Oil's Finnish refineries are located in Porvoo and Naantali. The Naantali refinery was commissioned in 1957, and it produces primarily traffic fuels and speciality products, such as bitumen, solvents and small-engine gasoline and products for the Porvoo refinery. The Porvoo refinery was commissioned in 1965, and it is focusing on producing premium-quality, low-emission traffic fuels. Neste has made important investments for both refineries during the past years in order to be able to grow in the global renewable based market. The Porvoo and Naantali refineries now form an integrated and complex system. Currently, Neste is the largest refinery producer of distillates from waste and residues. Neste's renewable diesel production is based on its unique and proprietary NEXTBL technology. Neste is also aiming to find renewable solutions for aviation. The annual renewable diesel production capacity of Neste, including its production facilities in Singapore and Rotterdam, is approximately 2.6 million tonnes.[216]

212. Government report on the National Energy and Climate Strategy for 2030/Publication of the Ministry of Economic Affairs and Employment 12/2017.
213. Statistics Finland 2016 and Finnish Customs 2016.
214. Government report on the National Energy and Climate Strategy for 2030.
215. *Ibid.*
216. 'Neste Oil Corporation Annual Report', 2016 and press release 9 Jan. 2018.

438. Sweden and Finland have, since the middle of 1990s, been the predecessors of environmental friendly oil products, providing tax incentives for qualified oil products. The investments in new technology in the Finnish refineries, together with the demand for high-quality oil products, have opened the markets for oil products exported from Finland. Approximately more than one-third of the refinery production in Finland was exported in 2016. Exports from Finland in 2016 amounted to approximately 2.9 million tonnes of motor gasoline in comparison with about 2.3 million tonnes in 2008 and approximately 3.8 million tonnes of middle distillates in comparison with approximately 3 million tonnes in 2008. The main buyers of the Finnish gasoline and middle distillates in 2016 were from the EU and North America.[217] Total value of exports of chemical products from Finland was approximately EUR 10.2 billion in 2016. The share of oil products of total chemical product exports from Finland in 2016 was approximately one-third.[218]

439. In the past, Neste Oil had oil exploration plans, but today the strategy of the Finnish oil refinery business is to be the world's leading supplier of lower-emission traffic fuels and renewable fuel. Accordingly, the purpose is to produce premium-quality, lower-emission traffic fuels from a broad range of low-cost feedstock and renewable sources. This strategy has been reflected in the investment plans of the two refineries in Finland. The rapid rise of renewables has benefited the Finnish oil industry, and investments in production capacity for renewables have been based on rational assumptions. The legal requirements to have renewable components in the transport fuel have made investments in modern refinery capacity well founded for the long-term. There are reasons to expect that such investments may provide competitive rate of return for the company and secure its position in the equity market provided that the definitions for the renewable sources and products and the legal requirements will comply with basis of the investment plans.[219] It is evident that the oil industry is a business requiring decisions to be made on a long-term basis and having capabilities to meet the global environmental challenges and benefiting from the requirements to reduce CO_2 emissions by replacing oil components partly with renewables components.

217. Finnish Customs 2016.
218. Finnish Customs 2017.
219. Neste Oil Corporation Press Release, issued January 2018.

Chapter 3. Consumption and Distribution

440. Finland's biggest energy consumer has traditionally been the industry sector. This, however, is not the case for oil products. Here, the transportation market represents close to half of the total oil consumption in Finland. The share of lubricants and other oil products is about one-fifth, while the other consumption sectors are industry, heating, farms and building. Finland's large geographical area continues to require efficient transportation networks. Currently, Finland has about 78,000 km of main roads, which illustrates the future need for an efficient oil supply network to meet local transportation requirements.

441. Two of the key issues in the distribution of oil are terminal capacity and secured supply chains. The two refineries in Finland are ideally located at the sea and are supplied by ships carrying crude oil. Helsinki harbour used to be the major oil terminal in Finland, having the capacity to serve southern Finland in particular. As a result of a decision by the city of Helsinki, the lease agreements with the city was terminated at the end of 2010, and, in line with the zoning requirements, the harbour area was utilized mainly for residential purposes.[220] Important oil terminals are located in HaminaKotka, Inkoo, Turku, Rauma, Pori, Vaasa, Pietarsaari, Kemi and Oulu and inland at Joensuu, Kuopio and Varkaus.

442. Coal is primarily being used in the power plants for generation purposes. There are currently about ten power plants having coal as one of their energy sources.[221] Almost all of the power plants are located at the seaside, as the most practical and economical transport of coal is by ship. Coal-driven power plants are also significant for reserve capacity. The oldest plants are kept as reserve plants and used depending, among other factors, on the availability of hydro energy. In addition, coal is used by industry for manufacturing processes. Most of the current power plants using coal were built in the 1970s[222] when the global oil crises drove Finland to adopt an energy strategy based on coal instead of oil. Since that time, the energy strategy in Finland has changed dramatically and as coal is striking out globally and also in the Finnish Government's National Energy and Climate Strategy, the share of coal is going down with an aim to not be used for energy purposes by 2030. There are requirements to close the energy use of coal in Finland ever earlier, by 2025.[223]

443. In the past, it was possible to establish oil terminals in areas that had no master plan or city plan. However, the current practice has been to have highly detailed zoning requirements, including obligations for various operations.[224] Oil terminals have to be in compliance with these zoning requirements and have to

220. City of Helsinki.
221. Hiilitietory.
222. Huoltovarmuuskeskus.
223. Government report on the National Energy and Climate Strategy for 2030, press release by the Ministry of Economic Affairs and Employment 5 Jan. 2018.
224. Act on Land Use and Building.

acquire the necessary building permits in line with the Act on Land Use and Building. This Act covers all levels of zoning plans from the general level to the detailed master plan. Drafting the master plan requires healthy and safe environments, and, therefore, the environmental effects should already have been taken into account at least in the most recent master plans. A case illustrating this change is the above-mentioned case of Helsinki. While the oil terminal had been located in the harbour of Helsinki for several decades, the City Parliament decided in the 1992 master plan to rezone the area for residential purposes in case the services for infrastructural purposes moved from the area.[225] The far-reaching and long-term effects of the locations of the major oil terminals are illustrated in the report of the Finnish government of 30 November 2000, requesting an alternative location for the Helsinki oil terminal if the terminal activities are moved from the current location.[226] In the consulting studies, it was concluded that alternative locations for oil service infrastructure were Porvoo, where Neste's refinery is located, and the harbour of Inkoo. Finally, in 2008, the City Parliament decided on the partial master plan providing for residential use of the oil terminal area.[227] The Helsinki case illustrates the practice of changing the zoning requirements of established oil terminal areas to serve other purposes, often for residential purposes. This trend raises several questions on liability for possible pollution of soil and water. This means substantial potential costs for terminal areas, but the same concern is linked to the more minor areas, such as service stations. The Supreme Administrative Court has taken the position that rezoning of the former service station master plan to the current residential master plan requires particular terms to ensure the quality of the soil.[228] Buildings on the terminal areas and service station areas require building permits in line with the Act on Land Use and Building.[229]

444. The Act on Environmental Protection[230] and the Decree on Environmental Protection[231] with subsequent legislation are the basis for the health and safety requirements for fuel operations in order to avoid pollution of the environment. Accordingly, terminals need to have environmental permits for their operations in line with the Act on Environmental Protection. Oil terminal operations in harbours require environmental permits for the harbours as a whole, and in addition, the various operators in the harbour, such as oil terminal operators, need environmental permits for their particular operations. An environmental permit is needed where terminal operations include the risk of environmental pollution[232] or where the tank capacity is at least 10 m^3 in the case of distribution sites and at least 100 m^3 in the case of other terminals.[233] In addition, large-scale storage of dangerous chemicals

---

225. Kruunuvuorenranta, Laajasalon länsiosien suunnittelun aloitusvaiheen taustatietoja, lähtökohtia ja ideoita, 31 Dec. 2002.
226. *Ibid.*
227. Helsingin kaupunginvaltuusto, 10 Dec. 2008 Kruunuvuorenrannan osayleiskaava.
228. Supreme Administrative Court, KHO:2004:84, 6 Sep. 2004.
229. Section 125 of the Act on Land Use and Building.
230. Act on Environmental Protection.
231. Decree on Environmental Protection.
232. Section 27 of the Act on Environmental Protection.
233. Section 27 of the Act on Environmental Protection.

requires a permit from the Safety Technology Authority; in the case of minor storing, providing information to the Authority is sufficient.[234] The major regulatory framework for terminal operations is codified in the Act on Environmental Protection, Act on Chemicals and Act on Water, including subsequent changes.[235] The national guidelines and practices for oil harbours date back to the 1970s. Obviously, there have been significant changes in terminal equipment, practices, vessels and transportation models since then, which has led to the need to update the standards to be in used in the Finnish oil harbours or to adopt the corresponding international standards for local purposes.

445. Recognizing the potential risk to health, safety and the environment of oil terminals and storage, legislation on chemical safety is of vital importance for the oil operators in the oil distribution chain. Therefore, implementation of Council Directive 2012/18/EU on the control of major-accident hazards involving dangerous substances is at the centre of legislative measures to prevent risks resulting from dangerous substances.[236] The Safety Technology Authority supervises such large-scale activities, and regional rescue authorities supervise small-scale activities.

446. Large-scale storage of dangerous chemicals requires a prior licence from the Safety Technology Authority.[237] The Authority is also authorized to inspect these operations. Further, any major modification and/or expansion require a licence and inspection by the same Authority. Large-scale storage facilities are also subject to periodic inspections by the Safety Technology Authority. It follows from the legislation that the operator of such large-scale facilities needs to be fully acquainted with the features and characteristics of the dangerous substances being stored. In addition, the operator has to appoint an individual who is familiar with the respective legislation and regulations.[238] The largest establishments are obliged to produce a safety report of the operations describing the establishment, the environment, the safety management system, possible safety hazards and accident scenarios. Large-scale establishments also have to draw up internal emergency plans. Joint storage areas that are shared by several operators need to have the area confirmed as a specific storage area if the operators share collective areas and fire-extinguishing equipment in order to define the obligations of the operators.

447. Those providing maintenance services relating to storage equipment, pipelines and oil tanks are subject to particular legal requirements and have to be licensed by the Safety Technology Authority. Underground tanks in important groundwater areas or in areas otherwise suitable for water resources have to be periodically inspected, and, in addition, environmental permits tend to expand the scope

234. Section 23 of the Act on Safe Use of Dangerous Chemicals and Explosives.
235. Act on Environmental Protection; Act on Chemicals; Act on Water.
236. Council Directive 2012/18/EU on the control of major-accident hazards involving dangerous substances.
237. Section 23 of the Act on Safe Use of Dangerous Chemicals and Explosives.
238. Section 29 of the Act on Safe Use of Dangerous Chemicals and Explosives.

of inspection requirements to include tanks located in less sensitive areas.[239] The inspection of underground tanks has raised different views, as such inspection may result in serious risks for the inspector.

448. Like oil terminals, power plants using coal have to be in compliance with zoning, environmental protection and waste legislation. Accordingly, environmental permits are required for power plants using coal, and, in addition, environmental permits are required for the stockpiling of coal. Essential disadvantages of the use of coal are the CO_2 emissions and other emissions, such as sulphur dioxide emissions, and, therefore, new power stations and new technology are very much needed as part of the best available techniques for LCPs in order to improve the environmental image of coal.[240] The separation of CO_2 emissions by new technology and more efficient coal-fired power stations could improve the position of coal as an energy source. As for the stockpiling of coal, the geographic location of the storage is important as emissions to groundwater or soil are among the potential environmental risks of coal. The current practice is to keep coal in underground storage.[241]

449. As the transportation market is the primary oil-consuming market in Finland, the networks of stations are of particular significance for the industry. In Finland, there were (in 2014) about 3.7 million registered vehicles, out of which about 3.2 million were passenger cars. Largely because of the changes in fuel taxes, the former increase of the share of diesel cars has not continued mainly due to the demand for hybrid cars and balanced consumer prices for gasoline and diesel fuel. In 2017, diesel cars made up about 30% of all passenger cars and of all new passenger car registrations.[242]

450. The total number of service stations in Finland has been slightly declining over the last decades. Although the demand in southern Finland for motor fuels goes clearly beyond the needs in other parts of the county, long distances across the whole country require an extensive network of distributors throughout Finland. The distribution networks have also been diversified. At the end of 2016, there were 1,857 distribution stations in Finland, of which 792 were manned service stations and 1065 were unmanned stations. The share of unmanned stations has continued to increase, reflecting the market requirement to reduce costs and increase efficiency. This market trend is seen in the 2016 figures, showing that unmanned stations accounted for about 57% of gasoline stations. On the other hand, the traditional service stations have expanded their services by providing convenience stores and, e.g., mail services as the tight fuel margins have challenged their position. The increase in the convenience store business is seen particularly in the expansion of the local cooperatives and by the cooperation of the oil companies

239. Section 54 of the Act on Safe Use of Dangerous Chemicals and Explosives.
240. European Union Reference Document on Best Available Techniques for Large Combustion Plants.
241. Helsingin Energia.
242. Autoalan tiedotuskeskus 2017.

with grocery retailers.[243] However, the liberalization of the opening hours for retail shops may have influenced the competitive edge of the convenience stores.[244]

451. Service stations and unmanned sites have to be in compliance with zoning legislation.[245] Therefore, if a city has a zoning plan in place, it is not legal to have a service station or unmanned station in an area that has not been zoned for fuel distribution purposes unless an exemption has been granted under the law. In the past, it had been unclear if unmanned stations could get more favourable treatment, but the current status has been made clear by the Supreme Administrative Court. In its judgment from the mid-1990s, the Supreme Administrative Court concluded that it was not possible to grant minor permits for unmanned sites when the site was zoned for office purposes in the city plan.[246] As a natural result, the establishment of new fuel distribution sites in city areas has become more demanding because of rezoning requirements.

452. In addition to the zoning requirements, the service stations and unmanned stations need to have environmental permits. According to the Act on Environmental Protection, operations that may lead to pollution have to be located in such a way that there will be no pollution or danger of pollution and that pollution can be prevented.[247] In the Government Bill for the Act on Environmental Protection, it was stated that locating fuel distribution sites on groundwater areas or near otherwise important water purchase sources would create such a danger.[248] This change has made it more difficult to open new fuel distribution sites, particularly as large parts of Finland are on groundwater areas. The changed legislation has also led to the curious situation where an established service station site can be zoned for service station purposes, but where no environmental permits are granted, making it impossible to continue with the old, established business in line with the zoning plan. Underground tanks on fuel distribution sites are subject to the Act on Use of Dangerous Chemicals and Explosives.[249] Such tanks have to be regularly inspected if they are located in important groundwater areas or in areas otherwise suitable for water purchases.[250] Environmental authorities are authorized by the Act on Environmental Protection to constantly review the site's operational standards, to measure the results and to give information to the respective authorities. It is a common practice to include various conditions in the environmental permits, which leads to a stricter environmental control system than that which is based directly on regulations.[251] As a common practice, underground tanks are often subject to regular controls even when they are not located in areas suitable for water purchases.

243. Finnish Petroleum and Biofuels Association excluding statistics of minor operators.
244. Repeal of the Act on opening hours for retail shops.
245. Act on Land Use and Building.
246. Supreme Administrative Court KHO:T:199, 24 Jan. 1995.
247. Act on Environmental Protection.
248. Government Bill HE214/2013.
249. Act on Safe Use of Dangerous Chemicals and Explosives.
250. Section 54 of the Act on Safe Use of Dangerous Chemicals and Explosives.
251. Examples are Espoo ympäristönsuojelulautakunta, City of Espoo Committee on Environmental Matters. Supreme Administrative Court KHO 5974/2017, 20. Nov. 2017.

453. The Finnish oil market faced historical restructuring when two major international oil companies exited from the Finnish gasoline and diesel oil market. Following the structural changes, the established local cooperatives increased their share in the Finnish oil market. In addition, the new emphasis on the development of bioenergy has had its effects., Neste Oil has the largest network of manned and unmanned sites (approximately 461 sites of which about 218 unmanned sites) but the number of stations of competing companies' sit is almost the same; ABC – chain of cooperatives (approximately 445 sites of which about 321 unmanned sites), St1 (approximately 244 sites of which about 187 unmanes sites) and Teboil (approximately 327 sites of which about 213 unmanned sites), Shell (approximately 171 sites of which about 55 unmanned sites) and SEO (approximately 200 sites of which 110 unmanned sites). In 2016, Neste Oil and ABC – chain of cooperatives accounted together about one-half of the manned and unmanned sites network.[252]

454. Oil has also been important in residential heating, although the share of new houses using oil heat has continued to drop significantly although hybrid energy houses have been popular.[253] District heating in urban areas challenges oil heating systems in particularly because in line with the Act on Land Use and Building, it is possible to require mandatory joining to the district heating system in the city plan if this is necessary to use energy efficiently, to meet air quality targets or to achieve other objectives in the city plan.[254] Solutions for zero energy houses and renewable energy solutions have become popular. Still, it is estimated that approximately 190,000 Finnish residential houses use heating oil in comparison with approximately 250,000 houses in 2005. The annual heating oil consumption of residential houses has been approximately 460 million litres, being approximately 2% of the Finnish total annual energy consumption.[255] Residential heating oil tanks in important groundwater areas are subject to regular control, and the owner of the tank can be held liable for oil pollution resulting from leakage of the tank based on the Act on Environmental Protection. Heating oil tanks are still being manufactured and installed, and, as the current standard dates back to 1974, this exposes current owners of the tanks to potential liabilities.

455. The use of oil by industry, airplanes and marine vessels is clearly essential, but will not be covered in this part. Industry and agriculture use oil for heating and power generation purposes. Heavy fuel is often used as a backup source of power for other forms of energy production. Here, oil is competing mainly against natural gas and domestic fuel sources. The jet fuel business at airports around the world is an essential part of the global business of commercial airlines, general aviation and the military. Here, the key players are the Finnish airports and the few jet fuel suppliers in Finland.

252. 'Finnish Petroleum and Biofuels Association'.
253. Combination of oil heating with other energy sources has been expanding. In particular, the oil industry has promoted the use of heating systems that combine oil and solar energy and other renewable energy sources.
254. Section 57a of the Act on Land Use and Building.
255. Finnish Petroleum and Biofuels Association.

456. Oil pollution fees have to be paid for crude oil and oil products imported to Finland or transported via Finland. The fee is deposited in the Oil Protection Fund,[256] which is a government fund outside the state budget. The purpose of the Fund is to take care of the costs of oil spills when the polluter is unknown or is not in a position to compensate for the damage. The Fund has been a major financier of purchases of municipal equipment for potential oil accidents. In addition to the preventive measures for oil accidents, the Fund has been contributing to the investigation and cleanup costs of oil-polluted soil and water. For example, since 1996, the fund was cooperating with the Finnish Petroleum and Biofuels Association in a joint programme to clean up oil-polluted sites.[257] The programme undertook restoration work on close to about 600 sites financing approximately EUR 50 million. The programme was terminated by the end of 2015 but a new programme was launched to investigate polluted sites without known polluters. The programmes have had an important role in supporting the cleanup of polluted service station sites in Finland, using the government Fund and the voluntary contributions of the oil industry. In the future, the funds from the oil pollution fee will also be used for the acquisition of new equipment for regional rescue services to safeguard the Gulf of Finland from the potential risk of oil damage, as the transportation of oil in the Gulf has continued to increase.

256. Act on Oil Protection Fund.
257. Financial Statements of Oil Protection Fund 2016.

Chapter 4. Quality

457. The former popularity of diesel-driven cars in comparison with cars using gasoline in Finland has been slightly diminishing since hybrid cars are entering the market as well. However, approximately 3,000 million litres of diesel oil were sold in 2016, showing a slight increase from previous years. Approximately 2,000 million litres of gasoline were sold in 2016, which was a slight decrease from the previous year.[258] In order to reduce greenhouse gas emissions that cause harm to people's health and pollute the environment, the need to replace oil by biofuels is encouraging research and production of biofuels and hence the mixture of conventional energy with biofuels is supporting the targets for better climate. The Act on Environmental Protection authorizes the government to regulate the content and marking of such substances to be manufactured, marketed, imported, exported or used in Finland. Hence, the government has decided on quality requirements that apply to motor gasoline and diesel marketed in Finland for use in motor vehicles.[259] The quality requirements have been changing in line with the EU legislation. It is prohibited to market leaded motor gasoline. The Ministry of the Environment is authorized to grant temporary exemptions from the quality requirements. The manufacturers and importers of motor gasoline and diesel have to provide annual reports to the Ministry of the Environment confirming that all motor gasoline and diesel provided by them to the market was in compliance with the quality requirements. The Act on Excise Taxes on Fuels defines the fuel qualities with corresponding tax obligations.[260]

458. The global concern over the dependency on conventional energy sources and the need to reduce greenhouse gas emissions has affected both the volume of energy used and the types of energy sources promoted. The share of biofuels in comparison with other energy sources and the pressure to support renewable energy and subsidies for biofuels has continued to increase the share of biofuels used in Finland as anticipated. It is expected that renewables will globally cover over 60% of power generation by 2040.[261]

459. Finnish oil refining has taken up the challenge of renewable fuels and has been investing in renewable diesel and biofuels production. Renewable diesel is blended with conventional diesel. In the past, the raw materials used for renewable diesel were vegetable oil and animal fat, but following research and EU directives, new raw materials in compliance with EU sustainability criteria, particularly waste, scrapand lignocellulosic material are also used for biofuels. Neste Oyj has even launched a product called Neste MY which is to be used as conventional diesel. The Neste MY diesel is made 100% of waste and scrap.[262]

258. Finnish Petroleum and Biofuels Association.
259. The Council of State Decree 1206/2010 on quality requirements for motor gasoline and diesel oil.
260. Act on Excise Taxes on Fuels.
261. International Energy Agency World Energy Outlook 2017.
262. Neste Oyj.

460. The Renewable Energy Directive of the EU sets out biofuels sustainability criteria for all biofuels consumed or produced in the EU to ensure that they are produced in a sustainable and environmentally friendly manner. Companies can show that they comply with the sustainability criteria through national systems or voluntary schemes recognized by the European Commission[263] in line with the revised Renewable Energy Directive, the aim is to make the EU a global leader in renewable energy and to ensure that the target of at least 27% renewables in the final energy consumption in the EU by 2030 is met. The Directive 2009/28/EC, which promotes biofuels and renewable energy, contains mandatory national targets from 10% to 49% for the share of renewable energies within total energy consumption and has particularly effected the quality requirements of fuels in Finland.[264] According to the directive 2009/28/EC, each Member State has to ensure that the share of energy from the renewable sources of transport in 2020 is at least 10% of the final consumption in energy transport in that Member State. The blending of biofuels with gasoline and diesel oil is one method to meet the target. The Renewable Energy Directive sets out biofuels sustainability criteria for all biofuels produced or consumed in the EU to ensure that they are produced in a sustainable and environmentally friendly manner. Hence advanced biofuels, such as those made from wastes and algae, provide high greenhouse gas emission savings with a low risk of causing indirect land use change and do not compete directly for agricultural land for the food and feed markets.[265] Finland has implemented the respective EU directives in the Act on promoting the use of biofuels in traffic[266] and the Act on biofuels and bioliquids.[267] The target of the Act on promoting the use of biofuels is to replace gasoline and diesel oil by biofuels. The Act sets mandatory obligations on distributors on the share of biofuels in gasoline and diesel oil provided for consumption. The share of biofuels increases annually and is expected to be 20% in 2020. In Finland, the share of biofuels has already been higher than the mandatory limit. In 2015, the share of biofuels used in traffic fuels was on average 24%.[268] Minor distributors are not covered by the Act and hence in 2015 four distributors[269] were subject to the obligation. The Act on biofuels and bioliquids defines the sustainability criteria regarding the reduction of greenhouse gas emissions for the life cycle in comparison with fossil fuels and the origin of biofuels in order to minimize the risks on indirect land use change. The operators need to have a system in place for sustainability in order to prove compliance with the Act and have to apply for the approval of the system from the Finnish EA. Alternatively, the operators may have voluntary systems in line with the systems approved by the European Commission.

461. Promotion of biofuels continues to require cooperation with car manufacturers in order to ensure suitability of the fuel with different modern engines. In

263. Renewable Energy Directive (2009/28/EC).
264. Directive 2009/28/EC on the promotion of energy produced from renewable energy sources.
265. Directive 2015/1513/EU amending Directive 98/70/EC and Directive 2009/28/EC.
266. Act on promoting the use of biofuels in traffic 446/2007 as amended.
267. Act on biofuels and bioliquids 393/2013 as amended.
268. Government Bill HE 184/2017.
269. Neste Oyj, North European Oil Trade Oy, Oy Teboil Ab and Suomalainen Energiaosuuskunta (SEO).

addition, taxation policy, research to identify the best available raw materials, further study of developed technology, investment and means to ensure the supply chains are essential to ensure the competitive availability of modern motor fuels. Development of biofuels as a mixture of gasoline and diesel oil is supporting the position of gasoline and diesel oil while competing with electricity-driven engines.

Chapter 5. Transportation

462. Transportation of oil and oil products to or through Finland takes place mainly by vessels and rail. The international conventions are of primary importance in the international trade. With respect to domestic deliveries, the Act on Transport of Dangerous Goods,[270] covering transport by truck, rail, vessel and plane, is of essential importance. The international European Agreement concerning the International Carriage of Dangerous Goods by Road (ADR) and the Regulations concerning the International Carriage of Dangerous Goods by Rail (RID) have been incorporated into local legislation. Transportation by road also has to be in compliance with the Act on Road Transportation.[271] The Act regulates the mandatory information needed for the consignment note. The consigner is liable to the carrier for costs and damage resulting from incorrect or missing information in the consignment note. The implementation of the Directive on the inland transport of dangerous goods has introduced more detailed safety requirements into the transport regulations covering packaging, tanks and bulk containers.[272] Accordingly, the transporter and the driver have to ensure that it is legal to carry dangerous goods on the planned roads, that the vehicle has the necessary documents, that the vehicle has no leakages or lack of equipment, that the control dates of the tanks are not overdue, that the volume and weight do not exceed the regulatory limits and that the safety guidelines are in the vehicle. The law also requires the operator to appoint one or several qualified safety advisors.

270. Act on Transportation of Dangerous Goods.
271. Act on Road Transportation.
272. The Council of State Decree to Amend the Council of State Decree on Transportation of Dangerous Goods 236/2009.

Chapter 6. Security of Supply

463. The security of the energy supply is one of the relevant issues to consider before crisis situations arise, in order to safeguard the critical infrastructure of society. The Finnish approach to emergency supply is based on national preparedness, measures implemented by the EU, the agreement on the International Energy Program and bilateral and multilateral agreements with other countries. The structure and basis for emergency situations in Finland are defined in the Readiness Act.[273] The purpose of the Act on Safeguarding Security of Supply[274] is to define how to ensure the continuation of critical operations and services in the society in an emergency situation. The interpretation of emergency covers serious interruptions in normal situations. The government body empowered to safeguard the supplies of necessary material and stocks and to coordinate the cooperation between the public and private sectors is the National Emergency Supply Agency. As part of its tasks, the Agency manages national emergency fuel stores. The cooperation between the public and private sectors in oil-related emergency matters takes place in the oil pool, which consists of representatives from the National Emergency Supply Agency and the member companies of the Finnish Petroleum and Biofuels Association. The purpose of the pool is to draft plans on the distribution of fuel, gas and lubricants during emergency situations.

464. Based on the International Energy Program and the EC directive,[275] Finland needs to have ninety days' worth of oil imports stored under the control of the authorities. This obligation on oil storage is implemented by the compulsory stockpiling of imported fuels and national emergency fuel stores. As a result of special circumstances in Finland, the level of energy security is likely to exceed the EU obligations and the obligations of the International Energy Program. Therefore, stockpiles of imported fuel stocks are likely to correspond to five months' worth of normal consumption. The stockpiling of fuel products also covers natural gas. The government has established the targets of security of supply.[276] The purpose is to promote energy production based on several fuels and procurement sources and to develop the use of domestic fuels and of municipal waste. Regarding the dependence on imported energy and the need to comply with international contractual obligations, imported fuels will be stockpiled in an amount corresponding on average to five months' worth of normal consumption. According to the government targets, domestic storage of imported energy fuels has to correspond at least to four months' worth of normal consumption of imported energy fuels. Stockpiles of coal by the National Emergency Supply Agency are needed for supporting the total target of energy security.

273. Act on Readiness 1552/2011.
274. Act on Safeguarding the Emergency Supplies 1390/1992.
275. International Energy Program 1682/1991; EC Directive 2009/119/EC, European Energy Security Strategy 28 May 2014.
276. The Council of State Decision on the Objectives of the Emergency Situations.

465. The Act on Compulsory Stockpiles of Imported Fuels requires that the oil-importing companies in Finland have a compulsory stockpile corresponding with two months' worth of average oil imports. The obligations of the importers are calculated on the basis of imported volumes for the previous year. Imports of both crude oil and oil products are similarly covered by the stockpiling obligations. Subject to permit, the compulsory stockpiles can be located outside Finland in other EU countries or in Norway, provided that the National Emergency Supply Agency can control the storage and that bilateral treaties are in place with the respective countries. The permit on stockpiling outside Finland can be unilaterally withdrawn in case of changes in the Finnish security-of-supply situation. The alternative to fulfil the compulsory stockpiling obligations by a network of agreements may give fuel importers more flexibility in terms of financing possibilities.

466. Compulsory stockpiles of coal amount to three months' worth of average use or import of coal during the previous three years. Coal is considered to be a practical and useful alternative to other energy sources for emergency situations due to its availability in the global markets and stockpiling possibilities. Hence, the emergency stockpiling of coal also partly covers other imported fuels. If the use of coal is limited for environmental reasons, energy security in emergency situations will also be hampered because of the lack of adequate storage capacity and logistics.

467. In the European Energy Security Strategy,[277]the European Commission is pointing to the common European energy policy and strengthening the EU´s energy security. The Commission underlines collective approach through a functioning internal market and cooperation at regional and European levels. The EU´s energy security is fostered by the target to move to a low-carbon economy. The European Energy Security Strategy is thus an integral part of the 2030 policy framework on climate and energy. The use of renewable energy and sustainable production of competitive fossil fuels are essential elements in the energy security strategy in the future.

468. In addition to the compulsory stockpiling preparedness for emergency situations, the oil market is subject to the compulsory strategic stockpile fee. The fee is collected together with fuel taxes from oil companies.

277. European Energy Security Strategy dated 28 May 2014.

Chapter 7. Conclusion

469. One of the key targets of the long-term climate and energy strategy report of the Finnish government, in addition to the promotion of renewable energy, is the improvement of energy efficiency. The EU Energy Services Directive was implemented in Finland largely through voluntary agreements as part of a network of agreements.[278] Similarly, the EU Energy Efficiency Directive has been implemented mainly through voluntary agreements in the networks.[279] The target of the Government is that at least a one-half of the binding reduction targets for Finland in the EU Energy Efficiency Directive will be fulfilled through voluntary agreements. The Finnish oil and biofuel industry had made an agreement with the government on an energy conservation programme relating to heating and transport fuels for 2008–2016 and has made a new agreement for the period 2017–2025. With respect to oil heating, the objects of the agreement are energy savings, an increase in the use of bio heating oils and promotion of the use of other renewable energy forms. The target for the new period in the oil and biofuel industry is that at least one-half of the real estate using heating oil will be using also renewable energy.

470. The oil industry continues to be subject to strong demand for changes, and, hence, there can be overlapping and conflicting legislation. As a result of the global target to reduce greenhouse gas emissions, legislators are trying to reduce the use of oil, promote alternative energy sources and enhance energy efficiency. Biofuels are renewable substitutes for fossil fuels and hence can support greenhouse gas emission reductions. The share of biofuels used in the transport sector is increasing and requires cooperation between the oil industry and the car industry to ensure that the fuels fulfil all quality and safety requirements. The increase in the share of biofuels will also affect logistics and the whole distribution chain, as the equipment is to be compatible with the new products. The sustainability criteria for biofuels are of significant importance while analysing investments in the renewable biofuel industry. Hence, the future of conventional gasoline and diesel oil mixed with biofuels in competition with electricity-driven cars is also dependent on the new legislation and its consistent implementation in the Member States. The target of the Government of Finland is to reduce the import of oil for domestic purposes and to have at least 30% biofuels in the fuels for transport by 2030. The increased share of biofuels also supports the aim to promote local industry and to increase the share of domestic components in the fuel. This chapter has dealt with oil, and, although oil will continue to be an important energy source, particularly for traffic, in the foreseeable future, the share of biofuel in the fuel will increase.

471. The traditional oil market in Finland is in a new situation. The country is heavily dependent on energy supplies, and, due to the country's large area, gasoline and diesel oil have been necessary in order to ensure safe, secure and flexible transportation for people and deliveries. However, the supplies of oil used in residential

278. European Energy End-Use Efficiency and Energy Services Directive 32/2006/EC.
279. European Directive on Energy Efficiency 2012/27/EU. European Energy End-Use Efficiency and Energy Services Directive 32/2006/EC.

heating and in industries need proper attention. European overinvestments have resulted in depressed oil markets and structural changes. Also, the oil industry in Finland has faced major changes in the past years. Now the changing product demand, quality requirements and emission legislation require traditional oil to be blended with biofuels and may thus introduce incentives for new investments.

472. The environmental challenges for coal are also significant in Finland and in spite of its position as alternative energy source particularly in emergency situations, and its stable prices, it is evident that the use of oil will also heavily decline in Finland.

Part IV. Interaction Between Energy Law and Environmental Law

Chapter 1. Introduction

473. Modern environmental law has originated from land and water law, consisting of land law (law related to real estate, parcelling, surveying, etc.), planning and building law, water law, and nature conservation and pollution control law. The focus has shifted over time. Environmental law, in its modern context, focuses on environmental quality, safety, liability and conservation of the natural and cultural environment.

474. Finland has never enacted a comprehensive code that incorporates all environmental regulation into a single statue. Instead, there are several important statutes such as the Environmental Protection Act, the Nature Conservation Act, the Water Act, and the Land Use and Building Act. Furthermore, there are dozens of other regulations that deal with some minor sector of the environment.

475. Traditionally, systems of regulation are divided into legal-administrative, economic, and informative regulation. In the Finnish environmental law system, the legal-administrative regulation is the most important form of regulation, and various types of plans and especially various permit procedures are used to regulate activities that can have a major impact on the environment. However, the significance of economic regulation has been on the rise, and the emissions trading scheme, in particular, is of great importance in the energy sector. There are also some initiatives towards informative regulation, such as various types of certifications and eco-labelling systems – either voluntary or involuntary.

476. Finland has been a Member State of the EU since 1995, and several EU directives have had a considerable impact on Finnish environmental legislation. In some sectors of environmental law, most of the pressure for new environmental legislation comes from the EU. Also, measures at the international level have had a significant impact on Finnish environmental law, and Finland is a party to several international environmental conventions and agreements. There are also some bilateral agreements between Finland and its neighbouring countries.

477. All generation of energy, and almost all conversion, transmission and use of energy as well, gives rise to some form of environmental impact. The combustion of different kinds of fossil fuels increases the concentration of greenhouse gases in the atmosphere and might cause pollution of air, water, and land. Hydropower, wind power, and energy transmission can have a significant impact on the environment in the form of their effects on nature and the landscape. Several energy processes produce waste – for example, ashes from the combustion of fossil fuels and spent nuclear fuel from nuclear power plants.

478. This part does not provide a comprehensive overview of Finnish environmental law but concentrates on interactions between energy issues and environmental law.[280] The areas that are the most significant from an energy sector perspective are decision-making and public participation (Chapter 2), emissions trading (Chapter 3), environmental pollution control and waste management (Chapter 4), land use and expropriation (Chapter 5), nature conservation (Chapter 6) and use of water resources (Chapter 7).

280. More detailed information about Finnish environmental law in general, *see* Vihervuori, Pekka, Environmental Law – Finland. Kluwer Law International.

Chapter 2. Decision-Making and Public Participation

§1. General Overview

479. According to section 20 of the Finnish Constitution, nature and its biodiversity, the environment, and the national heritage are the responsibility of everyone, and the public authorities must endeavour to guarantee for everyone the right to a healthy environment and the opportunity to influence the decisions that concern their own living environment. Thus, the goals of increasing citizens' opportunities to influence and participate in decision-making and of ensuring that information is widely available to citizens are among the key objectives behind the new environmental legislation enacted.

480. The 1998 Aarhus Convention on Access to Information, Public Participation in Decision-Making and Access to Justice in Environmental Matters has also had an effect on Finnish environmental legislation. The same applies to the Public Participation Directive.[281]

481. As a result, the central Finnish environmental legislation includes provisions for a possibility of interested persons to influence legal decision-making in advance. This applies to, for example, the Environmental Protection Act, Land Use and Building Act, and Nature Conservation Act.

482. Furthermore, a separate EIA is needed for all significant projects, and, in those cases, it is probably the most important legal procedure in terms of ensuring public participation. The EIA aims at integrating environmental considerations into the preparation of projects, plans, programmes and policies in early phases of planning. Consultation with stakeholders and public participation are an integral part of the assessment.

483. The current Act on EIA Procedure (Laki ympäristövaikutusten arviointimenettelystä; 252/2017, as amended) came into force in 2017. It is based on the EU Parliament and Council directive on the assessment of the effects of certain public and private projects on the environment (EIA Directive; 2011/92/EU).

484. In addition to the project based EIA, there is also EIA at the strategic planning level. The corresponding directive 2001/42/EC has been implemented by the Act on the Assessments of the Environmental Impacts of the Plans and Programs of Authorities (200/2005, as amended).

281. Directive 2003/35/EC of the European Parliament and of the Council providing for public participation in respect of the drawing up of certain plans and programmes relating to the environment.

§2. EIA Requirement

485. Based on Annex 1 of the Act on EIA Procedure, the following energy-related activities are, at the time of writing, subject to the EIA procedure:[282]

- boiler and power plants with a gross output of at least 300 MW;
- nuclear power plants and other nuclear reactors, including the demolition or decommissioning of these plants and reactors, except for research facilities;
- wind power plants involving a minimum of ten wind power turbines or a total power generation capacity of 30 MW or more;
- main pipelines intended for the long-distance transport of oil and liquids other than water or wastewater;
- gas pipelines with a diameter of more than 800 mm and a length of more than 40 km;
- overhead power lines carrying at least 220 kV and with a length of more than 15 km; and
- storages for oil, petrochemical products and chemical products when the total volume of the storage tanks for these substances is at least 50,000 m^3.

486. In addition, the assessment procedure must be applied to individual projects that will probably have a significant adverse environmental impact, also taking into account the combined impact of different projects. This responsibility covers all projects, irrespective of whether they have been mentioned in Annex II of the EIA Directive.

487. As a result, an EIA might be needed, as determined on a case by case basis by the Finnish Supreme Administrative Court, in projects that are smaller than those mentioned above, and also in more cases than necessary according to the Directive. The Finnish Supreme Administrative Court has decided that an EIA was needed for a natural gas pipeline with a length of 90 km, even when the diameter of the pipeline was only 500 mm (SAC 1633/2008, 3 June 2008). An EIA was needed as well for a 110 kV power line as well due to the significant landscape and natural, cultural and historical values (SAC 21.3.2012 t 647, 21 March. 2012).

§3. EIA Procedure

488. The concept of environmental impact is adopted in the legislation is broad. Environmental impacts encompass both direct and indirect impacts. The concept covers impacts not only on the environment, but also, for example, on living conditions and comfort, cultural heritage, and the utilization of natural resources (section 2 of the Act on EIA Procedure (252/2017, as amended).

282. Please note that certain activity descriptions may have been shortened and simplified here.

489. The project developer is responsible for carrying out the EIA. In the first phase, an EIA programme is drafted. That is a working programme for implementing the EIA procedure. In the programme, for example, project alternatives should be covered, one of which must be abandoning the project (the so-called *zero alternative*).

490. The EIA programme is submitted to the so-called *liaison authority*, which is usually the Centre for Economic Development, Transport and the Environment. However, in the case of nuclear power plants, the liaison authority is the Ministry of Employment and the Economy (section 10).

491. The liaison authority ensures that citizens and organizations in the area affected, as well as various authorities, have an opportunity to express their views on the EIA programme. The liaison authority also expresses its own opinion on the contents of the EIA programme.

492. Following the liaison authority's opinion, the project developer assesses the environmental impacts of the project and its alternatives and prepares an assessment report. After that, the stakeholders have a second opportunity to give statements and opinions, and the liaison authority gives its official final statement on the assessment report (section 23).

493. No authority may grant a permit for implementation of a project or make any other comparable decision before it has obtained the assessment report and the liaison authority's final statement on it. The permit decision on a project must state in what way the assessment report and the liaison authority's final statement on it have been taken into account (section 25). This applies for all environmental permits, including environmental permits under the Environmental Protection Act, water permits under the Water Act, and building permits under the Land Use and Building Act. This also applies to certain primarily non-environmental permits such as permits for the construction of high-voltage power lines under the Electricity Market Act.

494. The Act on EIA Procedure also applies in a transboundary context. Assessments of international environmental impacts are regulated by the Espoo Convention on Environmental Impact Assessment in a Transboundary Context and the EIA Directive. According to the Espoo Convention, signatory states must offer other states an opportunity to hold international negotiations on the potential transboundary impacts of projects in their territory, and on possible measures to reduce or prevent such impacts. Other signatory states to the convention have the right to participate in any EIA procedure conducted in Finland for projects that can be expected to have significant environmental impacts in their territory. The Ministry of the Environment looks after the notifications and negotiations required for a transboundary EIA procedure. International hearings must also be suitably scheduled within the timeframe of the national EIA procedure, especially based on the Espoo Convention on Environmental Impact Assessment in a Transboundary Context. Other states are entitled to participate in the EIAs conducted in Finland that are likely to cause significant adverse environmental impacts in their territories. Finland has a corresponding right to participate in assessments conducted in other countries whenever the projects under assessment are likely to have such impacts in Finland.

495. One example of an EIA in a transboundary context is the Nord Stream Extension, a project to construct and operate a natural gas pipeline through the Baltic Sea. On the one hand, an EIA is carried out in Finland, and it is possible for other states to participate in this. On the other hand, Finland has indicated willingness to participate in the other countries' respective EIA processes.

496. The EIA is not a permit procedure, and from the environmental point of view, a question is sometimes raised whether all environmental impacts assessed are fully taken account in the permitting. From the developer's point of view, the main problems with the EIA are that the assessment responsibility is very broad and that the assessment includes several phases that must be completed prior to the permitting procedure. In practice, an EIA procedure takes about a year. As a result, for example, a power plant or power line project with an EIA takes significantly longer to complete than a project that does not require an EIA.

Chapter 3. Emissions Trading

§1. Background

497. The EU greenhouse gas emissions trading scheme is based on the Directive 2003/87/EC, which entered into force on 25 October 2003.[283] The emissions trading scheme is the main instrument used by the EU to reduce greenhouse gas emissions cost-effectively, although several other initiatives exist as well. The current phase 3 (2013–2020) is based especially on the amendment 2009/29/EC of the Directive.

498. The EU emissions trading scheme works on the 'cap and trade' principle. A cap is set on the total amount of certain greenhouse gases that can be emitted by installations covered. The cap is reduced over time so that total emissions fall.

499. Within the cap, companies receive or buy emission allowances which they can trade with one another as needed. The limit on the total number of allowances available ensures that they have a value. After each year, a company must surrender enough allowances to cover all its emissions. If a company reduces its emissions, it can keep the spare allowances to cover its future needs or else sell them to another company that is short of allowances.

500. Basically, the EU emissions trading scheme ensures that the total emissions from the installations covered by the scheme do not exceed an overall limit set by the governments of the Member States. Allowing participating companies to buy or sell emission allowances should ensure that the targets can be achieved at the least cost.

501. Finland has implemented the Directive with the Emissions Trading Act (Päästökauppalaki; 311/2011, as amended). There are also several decrees covering, i.e., authorizing of verifiers (667/2013), monitoring and reporting (28/2013), new entrants (598/2012), applications for emissions permit (541/2012), and applications for free allowances (544/2011). In spite of the number of decrees, the role of the national legislation is moderately low due to the detailed EU level harmonization.

§2. Scope of the Act

502. According to the Emissions Trading Directive, all CO_2 emissions from combustion installations with a rated thermal input exceeding 20 MW, except hazardous or municipal waste incineration installations, are within its scope. This is also the basis of the Finnish Emissions Trading Act (section 2).

---

283. Directive 2003/87/EC establishing a scheme for greenhouse gas emission allowance trading within the Community and amending Council Directive 96/61/EC.

503. Under Article 24 of the Emissions Trading Directive, the Member States may apply the EU's emissions trading scheme to installations that are not listed in the Directive, provided that the inclusion of such installations is approved by the Commission (so-called *opt-in installations*). In Finland, all heat-generating installations that form a part of a district heating network are within the scope of the Emissions Trading Act whenever at least one of the installations forming the heat distribution network has an input of more than 20 MW. This aims to lead to an unbiased treatment of all installations generating heat for the same district heating network. Installations in the same network generate heat in a priority order based on their variable costs, and if only one or some of the installations were subject to emissions trading, this might affect their mutual financial priority order and competitive situation.

§3. Emissions Permit

504. Every installation within the scope of the Emissions Trading Act must have an emissions permit (section 8). The responsibility for issuing the permits lies with the EA, which is the national emissions trading authority in Finland.

505. To obtain a permit, the operator must be capable of monitoring and reporting emissions in a reliable manner. Furthermore, the grant of a permit for CO_2 emissions requires that the necessary permits under the Environmental Protection Act or an older environmental legislation be granted with respect to the installation in question (section 10). In other respects, there is no relationship between emission permit according to Emission Trading Act and other environmental permits.

506. The EA will annul a greenhouse gas emissions permit if the environmental permit of the installation has expired or has been annulled, (the installation) has been permanently decommissioned or the permit holder announces that operations will not be started. Furthermore, a greenhouse gas emissions permit could be annulled if the permit holder has essentially infringed its obligations (section 16). In the case of annulment of the permit, the emission allowances allocated to the installation are no longer registered on the operator's emissions trading account (section 50).

§4. Auctioning of Allowances

507. Auctioning is the default method of allocating allowances within the EU emissions trading system. Approximately more than 50% of EU Allowances will be auctioned during the trading period 2013–2020.

508. The auctioning of allowances is governed by the EU ETS Auctioning Regulation (1031/2010). This covers the timing, administration and other aspects of auctioning to ensure it is conducted in an open, transparent, harmonized and non-discriminatory manner.

509. The auctioning method is the single-round, sealed-bid auction. Bidders submit their proposals unaware of the bids of others, and the auction clearing price is determined by the lowest bid. All winning bidders will ultimately pay an equal price for their allowances.

510. Only few Member States (Germany, the United Kingdom and Poland) have elected to organize their own auctions. Finland's auctionable allowances are sold at a common auctioning platform, the Leipzig-based European Energy Exchange (EEX). The competent authority for organizing the auctions and for crediting auction revenue toward the state budget in Finland is the EA.

§5. Free Allocation of Allowances

511. Unlike during the period of 2008–2012, in the period of 2013–2020, free allowances are no longer allocated to electricity production. Only eight Member States which have joined EU since 2004 are allowed to continue granting limited number of free allowances until 2019 for electricity production and Finland is not among these Member States. Instead, Finnish power plants operators have to purchase all the allowances they need at auctions or from the market.

512. Heat production and various industries continue to receive a share of their allowances for free, but free allocation will decrease in linear fashion during the period 2013-2020. Unlike in the period of 2008–2012, national allocation plans are no longer used. Instead, the allocation of free allowances is based on harmonized allocation methodologies. EU-wide harmonized rules for free allocation are set out in the European Commission's 2011 Benchmarking Decision (Decision 2011/278/EU determining transitional Union-wide rules for harmonized free allocation of emission allowances pursuant to Article 10a of Directive 2003/87/EC of the European Parliament and of the Council).

513. In Finland, the free allowances are applied to the Ministry of Economic Affairs and Employment, which calculates initial amounts of allowances and presents information to the Commission. In 2013–2020, a total of 450 installations located in Finland will receive free allowances. Their total free allocation is equivalent to an average of 19.7 million tonnes of CO_2 per year.

514. Due to the decisions concerning free allocation of allowances in the period 2013–2020, four appeals were directed to the Supreme Administrative Court of Finland. It decided to ask for preliminary ruling of the European Court of Justice especially on the validity of the acts of the Commission. The European Court of Justice replied that Article 4 and Annex II (cross-sectoral correction factor) to Commission Decision 2013/448/EU were invalid (C-506/14). However, the temporal effects of the declaration of invalidity were limited so as to enable the Commission to adopt the necessary measures. This decision has no impact on energy production.

§6. Transferring, Registering and Trading of Allowances

515. The emissions trading scheme requires that ownership, transfer and annulment of allowances be registered. Provisions to this effect are set forth in the Chapters 8 and 9 of the Emissions Trading Act. The EA acts as the keeper of the national register, and the national register is connected to the central register of the European Commission, which conducts automatic checks of each entry in the register in order to ensure that the annual registration, transfer and annulment of emission allowances comply with the regulations in force.

516. An emission allowance represents an economic value and may be transferred and traded as soon as it has been issued. A natural or a legal person may possess emission allowances whether /it is an operator within the scope of the emissions trading scheme or not. Emission allowances can be transferred between persons and entities.

§7. Monitoring and Verification of Emissions and Surrendering Allowances

517. The operator must monitor its emissions within the scope of the Emissions Trading Act in a consistent, reliable and accurate manner and draw up a report on them for each calendar year in compliance with the Act and the provisions laid down by virtue of it and the conditions set in the greenhouse gas emissions permit issued by the Finnish EA (section 56).

518. In emission report verification, the operator must use a verifier that is authorized in Finland under the Emissions Trading Act or a verifier that is authorized in another state belonging to the EEA. The verification focuses on the reliability, credibility and accuracy of the monitoring system as well as the emission figures and information provided. The verifier draws up a statement on the emission report in which it states whether the emission report is satisfactory. An emission report can be considered satisfactory if the emissions have been monitored in accordance with an approved monitoring plan, including all emission sources, and the emission report does not include any essential misinterpretations.

519. The operator must ensure that the report drawn up on the emissions annually and the verifier's statements on the report are delivered to the EA by the 31 March of the following year. On the public website, citizens are given an access to the information of the Finnish emissions permits, emission reports, verifier permits and verifier reports (www.paastokauppa.fi).

520. The operator has to surrender enough allowances to cover their total emissions by 30 April of the following year. The excess emissions penalty is EUR 100 for each tonne of CO_2 equivalent emitted by that installation for which the operator has not surrendered allowances, and the payment of the excess emissions penalty shall not release the operator from the obligation to surrender an amount of allowances equal to those excess emissions. According to a decision by the Finnish Supreme Administrative Court (2009:78), the penalty fee cannot be moderated.

Chapter 4. Environmental Protection and Waste Management

§1. General Overview

521. The Environmental Protection Act applies to all activities that lead or may lead to environmental pollution. It covers emissions to the air, water and ground. The Act also applies to activities that generate waste and to the recovery and disposal of waste (section 2). The Act does not apply to the prevention of the harmful effects of radiation insofar as it is addressed in the Nuclear Energy Act (990/1987 as amended) or the Radiation Act (592/1991, as amended).

522. The environmental permit system is the main tool for pollution control under the Environmental Protection Act. It is based on case by case decision-making, but there are numerous technical provisions that must be taken into account. These cover, e.g., emission limit values and environmental quality standards. As part of the permit assessment procedure, the parties who might suffer inconvenience due to pollution, as well as other interested parties, may express their opinion. In addition, the Environmental Protection Act regulates accidental and temporary activities and the prevention and restoration of polluted soil and groundwater.

523. Even if combating climate change has been mentioned as an objective in the Environmental Protection Act, climate effects cannot be regarded as relevant pollution in single permit cases. The Act and the permit system is based on the idea of concrete polluting effects, and the Supreme Administrative Court has consistently held that in an individual environmental permit case, greenhouse gas emissions cannot be regarded as environmental pollution in the context of the Environmental Protection Act.

§2. Requirement for Environmental Permit

524. Under the Environmental Protection Act, essential activities causing the risk of pollution to the environment are subject to advance supervision, and an environmental permit is required. The need for an environmental permit is regulated by section 27 of the Environmental Protection Act and concretized in Annex I.

525. An environmental permit is needed for all *directive installations*, following the Annex I of the Directive on Industrial Emissions (2010/75/EU), such as combustion of fuels in installations with a total rated thermal input of 50 MW or more.

526. There are also some other installations mentioned in the Annex I of the Environmental Protection Act such as combustion units with a rated thermal input of 20 MW or more, fuel stations for the distribution of liquid fuels where the capacity of the storage tank is at least 10 m^3, coal storage and peat production and related drainage work where the production area exceeds 10 hectares. Even though these are not directive installations, they still require an environmental permit.

527. There are some additional situations designated by law. An environmental permit is required for activities that may place unreasonable burden on the surroundings, as referred to in section 17(1) of the Adjoining Properties Act (Laki eräistä naapuruussuhteista; 26/1920). The requirement for a permit for these kinds of activities is based on their estimated adverse effects, and the need for a permit is determined case by case. In some cases, it has been deemed that a wind power plant near a residential area needs an environmental permit. A permit is also required for any significant alteration of an activity.

528. It should be kept in mind that the term *environmental permit* is used here in a narrow sense, referring solely to the permit mechanism regulated in the Finnish Environmental Protection Act. Gas pipelines, power lines, and wind power plants, for example, always require permits with environmental considerations, but not necessarily according to the Environmental Protection Act.

529. Nuclear power plants need an environmental permit. Nevertheless, the environmental permit does not control nuclear-specific issues such as radioactive emissions and radioactive waste, but rather only general pollution – in particular, whether the fish and aquatic ecosystems are threatened due to the discharge of warmed cooling water.

530. Previously, small combustion plants from 5 MW to 20 MW were within the environmental permitting system. Nowadays, instead of applying for an environmental permit, these operators must submit an announcement to register the operation in the environmental data system no less than ninety days prior to commencing the operation.

§3. Permit Procedure

531. There are two kinds of environmental permit authorities in Finland at present: six Regional State Administrative Agencies (*aluehallintovirasto*) and more than one hundred municipal environmental authorities. The Regional State Administrative Agencies process the permit applications of projects with the most substantial environmental impacts, and municipal environmental authorities process all other projects.

532. An operator has to submit a permit application to the competent permit authority. Applications must include a report on the activity, its impact, the parties concerned, and other matters relevant in the permit consideration; requirements are set out in more detail in Chapter 2 of the Environmental Protection Decree. The EIA report, if required, must be presented to the permit authority as well.

533. The permit authority must request an opinion on the permit application from the regional environmental authority and from the municipal environmental protection committee. In some cases, the permit authority must also request an opinion from other authorities (section 42). Furthermore, the permit authority must provide those, whose rights or interests might be concerned, with an opportunity to lodge a complaint regarding the matter. Also, other persons are provided with an opportunity to state their opinion. The application must usually be announced in at least one newspaper in general circulation, and parties especially concerned by the matter must be notified separately. In addition to these individuals, various types of organizations have the opportunity to express their opinions.

534. Often there is a great deal of interaction among the applicant, the permit authority, and any interested third parties during the permitting procedure. It is even possible that the permit authority will give the applicant the opportunity to complement its application in order to fulfil the requirements before the final decision is given.

535. There are no time limitations regarding the authority's actions that would ensure that the permit application is processed within a certain time. As an average, an environmental permitting procedure without appeals takes a little over a year.

536. The decision granting or denying a permit can be appealed. The first level of appeal is the Vaasa Administrative Court. The second and final level is the Supreme Administrative Court, but an appeal requires a leave of appeal. In addition to the applicant, the right to appeal accrues to other persons whose rights or interests may be affected by the matter (typically neighbours); registered associations or foundations whose purpose it is to promote environmental, health or nature protection or the general amenity of the environment and whose area of activity is subject to the environmental impact in question; and some authorities. The average length of appeal proceedings in environmental matters is a little over a year in the Vaasa Administrative Court and about a year in the Supreme Administrative Court.

537. The costs of the permitting procedure vary considerably depending on the magnitude of the project and the permit authority in question. For instance, the current permit processing fee for combustion plants over 300 MW is EUR 21,700. This does not include the operator's own expenses, such as the cost of assessing the environmental impact of the project.

§4. General Permit Assessment

538. As preconditions for granting an environmental permit, the activity cannot, by itself or together with other activities, cause:

(1) harm to health;
(2) other significant environmental pollution or risk thereof;
(3) a consequence that would contradict the bans on polluting the soil, groundwater and sea;

(4) deterioration of special natural conditions or risk to water supply or other potential use, important to the public interest in the activity's area of impact;
(5) any unreasonable degree of nuisance to neighbouring properties; and
(6) a substantial weakening of the prerequisites to maintain and develop Sámi culture (specified in more detail in section 49 of the Environmental Protection Act).

539. Additionally, activities may not be located so that they will conflict with the detailed local plan for the area, and they must be located so that they will not cause pollution or pose a risk thereof and so that pollution can be prevented, whenever feasible (sections 12).

540. Permit's regulations concerning each permit must cover emission limit values, wastes and reduction of their generation and harmfulness, action to be taken in case of a disturbance or in other exceptional situations and measures to be taken after cessation of operation such as remediation of the area and prevention of emissions. When permit regulations are issued, the nature of the activity, the properties of the area where the impact appears, the impact of the activity on the environment as a whole, the significance of measures intended to prevent pollution of the environment as a whole and the technical and financial feasibility of this action must be taken into account. Permit regulations concerning emission limit values and the prevention and limitation of emissions have to be based on the best available technology (section 52).

541. In the case of directive installations, the EU level best available technique (BAT) conclusions shall be the reference for setting the permit conditions. Under normal operating conditions, emissions are not allowed to exceed the emission levels associated with the best available techniques as laid down in the decisions on BAT conclusions, as required in the Industrial Emissions Directive (Article 15). However, the authority may, in specific cases, set less strict emission limit values.

542. With regard to the generation of energy, permit regulations cannot concern production volume or, as a general rule, fuels (section 52). Thus, it is the operator – not environmental authorities – that defines the fuels used (coal, natural gas, biomass, peat, etc.) and the amount of energy produced.

§5. Combustion Plants

543. With regard to combustion plants, it is important to notice that the first BAT conclusions were published on 17 August 2017 in the Official Journal of the EU (2017/1442/EU). Because of this, the environmental permits of the directive installations are subject to a review process within six months after revision of the BAT conclusions, as required in section 80(1) of the Environmental Protection Act. Based on the review, it might be necessary to apply for the review of the environmental permit. A new environmental permit based on the new BAT conclusions may be issued, and the operator must comply with the new emission limits within four years after the revision of the BAT conclusions.

544. In addition to the BAT conclusions, certain government decrees are of great importance. These include Decree 936/2014 on large combustion plants, Decree 165/2017 on medium-sized combustion plants and Decree 151/2013 on waste incineration, which set specific limits for several types of emissions. The limit values are based mainly on Chapter III and Chapter IV on the Directive on Industrial Emissions, and Directive 2015/2193/EU on the limitations of certain pollutants into the air from medium combustion plants. A permit regulation may be stricter than a specific minimum environmental protection requirement contained in a government decree in order to meet the preconditions for granting a permit, to ensure that environmental quality requirements issued by decree are met to protect waters or to require use of the best available technology (section 70 of the Environmental Protection Act).

§6. Peat Production

545. In Finland, peat extraction sites cover about 70,000 hectares in total. An environmental permit is needed if a production area exceeds 10 hectares.

546. The Environmental Protection Act applies to water pollution, including the drainage stage of peat production. The Act also covers the harmful dust caused by peat extraction. Previously, the environmental permit considerations did not include impacts on nature or landscape, if affected physically by the project but not through pollution. This changed in 2014, and according to the section 13 of the current Environmental Protection Act, peat production location decisions must not result in damage to nature value of national or regional significance.

§7. Noise Pollution

547. In addition to other pollutants, noise abatement is also largely covered by the Environmental Protection Act, and noise is, by definition, one form of pollution. Limits of allowed noise and the allowed times of a day or a week for causing noise are typical items of environmental permit provisions.

548. In practice, the non-binding starting point of the noise provisions in environmental permits is the Government Decree on Noise Level Guidelines (993/1992). The guideline value for daytime is 55 dB, which applies in areas in use for dwelling, recreational areas in built-up areas, and their immediate vicinity, as well as in areas serving care or educational facilities. The corresponding night-time guideline value is 50 dB for existing areas and 45 dB for new areas.

549. In August 2015, the Government Decree on Guideline Values for Outside Noise Levels of Wind Turbines (1107/2015) was adopted, and the guideline values set out are stricter than those provided in the Government Decree on Noise Level Guidelines. According to the Decree on Guideline Values for Outside Noise Levels of Wind Turbines, the noise of wind farms shall not exceed 40 dB at night and 45 dB at daytime outdoors in permanent or holiday residential areas. The guideline value at educational institution and recreational areas shall not exceed 40 dB during daytime. The reference value set for national parks is 40 dB, which applies both during day and night time. Even if an environmental permit is not needed for a wind power plant, the noise abatement is taken into account in the Land Use and Building Act procedures for wind turbines.

§8. Waste

550. In environmental permits, there are provisions on the waste resulting from the activity. A separate permit according to the Environmental Protection Act is generally needed also for any installation-scale or professional refuse or recovery of waste. However, according to the Decree on the Recovery of Certain Waste in Earth Construction (843/2017), no environmental permit is needed in certain cases, if waste quality control and recovery is arranged, and is notified to the environmental protection database. The Decree applies to fly ashes from the combustion of coal, peat and wood-based material, bottom ash, and fluidized bed sand. An essential condition is that the leaching and content of the harmful substances in the waste shall not exceed the limit values set out in the Annex II of the Decree.

551. Waste tax under the Waste Tax Act (1126/2010, as amended) is also worth mentioning here. The tax is levied on waste that is delivered to a landfill. At present, the tax rate is EUR 50 per tonne of waste. The costs can be significant for combustion plant or waste incineration plant operators, if disposal in the landfills is needed.

§9. Control

552. Permit supervision is conducted by municipal authorities and by the Centres for Economic Development, Transport and the Environment. The supervisory authorities have been granted rights to carry out inspections and get access to information that is necessary for supervisory control (section 172 of the Environmental Protection Act). The permit and supervisory authorities also have widespread options in case of violation: they can, for example, order an operator that violates permit regulations to fulfil its duty, to restore the environment to the state it was before or eliminate the harm caused to the environment by the violation or to conduct an investigation on a scale sufficient to establish the environmental impact of its operations (sections 179 and 181).

553. The authority who granted the permit also amends it if needed, for example, when the pollution is substantially different than what was expected or the circumstances have changed substantially since the granting of the permit (section 89).

554. The permit may be revoked if the operator has provided erroneous material information or if the permit regulations have been violated repeatedly despite a written reminder (section 88).

Chapter 5. Land Use and Expropriation

§1. General Overview

555. The Land Use and Building Act (Maankäyttö- ja rakennuslaki; 132/1999, as amended) came into force in 2000. The Act regulates land use planning and building activities. The objective of the Act is to ensure that the use of land and water areas and building activities on them create preconditions for a favourable living environment and promote sustainable development ecologically, economically, socially, and culturally. The Act also aims to ensure that everyone has the right to participate in the preparation process (section 1).

556. One of the key principles behind the Land Use and Building Act is municipal decision-making. The State has no direct control over individual planning decisions, whereas the municipalities do have direct responsibility for their environment, land use planning, and building supervision. At the national level, the functions of the Ministry of the Environment include the general development and guidance of land use planning and building activities as well as the promotion, steering, and monitoring of regional planning. The national land use objectives are also decided at the national level by the Council of State.

557. Actual plans are divided into two categories: general and detailed plans. There are two types of general plans: a regional plan and a master plan, but only one type of detailed plan: the local detailed plan. This has two subtypes: the normal local detailed plan and the detailed shore plan.

§2. National Land Use Objectives

558. There is no national spatial plan in Finland,[284] but the national land use objectives are decided upon by the Council of State (section 22 of the Land Use and Building Act). The Ministry of the Environment is in charge of drafting national land use objectives in collaboration with the other ministries, regional councils and other authorities and parties (section 23).

559. Energy aspects play some role in the national land use objectives. According to the objectives, land use should satisfy the national needs for energy supply and promote the possibilities of utilizing renewable energy sources. Power lines and gas pipelines important for the national energy supply should be taken into account. It is also stated in the objectives that the locations of wind power works should primarily be concentrated so as to combine several works.

284. The Ministry of the Environment prepares non-binding national strategies, and there are also special programmes on, e.g., forests, shoreline management, cultural heritage, etc. There are also Natura 2000 areas, which are designated at the national level.

560. Government authorities must take national land use objectives into account, promote their implementation and assess the impact of their actions on local structure and land use. In regional and other land use planning, national land use objectives must be taken into account in a way that promotes their implementation (section 24).

§3. Land Use Plans

561. As mentioned above, all plans are drawn up by municipal bodies. Finland is divided into nineteen regions, each having a regional land use plan that covers the area of several municipalities. These regional land use plans are drafted and approved by the regional councils, which are made up of representatives from the municipalities. The contents of the master plan and the local detailed plan are a matter of municipal decision-making.[285]

562. Regional land use plans may be a comprehensive regional land use plans covering all major planning issues in the whole region, or a phased regional land use plans covering certain specific planning issues during each planning phase or sub-regional land use plans covering smaller sub-regions. There have been several regional plans in which only suitable wind power areas are reserved. It is also possible to draft a regional plan for a single project. This has been done, for example, for a nuclear power plant.

563. The regional plan is to be used as a guideline when other plans are drawn up and when any other measures are taken to organize land use. When planning land use in more detail, authorities must take the regional plan into account, seek to promote implementation of the plan and ensure that taking the measures under consideration does not hinder the plan's implementation. A building restriction is in force in areas designated by the regional plan as recreational or protected areas or areas for transportation or technical service networks. Where a building restriction is in force, a building permit may not be granted if it hinders implementation of the regional plan (section 33).

564. Usually, the master plan covers the entire area of the municipality. The minimum requirement for a municipality is to adopt a plan without legal impact – that is, to have a sketch for the future development of the area for the municipality's own purposes. A permit cannot be rejected by referring to such a non-binding plan.

565. There are also binding master plans that may directly affect individual cases, and in some cases, building permits may be granted on the basis of master plans. This applies especially to the wind power plant construction, and there is a specific regulation which allows the local master plan to be drafted specifically for

285. Local authorities may also cooperate in drawing up the joint master plan and delegate the approval of the plan to some joint body of the local authorities. A joint master plan that has legal consequences has to be submitted to the Ministry of the Environment for ratification.

wind power plant construction. The wind power local master plan only covers the project area and allows the building permits to be granted directly based on the master plan.

566. Earlier there were several categories of detailed plans, but in 2000, they were integrated into one category, the local detailed plan or town plan. The need for detailed plans depends on the stage of development and housing. However, the minimum requirements for plans are defined in the law. A local detailed plan must be drafted so that it guarantees the preconditions for a healthy, safe and comfortable living environment; for locally available services; and for traffic arrangements. The built-up and natural environments must be preserved, and their special values must not be destroyed.

567. Any activity subject to an environmental permit cannot be located in conflict with a detailed local plan. Consequently, in a power plant project, it is often necessary to change the detailed local plan prior to the environmental permitting procedure.

568. In some cases, construction might be possible without land use planning. Building permits without land use planning can be granted based on a so-called deviation permit, which allows the municipality to deviate from any land use purpose defined in a general or a detailed plan. It is also possible to grant a permit to build without a detailed plan, in spite of actual planning need, if the additional preconditions set forth in section 137 of the Land Use and Building Act are met. Land use planning may be deemed unnecessary for wind power projects when only few turbines are planned in a specific area. However, this option is very limited and there are several cases from the Supreme Administrative Court indicating that in normal situations, planning is needed. For example, in a case SAC 2013:183 the Court considered that it was not possible to grant a permit without planning for a wind farm of five turbines due to the potential disadvantage to future planning.

§4. Expropriation of Land

569. The ownership of real property is protected by the Constitution of Finland (section 15) as it is in most other countries. However, particularly with power line and natural gas pipeline projects, voluntary land acquisition is often impossible, and in those cases, the ability to expropriate land is essential. This has also been the case in a planned nuclear power plant project. The expropriation is regulated mainly under the Expropriation Act (Lunastuslaki; 603/1977, as amended).

570. The expropriation procedure has two phases. The expropriation permit is handled in an administrative procedure. After that, the compulsory purchase, including especially the determination of compensation, is executed in an expropriation proceeding. In high-voltage power line projects, an EIA (*see* Chapter 2) and a permit under the Electricity Market Act are required prior to the expropriation procedure.

571. The expropriation permit is granted by the Council of State. The permit can be granted if the compulsory purchase is necessary for the public interest, if the purpose cannot be suitably achieved in some other way or if the harm caused to the private interest is not greater than the benefit to the public interest (section 4 of the Expropriation Act). Expropriation for an electricity plant is regulated separately in Act on Expropriation for Electricity Plant (168/1928, as amended).

572. The compulsory purchase is executed in the expropriation proceedings by an expropriation committee, which consists of a cadastral surveyor from a District Survey Office and two lay members. The post of a lay member is a municipal position of trust, and a lay member must be familiar with the local conditions and matters in real estate. The expropriation committee has the power to decide on all matters required to execute the decision of the Council of State. The committee confirms the expropriated object, maps and demarcates it, identifies and describes the property rights to be expropriated, carries out the necessary relocation of private roads, decides on the reparation of damages and so on. The committee is not bound by the claims of the parties, but all relevant material has to be acquired and taken into consideration by the committee. The decisions of the expropriation committee can be appealed to the Land Court, which is a special body in a few local courts. The decisions of the Land Court can be appealed to the Supreme Court if it grants a leave to appeal.

573. The entire expropriation process takes several years. Nevertheless, the common opinion in Finland is that compulsory purchase is relatively easy and fast compared to expropriation in many other countries. The expropriation process is quite rapid and flexible, and the costs of the proceedings are reasonable.[286]

286. Klaus Viitanen, 'Compulsory Purchase as an Administrative Procedure', 3rd FIG Regional Conference, Jakarta, Indonesia, 3–7 Oct. 2004.

Chapter 6. Nature Conservation

§1. General Overview

574. The present Nature Conservation Act (1096/1996, as amended) was enacted in 1996. It is a modernized version of the previous act of 1923, and the EU membership has profoundly affected the enactment process. The most important obligations implied by EU membership are contained in the Council Directive 92/43/EEC on the Conservation of Natural Habitats and of Wild Fauna ('the Habitats Directive') and the Council Directive 79/409/EEC on the Conservation of Wild Birds.

575. An important concept of the Nature Conservation Act is favourable conservation status, which is based on the Habitats Directive. In order to achieve the aims of the Act, nature conservation must focus on attaining and maintaining a favourable conservation status of natural habitats and of wild fauna and flora. The conservation status of a natural habitat is taken as favourable when its natural range and the areas it covers within that range are stable enough to ensure the long-term maintenance of the said habitat and of the structure and functions of its ecosystem, and when the conservation status of its typical species is deemed favourable (section 5).

576. The Act includes provisions on nature conservation planning and conservation programmes (sections 7–9), nature reserves (sections 10–28), conservation of natural habitats (sections 29–31), landscape conservation (sections 32–36) and protection of species (sections 37–49). There are also special provisions on the Natura 2000 network (sections 64–69).

577. The Nature Conservation Act was a step towards an integrated approach. There are several horizontal rules that must be respected in all permit procedures beyond the Nature Conservation Act itself, and nature conservation according to the Act is not built on nature reserves alone.

578. In the energy sector, almost all projects can face nature conservation issues. The area of greatest potential conflict lies within such projects as wind farms, power lines, and peat production, which all need large areas.

§2. Nature Conservation Planning

579. Nationwide protection programmes have been prepared in Finland for decades. The programmes cover mires, bird wetlands, eskers, herb-rich woodlands, shores, and old-growth forests. Previously the nature of the programmes has been ambiguous. In the absence of statutory provisions, these older programmes can be considered more as declarations rather than as regulations.

580. In contrast to the earlier programmes, the programmes established under the new Nature Conservation Act have legal effects. The Ministry of the Environment is responsible for the drafting of nature conservation programmes, and these programmes must be adopted by the Council of State (section 8). Any action that jeopardizes the conservation objectives of a site included in a nature conservation programme adopted by the Council of State is prohibited. However, the regional environmental authority (the Centre for Economic Development, Transport and the Environment) may grant derogations from the restriction, provided that the conservation objectives of the site are not jeopardized to any substantial degree. The programmes set guidelines for planning as well (section 9).

§3. Nature Reserves

581. Under the Nature Conservation Act, nature reserves can be national parks, strict nature reserves or other nature reserves.

582. A national park has to be at least 1,000 hectares in size. The area should hold general interest as a natural attraction or be designed to raise general awareness of or interest in nature. A strict nature reserve should hold significance as a means of safeguarding undisturbed natural development or furthering scientific research or education. National parks and strict nature reserves can be established only on state-owned land. Any action altering the natural surroundings in a national park and in a strict nature reserve is prohibited (sections 12–13).

583. Other nature reserves are often conservation areas on private land. These are normally established on application or with the consent of the landowner. However, the regional environmental authority may designate a nature reserve on private land without the landowner having applied for it or given his consent if the land in question falls within the bounds of a nature conservation programme adopted by the Council of State (section 24).

584. Energy sector projects are seldom placed in nature reserves, but sometimes this cannot be avoided. For a national park or a strict nature reserve, derogations from protection provisions may be enacted by decree, provided that the conservation objectives are not jeopardized (section 16). The regional environmental authority is authorized to lift a protection order on private land or to grant derogations from it, provided that the ecological value of the site has declined substantially or its protection prevents the implementation of a project or plan of overriding public interest (section 27).

§4. Conservation of Natural Habitats and Biotopes

585. Section 29 of the Nature Conservation Act lists protected biotopes that should not be endangered. These include wild woods rich in broad-leafed deciduous species, hazel woods, common alder woods, sandy shores in their natural state, and the like. The prohibition takes effect when the regional environmental authority has set the boundaries of the natural habitat to be protected and has notified the site's owners and holders of its decision. In individual cases, the regional environmental authority may grant derogations from the prohibition if this does not seriously jeopardize the conservation objectives of the natural habitat type in question or if its protection prevents the implementation of a project or plan to override public interest (section 31).

586. Also, the destruction and deterioration of breeding sites and resting places used by specimens of certain animal species are prohibited (section 49). These animals are defined in Annex IV(a) of the Habitats Directive. In special cases, the regional environmental authority is authorized to grant derogations from the prohibition on grounds set forth in the Habitats Directive. The derogation has been granted, for example, for a hydropower company due to rare butterfly, scholarly herd (*Capricornia boisduvaliana*), found on a sandy bank of a river and threatened by the planned power plant construction.

587. Both regulatory orders mentioned above have a horizontal function, and the protection must be respected in all decision-making procedures (planning, environmental permit, expropriation permit, etc.). In practice, the most common habitats and biotopes protection issue in energy sector projects has been the protection of the Siberian flying squirrel (*Pteromys volans*), which is mentioned in Annex IV(a) of the Habitats Directive. It lives within a range from western Finland and the Baltic States to the Pacific coast. The International Union for Conservation of Nature (IUCN) has classified the Siberian flying squirrel as 'near threatened', but the EU has classified it as 'vulnerable'. In several decisions, the Supreme Administrative Court has evaluated whether or not the permit for a project should be annulled due to its impact on the breeding site of the flying squirrel.[287]

§5. The Natura 2000 Network

588. The Natura 2000 network is an instrument of the Habitats Directive. In Finland, the rules for the enactment of the network are provided in the Natural Protection Act (sections 64–69).

589. If a project, either individually or in combination with other projects, is likely to have a significant adverse effect on the ecological value of a site included in the Natura 2000 network, and the site has been included in the network for the purpose of protecting this ecological value, the project's planner is required to conduct an appropriate assessment of the project's impacts. The same applies to any project or plan that is outside the Natura 2000 site, but that is likely to have a significantly harmful impact on that site (section 65).

---

287. Supreme Administrative Court, KHO:2007:41, KHO:2003:38 and KHO:2002:78.

590. The authority in charge of granting the permit or approving the plan must ensure that the assessment is carried out. The authority must then request an opinion from the regional environmental authority and the authority in charge of the Nature 2000 site in question.

591. No authority is empowered to grant a permit for the implementation of a project or to adopt or ratify a plan if the assessment indicates that the project or plan would have a significant adverse impact on the particular ecological value that is the reason the site has been included in the Natura 2000 network. However, a permit can be granted and a plan can be adopted or ratified if the Council of State decides that the said project or plan must, in the absence of alternative solutions, be carried out for imperative reasons to override public interest (section 65). In practice for example, the Natura assessment of power plant air emissions was found not to be necessary when the Natura network area was about 3.5 km from the plant.[288]

288. Supreme Administrative Court, 27 Dec. 2006, KHO:2006:101.

Chapter 7. Use of Water Resources

§1. General Overview

592. Water law is maybe the most traditional field of environmental law in Finland. The current Water Act (587/2011, as amended) contains provisions for the regulation of water management, associated permits, compensation issues and permit procedures. The Water Act does not regulate the pollution of water caused by emissions (*see supra* Chapter 4 about Environmental Protection Act). However, the rules of the Water Act apply if water pollution is caused by water construction projects. Many installations may require a permit according to the Environmental Protection Act and the Water Act.

593. Typical-energy sector projects needing a permit under the Water Act are hydropower plants, underwater power lines, and natural gas pipelines. Furthermore, in other projects, some part of the project might have an effect on watercourses, which makes it necessary to have a water permit. For example, condensing power plants require cooling water, and often a permit is necessary for the intake of water. A water permit is also often necessary for offshore wind power plants.

594. The Water Act is applicable within the economic zone in Finland. For example, Nord Stream 2 AG submitted an application to construct and operate the Nord Stream 2 natural gas pipeline through the Baltic Sea in the Finnish EEZ in 2017. The competent authority is the Regional State Administrative Agency for Southern Finland. In addition to that, the company has submitted a separate permit application to the Finnish Ministry of Economic Affairs and Employment to use the Finnish EEZ in accordance with the Act on the Exclusive Economic Zone of Finland (463/1956, as amended).

595. It is important to note the Rapids Protection Act (35/1987, as amended) as well. The Act protects a total of fifty-three individual rapids, river portions or catchment areas against power station construction. Corresponding acts have been passed to protect the Ounasjoki and Kyrönjoki Rivers.[289] Most of the potential for new hydroelectric power-generating capacity is within these areas.

596. The Water Framework Directive (2000/60/EC) aims to achieve a good state for all waters within the EU by 2015. The Directive is implemented mainly by the Act on Water Resources Management (1299/2004, as amended), which came into force on 31 December 2004. Based on the Act, a management plan is to be drawn up for each water management area.

289. Act on the Exceptional Protection of the River Ounasjoki (703/1983); Act of the Exceptional Protection of the River Kyrönjoki (1139/1991).

§2. Permit Procedure

597. The permit procedure under the Water Act is largely comparable to that under the Environmental Protection Act (*see supra* Chapter 4). An operator has to submit a permit application to the competent permit authority. There are extensive opportunities for the public and the different interested parties to comment before a permit is granted. The permit decision can be appealed to the Vaasa Administrative Court and then to the Supreme Administrative Court.

598. The most significant special characteristics of the water permit procedure are as follows:

- In water permit decisions, damage compensation is provided ex officio. Compensation is paid to the owners of water areas as well as, for example, professional fishermen.
- In Finland, coastal and inland water areas are mainly privately owned, and most of these water areas are managed jointly by the individual owners. A water permit decision might include rights granted to the project developer for the expropriation of water areas to carry out the project.
- Complicated permit issues can be addressed to an inspection proceeding. In the proceeding, the surveyor officer and two lay members solve issues related to the permit application, especially damage compensation. There is at least one inspection meeting in which parties can present their opinions.
- The water permit is normally permanent, and there is no review of compliance with its provisions at any fixed time. There are some exceptions, however, and especially the fishery obligations can be changed if the circumstances change.

§3. Permit Assessment

599. An absolute prerequisite for the issuing of a water permit under the Water Act is that the activities subjected to the permit procedure does not jeopardize public health or safety, causes considerable detrimental changes to the natural state of the environment or the aquatic environment and its functions, or causes considerable deterioration to the local living or economic conditions. Permit applications are hardly ever refused on this basis. In 1992, for the first time since the entry into force of the Water Act in 1961, this section was referenced in denying a permit for the construction of the artificial lake of Vuotos. The Supreme Administrative Court considered that 'the effects of the project, when taking into consideration their extent and in particular, their depth and permanency in the basin area and the nature values within that basin area, must be considered as substantial as intended in the legal provision of the law previously mentioned and as extending over a wide area, as harmful changes in the natural relations in the environment and in water nature and its functions'.[290]

290. Supreme Administrative Court, KHO:2002:86.

600. With respect to building facilities that may cause alterations in the water, a permit is granted if the facility does not considerably infringe the public or private interest, provided that the facility, due to its useful or protective purpose, is necessary in order to enable the meaningful use of the water or the adjoining land or is necessary for some other justifiable economic activity. Permits for underwater power cables are often issued on the basis of this section.

601. Most projects fall between the two mentioned above. There is no detrimental effect that would require absolute denial of the permit, but the disadvantages are still not minor. These projects are subject to a weighing of their advantages and disadvantages (weighing of interests). A permit may be granted if the benefits from the project are significant compared to the damages, inconveniences, and other losses of benefit caused by it. Damages, inconveniences, and losses of benefit are among the adverse effects on both the public interest and the property of others. The construction costs are not taken into consideration in the weighing of interests. Environmental impacts are considered inconveniences even if they cannot be assessed in terms of money. In that case, the significance of the project and the benefit that would be lost if the permit was denied must be weighed from the point of view of the public interest.

602. As a part of weighting of interests, the river basin management plans which are based on the EU Water Framework Directive (2000/60/EC), have to be taken into account. This was stated especially in the case SAC 2017:87 regarding a new hydropower plant where the Supreme Administrative Court referred to the European Union Court decision C-461/13 (Weser). However, in this case the appeals were rejected, and the court held that the power plant did not jeopardizes the attainment of good surface water status or of good ecological potential and good surface water chemical status by the date laid down by the directive.

603. With energy sector projects, their benefits are often considered to be significant compared to their damages, and their permit applications are seldom denied. However, there are exceptions. In one of its decisions, the Supreme Administrative Court, by a 4–3 vote, refused to grant a permit to a hydropower plant project, since its benefits were minor due to low energy production, but it disadvantages were significant due to the reduced natural beauty and cultural-historical value of the place.[291]

291. Supreme Administrative Court, *Huopanankoski* 10 May 1978, KHO:1978 A II 123.

Chapter 8. Other Environmental Legislation

§1. Projects of Common Interest

604. PCIs are key infrastructure projects, especially cross-border projects, that link the energy systems of EU countries. EU Regulation 347/2013 lays down, *inter alia*, guidelines for the timely development of these projects. In Finland, the Regulation is implemented mainly by the Act on the Permit Procedure of Energy Projects Concerning the Common Interest of the European Union (684/2014, as amended).

605. Member States have to designate a national competent authority responsible for facilitating and coordinating the permit granting process for projects of common interest. In Finland the EA acts as a competent authority.

606. The PCI-project promoter must submit the permit applications and the related documents simultaneously to both the EA and the licensing authority responsible for this matter. This process covers the permits according to the Electricity Market Act, the Natural Gas Market Act, the Act on the Exclusive Economic Zone of Finland, the Water Act, the Land Use and Building Act, the Act on the Safety of the Handling of Dangerous Chemicals and Explosives, and the Expropriation Act. The EA facilitates the issuing of the comprehensive decision according to the collaborative scheme set out in Article 8(3)(c) of the Regulation. The Regulation sets an overall timetable of 3.5 years for the permitting process, with an indicative period of 2 years for pre-application procedures, and 1.5 years for determination of applications for permits. However, the Finnish law does not provide any instrument with which to ensure compliance with the limits set in the regulation.

607. The Member State or competent authority shall publish a manual of procedures for the permit granting process applicable to projects of common interest. The manual is published on the public website (www.energiavirasto.fi, in Finnish).

§2. Contaminated Land

608. The liability for contaminated soil and groundwater is mainly based on the public law system.

609. The provisions in Chapter 14 of the Environmental Protection Act apply only to cases in which the pollution is caused on 1 January 1994 or later thereafter. Any party whose activities have caused the contamination of soil or groundwater is required to restore that soil or groundwater to a condition that will not cause harm to health or the environment. Negligence is not a prerequisite for the liability. If the party that has caused the contamination cannot be reached or cannot be prevailed upon to fulfil its remediation duty, the holder of the area must restore the soil and the groundwater. However, this applies only as far as the holder of the area knew, or should have known, about the state of the area when it was acquired, and the duty is not clearly unreasonable. If the holder is not responsible for the remediation of the area, the municipality has to carry it out the remediation.

610. Prior to 1 January 1994, liability was based on the previous Waste Management Act (673/1979, as amended). The liability provisions of the Act shall still apply to soil contamination which occurred before 1 January 1994. The polluter or the current holder of the area is liable for the remedial costs.

611. The Decree on the Assessment of Soil Contamination and Remediation Needs (214/2007) lays down the procedures for the assessment of soil contamination and contains guideline values and criteria for risk assessment.

§3. Environmental Damage Legislation

612. The Act on Compensation for Environmental Damage (Ympäristövahinkolaki; 737/1994, as amended) entered into force in 1995. Compensation is paid for a loss defined as an environmental damage. Such damage can be caused by activities carried out in a certain area and can result from pollution of water, air or soil; noise, vibration, radiation, light, heat or smell; or other similar nuisance. The responsible party must pay the costs of environmental damage to people or property, and possibly economic losses. Additionally, the Act requires compensation for the costs of reasonable measures taken to prevent or limit environmental damage and for the costs of cleaning up and restoring the environment to its previous state.

613. The Environmental Damage Insurance Act (Laki ympäristövahinkovakuutuksesta; 81/1998, as amended) came into force on 1 January 1999. This Act guarantees full compensation for environmental damage in cases where those liable for compensation are insolvent or cannot be identified. Thus, the Act creates a complementary compensation scheme for environmental damage occurring in Finland. The scheme is financed by special insurance that is compulsory for the companies whose activities cause risk to the environment. All parties holding an environmental permit are obliged to take out the insurance.

614. The Act was amended in 2009 when Finland implemented Environmental Liability Directive (2004/35/EC) with regard to the prevention and remedying of environmental damage.[292]

§4. Environmental Criminal Liability

615. The Penal Code (Rikoslaki; 39/1889, as amended) was amended in 1995 with the new Chapter 49 containing provisions on environmental crimes that are

292. The period prescribed for implementation of the Directive expired on 30 Apr. 2007. The European Court of Justice declared in December 2008 that Finland has failed to fulfil its obligations under the Directive (C-328/08).

punishable by imprisonment. As a part of various environmental statutes, there are provisions that deal with crimes punishable only by fines.

616. The Penal Code includes special provisions concerning corporate criminal liability (Chapter 9 of the Code), and corporate fines can be imposed on corporate bodies for environmental offences committed during their operations. Such corporate fines are imposed as a lump sum and are at least EUR 850, but not more than EUR 850,000.

617. The case law in this area is quite limited. In 2008, the Supreme Court of Finland ordered a company to pay a EUR 500,000 corporate fine for negligence leading to environmental damage. About 300 m^3 of oil were spilled from a refinery, and the Court found that the company had failed to fit its oil transfer equipment with suitable alarms and redundancy systems.[293]

§5. Protection of Archaeological and Built Heritage

618. Antiquities are protected in Finland under the Antiquities Act (Muinaismuistolaki; 295/1963, as amended). Under the Act, 'fixed antiquities are protected as reminders of Finland's past settlements and history. Without permission granted under this act it is prohibited to dig, cover, modify, damage, remove or physically interfere with antiquities'. The Antiquities Act protects automatically, without separate measures, antiquities that are within the definitions of the Act and prohibits action that might endanger the preservation of the relics. There is no age limit for fixed relics. The Act refers to both prehistoric and historic objects. If a fixed archaeological relic is found during excavation work, the Act orders that the work is to be discontinued and that the National Board of Antiquities or the provincial museum is to be informed of the matter.

619. The cultural environment and architectural heritage are taken care of primarily through town planning and building guidance – that is, the Land Use and Building Act. This is complemented by the Act on the Protection of Buildings and the Decree on the State-Owned Buildings (480/1985).

§6. Chemicals and Safety

620. Based on the SEVESO III (Directive 2012/18/EC), regulations concerning the prevention of accident hazards have been incorporated in Finnish chemicals legislation. The most important general statutes are the Act on the Safety of the Handling of Dangerous Chemicals and Explosives (390/2005, as amended) and the corresponding Decree (59/1999). In addition, there is special legislation for liquefied petroleum gas (LPG), natural gas, and explosives.

293. Supreme Court, 13 Feb. 2008, KKO:2008:61.

621. Responsibilities according to the Act on the Safety of the Handling of Dangerous Chemicals and Explosives are determined by the extent of operational activity. The operational activities of establishments are divided into two groups by legislation: large-scale and small-scale establishments. Large-scale activities are supervised by the Safety Technology Authority (TUKES); small-scale activities are supervised by the regional rescue authorities. The category of an establishment is determined by the amount and classification of the chemicals it uses.

622. The main obligations that apply to all large-scale establishments are:

- a licence for a new establishment;
- a licence for a plant modification;
- a notification in the case of a significant change;
- a nominated chemical supervisor;
- periodic inspections; and
- internal emergency plans.

623. An additional obligation for the larger establishments is a major accident policy document. For the largest establishments, a safety report, compulsory public information and an external emergency plan are needed as well.

§7. Informative Regulation and Voluntary Schemes

624. In Finland, there is an ongoing voluntary agreement scheme on energy efficiency that was launched in 1997, and most of the energy producers and distributors have joined the scheme. A company joins the voluntary agreement scheme by signing an accession document, by which the company commits itself to implementing the measures included in the action programmes, such as analysing its own energy consumption and drawing up an action plan to implement cost-effective, useful efficiency measures. The Ministry of Employment and the Economy provides support for energy audits, analyses and energy conservation investments eligible for subsidies that are conducted by companies and communities adhering to the agreement.

625. The EU's eco-management and audit scheme (EMAS) is a management tool used by companies and other organizations to evaluate, report on and improve their environmental performance. EMAS has been available to companies since 1995.[294] To register for EMAS, an organization must conduct an environmental review, establish an environmental management system, carry out an environmental audit and provide a statement of its environmental performance. EMAS is not widespread in the Finnish energy sector, although use of the ISO 14001 environmental management system is common within the energy industry.

294. Council Regulation (EEC) No. 1836/93 of 29 Jun. 1993.

Chapter 9. Discussion

626. The basis of environmental policy is found in the Constitution of Finland, and in principle, all legislation can include environmental aspects. However, there is a certain section of the environmental law that focuses on environmental quality, safety, liability and conservation of the natural and cultural environment.

627. Energy projects have various types of environmental impacts. Perhaps the most significant effects of the environment are those related to power plants' emissions from the combustion of different kind of fossil fuels. These power plants increase the concentration of greenhouse gases in the atmosphere, and the emissions trading scheme has a strong effect on their economy. In addition, power plants emit, for example, nitrogen oxides, sulphur dioxide, and dust, and their emissions are regulated through environment permits. The emission limit values of power plants are commonly based on the EU directives, thus levelling the playing field for parties in the Nordic electricity markets. Environmental legislation concerning, for example, land use and nature conservation has to be taken into account as well, but in general, those factors do not play a central role in the decision-making. This is especially due to the fact that greenfield investments by large power plants are quite rare in Finland.

628. Environmental legislation concerning hydropower is totally different. Normally, there are no emissions to air, water or ground from hydropower plants, and, thus, an environmental permit under the Environmental Protection Act is not needed. Instead, the Water Act has a central role, and the questions related to fishing, nature and landscape conservation and the impacts of water regulation are important. In addition, the Rapids Protection Act protects most of the suitable rivers against new power station construction.

629. In a wind power project, the land use and planning legislation is essential. However, it is not possible to forget nature conservation, water law (for offshore wind farms), and prevention of pollution (noise). Several time-consuming permitting procedures might be needed for a wind power project.

630. Nuclear power production and issues related to nuclear safety and radiation are heavily regulated under the Nuclear Energy Act. However, several other pieces of environmental legislation should also be taken into account in relation to nuclear power plants. Intake of cooling water is regulated under the Water Act, warm cooling water emissions under the Environmental Protection Act, land use under the Land Use and Building Act and so on.

631. Environmental impacts of the transmission of energy are mainly related to the use of land for power lines and natural gas pipelines. Nature conservation is often a key environmental issue in these cases. Also, the possibility of expropriating land is a question of great importance. Expropriation procedures take several years, but expropriation is still relatively easy to carry out compared to the procedures in many other countries.

632. In Finland, peat is a significant local source of energy in district heating and electric power production. Peat production needs an environmental permit under the Environmental Protection Act, in which questions related to emissions to watercourses, dust, and noise are handled. Also planning and nature conservation issues have to be taken into account.

633. Mining legislation is not discussed in this book. This is due to the fact that there is no mining of fuels in Finland so far, though in recent years some companies have started to evaluate whether it would be possible to mine uranium in Finland. The most important Finnish mining products thus far are metals, limestone, talc, apatite, and soapstone.

634. The most important interactions between energy sector projects and environmental law have been identified in the following table:

	Emissions Trading Law	*Pollution Prevention Law*	*Land Use Law*	*Nature Conservation Law*	*Water Law*	*Nuclear Law*	*Mining Law*
Combustion plants (coal, oil, peat, gas, biomass, waste)	•••[1]	•••	•	•	•	–	–
Hydro power plants	–	–	•	••	•••	–	–
Wind power plants	–	•	•••	••	•	–	–
Nuclear power plants	–	•	•	•	•	•••	–
Power lines and natural gas pipelines	–	–	•••	••	•••[2]	–	–
Peat production	–	•••	•	••	•	–	–
Mining	–	••	••	••	•	••[3]	•••

[1] Except biomass combustion and waste incineration.
[2] Underwater/undersea cables and pipelines.
[3] Uranium mining.
Key: Importance of the sectors of environmental law in energy projects:
••• Very important.
•• Fairly important.
• Sometimes important.

635. The basic principle is that energy authorities and environmental authorities make their decisions independently. However, there are a few procedural interactions between environmental law and energy law. A permit for the construction of a high-voltage or cross-border power line cannot be granted under the Electricity Market Act before the permit authority has obtained an EIA report and the liaison authority's statement on it. According to the Act on Production Subsidy for Electricity Produced from Renewable Energy Sources (1396/2010, as amended), the electricity producer may not apply for a feed-in tariff before the building permits for wind turbines are legally valid.

636. It should also be noted that the lines between energy law and environmental law and between energy policy and environmental policy are not clear, especially in the case of climate change issues. The EU emissions trading scheme is primarily aimed at reducing CO_2 emissions, thereby indirectly encouraging the switch to renewable energy. However, the promotion of renewable electricity serves as well to achieve a variety of energy policy objectives and other policy objectives such as improving security of supply, generating jobs, contributing to rural development, and promoting an industry with export potential.

Part V. Interaction Between Energy Law and Tax Law

Chapter 1. Introduction

637. Energy taxation is a major source of financing for Finland. The state excise tax revenues amount to nearly EUR 4.7 billion annually.[295]

638. The current Finnish energy taxation system has been in use since 1997. In the EU Member States, including Finland,[296] excise taxation of mineral oils (liquid fuels) and, since 1 January 2004 of electricity, natural gas and coal is harmonized by Directive 2003/96/EC (hereinafter the Energy Directive).

639. In addition to the harmonized excise taxes, a national excise tax is levied in Finland on tall oil. With regard to other energy products in Finland, the excise taxation of wood, wood-based fuels and peat is not harmonized.

640. The energy tax in Finland is an excise tax, which is levied on transport and heating fuels and electricity. In addition to the excise tax, a security-of-supply fee[297] is charged on most of the energy products. The energy tax is divided into the basic tax and the additional tax. The excise tax is levied per unit of each energy product rather than being based on its price.

641. The basic tax is fiscal in nature and is levied only on oil products. The basic tax on gasoline and diesel is staggered on the basis of whether it is sulphur-free or not.

---

295. Data from the Ministry of Finance, budget for Republic of Finland 2018. The EUR 4.7 billion estimate is without the VAT and the security-of-supply fee. Of this amount, approximately EUR 2.7 billion is collected on traffic fuels. Other fuels yield EUR 0.8 billion and electricity approximately EUR 1.2 billion.
296. Finland became an EU member in 1995.
297. The costs associated with national security-of-supply are addressed by the extra-budgetary National Emergency Supply Fund, which covers the expenditure involved in the reserve stocks, auxiliary technological arrangements, and preparedness planning.

642. Additional tax is levied on fossil oil products, coal and natural gas. The additional tax is determined principally on the basis of their carbon content.[298] Electricity, tall oil and peat are exempted from additional tax.

643. Electricity is taxed based on consumption. The tax rate does not depend on the energy product used in generating electricity. The fuels used for electricity (power) generation are tax-exempt.

644. In general, excise tax is levied on products (subject to the excise tax) that are produced in Finland or received in Finland from another EU Member State or on products that are imported to Finland from outside of the EU. The excise tax is levied in the EU Member State where the products subject to excise tax are released for consumption.

645. Generally, the following are liable to pay excise tax: authorized warehouse-keepers, registered and non-registered traders (in the system of duty-suspension arrangement) and tax representatives. In addition, excise tax has to be paid by those who import excisable products from outside of the EU and by those who have acquired duty-exempt products that have not been used for duty-free purposes. Furthermore, persons who hold products already taxed in another EU Member State and intended for other than private use in Finland, those holding untaxed products for commercial purposes in Finland and those having received untaxed products for payment from another Member State are liable to pay excise tax.

646. The Act on Excise Tax on Liquid Fuels (Laki nestemäisten polttoaineiden valmisteverosta; 472/1994, as amended) and the Act on Excise Tax on Electricity and Certain Fuels (Laki sähkön ja eräiden polttoaineiden valmisteverosta; 1260/1996, as amended) provide the main legal framework with respect to energy taxation in Finland.[299] The provisions on the taxation procedure and also partly on exemptions from tax and on parties liable to pay tax are given jointly for all types of excise taxes in the Excise Taxation Act (Valmisteverotuslaki; 1469/1994, as amended) and will be dealt with briefly in the relevant chapter. The Finnish Tax Administration is responsible for levying taxes and paying tax supports and tax refunds.

647. The basic principles under the main tax statutes are described in Chapter 2 ('Excise Tax on Liquid Fuels') and Chapter 3 ('Excise Tax on Electricity and Certain Fuels'), whereas value added tax (VAT) issues are dealt with in Chapter 5.

298. The additional tax has also been called a carbon dioxide tax.

299. Also relevant are the Decree on Excise Tax on Liquid Fuels (Asetus nestemäisten polttoaineiden valmisteverosta; 1547/1994 as amended), the Decree on Excise Taxation (Valmisteverotusasetus; 1546/1994 as amended) and the Act on Refund on Certain Energy Products Used in Cultivation (Laki maataloudessa käytettyjen eräiden energiatuotteiden valmisteveron palautuksesta; 603/2006 as amended).

Subsidies relating to energy taxation are addressed in Chapter 4, and questions concerning the energy taxation system as an instrument for controlling energy production and energy use, especially with regard to future prospects, are addressed in Chapter 6.

Chapter 2. Excise Tax on Liquid Fuels

§1. General Principles

648. According to the Act on Excise Tax on Liquid Fuels, the excise tax (both basic tax and additional tax) and security-of-supply fee are levied on motor spirit, diesel oil, aviation spirit and jet fuel, as well as light and heavy fuel oil at the tax rates in the Tax Table attached to the Act.

649. According to a substitution principle, those liquid fuels for which there is no excise tax rate quoted in the Tax Table are taxed on the basis of their intended use according to the excise tax rate corresponding to motor or heating fuel in the Tax Table. In addition, any products used or intended or sold to be used as motor fuels or auxiliaries, additives or substances enlarging the volume of motor fuel are subject to this excise tax at the rate of the corresponding motor fuel.

650. In general, authorized warehouse-keepers and registered or occasionally unregistered entrepreneurs are required to pay excise tax.

§2. Tax Exemptions

651. Fuels entered in the reserve stock; fuels used as the energy source for the oil-refining process; fuels used as raw materials or auxiliaries in industrial production or in direct first use in the production of goods; fuels used in vessel traffic other than private leisure boating; fuels used to generate electricity;[300] and fuels used in aviation other than private leisure flights are exempted from the excise tax and security-of-supply fee.

652. The exemption requires permit to uphold a tax-exempt warehouse. In case such a permit has not been obtained, the exemption is carried out by a refund mechanism; that is, the consumer of the products has to submit an application in order to have the excise tax and security-of-supply fee refunded.

653. Section 16 of the Excise Tax Act includes additional exemptions from the excise tax that are not further discussed here.

300. Except when generating electricity with a generator having a power less than 100 kVA that is not transmitted to the electricity network and when generating electricity in a vessel, train, car or other transporting vehicle for its own use.

§3. Tax Rates

654. The prevailing excise tax rates and security-of-supply fee rates (per litre/kg) are set out in the Act on Excise Tax on Liquid Fuels (section 4 and the attached Tax Table).[301]

301. The current rates are valid as of 1 Jan. 2018.

Chapter 3. Excise Tax on Electricity and Certain Fuels

§1. General Principles

655. As mentioned in Chapter 1, the fuels consumed to generate electricity are exempt from the excise tax, while the electricity is taxable. The fuels used for heating and traffic are taxable.

656. According to the Act on Excise Tax on Electricity and Certain Fuels, the excise tax and security-of-supply fee are levied on electricity. In addition, all solid and gaseous hydrocarbons, with the exception of peat, that are used or meant or sold to be used for heating purposes are taxed; that is, the excise tax is also levied on coal, tall oil, natural gas and peat. Please note that security-of-supply fee is charged only to coal and natural gas.

657. As a basic rule, those liable to pay the electricity excise tax are the network operators and for-profit electricity producers. They have to register by filing a declaration with the Customs District for their domicile.

658. However, it is possible for the electricity consumer to become an electricity taxpayer. For example, if an electricity consumer has acquired electricity from the network and paid the excise tax of the lower (II) tax category, and uses or delivers electricity for a purpose of falling within the higher (I) tax category, the consumer is liable to pay the difference between the two tax rates.

659. Similarly, if a party other than the network owner receives electricity from another Member State for the purpose of making a profit or imports electricity from a non-EU Member State and the electricity does not pass through the electricity network in Finland, that party is liable to pay excise tax on the electricity received.

§2. Electricity Excise Tax Categories and Tax Rates

660. The electricity tax has been divided into two taxation categories: the lower category II tax (currently EUR cents 0.703/kWh) is paid by industry, data centres and professional greenhouse cultivation. Other consumers (e.g., private households and agriculture as well as forestry, construction and services) pay the higher category I tax (currently EUR cents 2.253/kWh).

661. By industry, it is understood as:

- excavation of minerals; as well as
- industrial production and processing of goods.

662. Comparable to industry are:

- minor supporting activities not belonging to industry that take place on the production site of an industrial company and are mainly connected with the company's own industrial production; and
- professional greenhouse cultivation.

663. The prevailing excise tax rates and security-of-supply fee rates are set out in the Act on Excise Tax on Electricity and Certain Fuels (section 4 and the attached Tax Table).[302]

664. The excise tax and security-of-supply fee are assessed for each tax period in accordance with:

- the quantity of electricity that the network owner delivers for consumption;
- the quantity of electricity produced by the producer;
- the difference between electricity tax categories I and II in cases where electricity purchased for a category II use was actually used for a purpose falling within category I; and
- the quantity of electricity received or imported by the electricity consumer without the use of the network in Finland.

The quantity of electricity delivered for consumption or consumed is the quantity for which the network owner, directly or through a marketing agency, charges the electricity consumer.

665. In the case of combined production of electricity and heat, section 10 of the Act sets out how the fuels are considered to have been consumed in the production of heat and electricity, respectively.

666. The combined production of electricity and heat means that the power plant produces both electricity and heat for utility purposes, either simultaneously or separately, during the same tax period of the plant. This means that, in terms of taxation, the production of a power plant may be interpreted differently during different tax periods. The decisive factor for excise taxation is thus what the plant was producing during the tax period, not the type of technology the plant is considered to represent.

667. The amount of fuel taxable as being used in heat production is obtained by multiplying the heat transmitted for consumption by 0.9.

668. The fuel used to produce heat in a combined production plant is defined on the basis of the heat transferred for consumption by applying effective heat values. Heat transferred for consumption is the quantity of heat transmitted from the power plant to the district heating and process steam network and to other corresponding utility purposes. Each fuel is assumed to have been consumed in the same proportions in the production of electricity and heat.

---

302. The current rates are valid as of 1 Jan. 2018.

§3. Exemption from Electricity Excise Tax

669. Electricity exempt from the excise tax and security-of-supply fee includes electricity:

- transmitted between electricity networks (from one network owner to another);
- delivered by the electricity producer to the electricity network;
- passed to non-EU Member States or delivered for consumption to a part of the EC other than Finland;
- delivered for the direct use of electrical rail traffic;
- consumed by the power plant's internal consumption machinery during the production of electricity or combined electricity/heat (Decree 309/2003 of the Ministry of Trade and Industry); and
- passed into the power plant network.

670. In addition, a party generating electricity with a generator having a power less than 100 kVA that is not transmitted to the electricity network and a party generating electricity in a vessel, train, car or other transport vehicles for its own use are not required to pay the excise tax and security-of-supply fee.

§4. Certain Fuels: Coal, Tall Oil, Natural Gas

671. Coal and natural gas are subject to the excise tax, additional tax and security-of-supply fee. Tall oil and peat are subject to the excise tax (basic tax) only.

672. For coal, the parties liable to pay the excise tax and security-of-supply fee are, in general, authorized warehouse-keepers as well as registered and non-registered traders.

673. Coal used in industrial production as a raw material or auxiliary or in direct first use in the production of goods is exempt from the excise tax and security-of-supply fee. Also, coal that is delivered by an authorized warehouse-keeper to parts of the EC other than Finland to be released for consumption and that is used in the generation of electricity is exempt. In addition, tax exemptions in accordance with section 16 (subsections 1, 3–5) of the Excise Tax Act apply to coal. As an exception to the tax exemption for generation of electricity, the obligation to pay the excise tax and security-of-supply fee applies to coal used to generate electricity with a generator having a power less than 100 kVA that is not transmitted to the electricity network and coal used for electricity generated in a vessel, train, car or other transport vehicles for its own use.

674. An entrepreneur engaged in industrial production is liable to pay the excise tax on tall oil used for heating purposes.

675. An importer of natural gas from non-EU Member States is liable to pay the excise tax and security-of-supply fee on natural gas. Natural gas used in industrial production as a raw material or auxiliary or in direct first use in the production of goods, as an energy source in the oil-refining process or in the production of electricity, is exempt from excise tax and security-of-supply fee.

Chapter 4. Subsidies Relating to Energy Taxation

676. After a state becomes a member of the EU, any state aid implications of its energy taxation system and changes to that system are subject to assessment by the European Commission in light of the EU state aid regulation (Articles 87–98 of the Treaty Establishing the European Community).

§1. Tax Refund to Professional Cultivators and Greenhouse Cultivators

677. Part of the excise tax paid for light and heavy fuel oil, biofuel and electricity used in professional cultivation and greenhouse cultivation may, on application, be refunded to such cultivators.

678. A cultivator is entitled to apply for and receive refunds of the excise tax paid on light fuel oil and biofuels in the amount of EUR cents 7.05 per litre and on heavy fuel oil in the amount of EUR cents 8.05 per kilo. A cultivator is entitled to apply for and receive refunds of the excise tax paid on electricity in category I tax in the amount of EUR cents 1.55 per kWh.[303] No refund is available for excise tax paid in category II tax for electricity.

679. The refund is not paid if the total amount of refund is below EUR 50.

§2. Tax Refund to Energy-Intensive Enterprises

680. Under the Act on Excise Tax on Electricity and Certain Fuels, the excise tax paid by an enterprise during one accounting period for (a) electricity, coal, natural gas and tall, (b) light and heavy fuel oil and (c) the excise tax included in the acquisition price of these products can be refunded. The amount of refund is calculated by comparing the excise taxes paid during one accounting period to 0.5% of the value add of the enterprise during the same period.[304] The enterprise is entitled to a refund in case the paid excise taxes exceed the amount of value added.

681. However, only 85% of the excess is paid in excise tax refund after EUR 50,000 lump-sum deduction.

682. In addition, the maximum refund payable may be only as high as the total excise tax paid for electricity, coal, natural gas, and tall oil plus the excise tax included in their acquisition prices. When assessing the amount of the excise tax paid, the enterprise may include the excise tax paid for the district heating and process steam it has acquired if it is able to provide reliable documentation of this tax.

303. The rates apply for energy products used on or after 1 Jan. 2017.

304. EBIT + depreciation + impairments + personnel costs less tax refund during the accounting period.

683. The application for a tax refund must be filed with the local Tax Office of the company's area of domicile within six months after the expiry of the accounting period.

Chapter 5. Value Added Tax

684. In Finland, the VAT Act (Arvonlisäverolaki; 1501/1993 as amended) covers VAT as it applies to the energy sector as well as other sectors of the economy.

685. The entire energy sector is subject to VAT with respect to sales within Finland. A tax exemption is available in certain situations regarding international trade in accordance with section 70 of the VAT Act.

686. VAT on electricity, heating, fuels and so on is levied in Finland at the standard VAT rate of 24%. The taxable base is the price of the commodity, including possible energy tax.

687. Directive 2003/92/EC of 7 October 2003 amending Directive 77/288/EEC with regard to the rules on the place of supply of gas and electricity was implemented in Finnish law as of 1 January 2005 (Act 935/2004 as amended). The Directive and its implementing legislation resolved the problem that arose from the earlier legislation concerning taxation of the country of supply for electricity and gas, since tracking electricity and gas was difficult. Therefore, a special regulation (section 63d of the VAT Act) was adopted, indicating that the country where these goods are seen as having been sold has the right to taxation. The taxation rules are different depending on whether the buyer is a distributor liable to pay VAT or another buyer.

688. Accordingly, in general, VAT is levied in Finland for electricity and gas (as well as for natural gas, biogas and gas produced from biomass) distributed through the natural gas distribution network and sold to a distributor liable to pay VAT when that distributor has an established business in Finland to which these goods (electricity and gas) are delivered. If the goods are not delivered to an established business in Finland, or elsewhere, the goods are seen as having been sold in Finland (and the VAT Act applies) if the distributor's domicile is in Finland. In case electricity and gas distributed through the natural gas distribution network are sold to a buyer other than such a distributor, then the decisive factor is basically the actual place of consumption or the country to which the products are delivered for consumption.

689. Because buying electricity and gas distributed through the natural gas distribution net from outside of the EU – for example, from Russia – is also based on the above principles (section 63d), import of these goods (import always meaning from outside of EU) has been exempted from VAT (section 94).

Chapter 6. The Energy Taxation System as an Instrument to Control Energy Production and Energy Use

690. The energy taxation system in Finland is, in addition to its fiscal purpose (public financing; *see* Chapter 1), a key instrument of energy and environmental policy. As such, it is used to prevent the growth of energy use and to guide energy production and use towards energy alternatives that will generate lower CO_2 emission and towards renewable energy sources. Regarding the aim of reducing CO_2 emissions, the excise tax rates are determined on the basis of, for example, carbon content, as mentioned in Chapter 1.

691. While the Ministry of Finance is responsible for legislation on energy taxation, the Ministry of Employment and the Economy participates in the preparation of the energy taxation scheme in order to ensure that it supports energy and climate policy goals as efficiently as possible.

692. The security-of-supply fee, which is a part of energy taxation, is collected to cover the expenses incurred by the State in establishing emergency energy supplies and taking other measures to secure energy supplies.

§1. Long-term Climate and Energy Strategy

693. In 2016, the Finnish government approved a new national climate and energy strategy (the 'Strategy') with detailed insights into climate and energy policy measures up to 2030 and suggestions up to 2050. The Strategy clearly proves that the objectives proposed by the European Commission for Finland regarding the reduction of emissions, promotion of renewable energy and enhancement of the efficiency of energy consumption cannot be attained without new, prominent climate and energy policy measures.[305]

694. The Strategy includes key steering methods to meet the aforementioned objectives.

695. The Strategy outlines the actions that will enable Finland to attain the targets specified in the Government Program adopted by the EU for 2030 and to systematically set the course for achieving an 80%–95% reduction in greenhouse gas emissions by 2050. With minor exceptions, Finland will phase out the use of coal for energy. The share of transport biofuels will be increased to 30%, and an obligation to blend light fuel oil used in machinery and heating with 10% of bioliquids will be introduced. The minimum aim is to have 250,000 electric and 50,000 gas-powered vehicles on the roads. The electricity market will be developed at the regional and the European level. The flexibility of electricity demand and supply

305. Ministry of Employment and the Economy Press Release issued 24 Nov. 2016, and 'Long-Term Climate and Energy Strategy, Government Report to Parliament on 24 November 2016' (an abstract of the Strategy is available in English).

and, in general, system-level energy efficiency will be improved. Technology neutral tendering processes will be organized in 2018–2020, on the basis of which, aid will be granted to new cost-effective electricity production methods from renewable energy. The share of renewable energy in the end consumption will increase to approximately 50% and the self-sufficiency in energy to 55%.

696. According to the Strategy, the energy taxation scheme will be developed in a way that will most effectively support the reduction of emissions and the increase of energy efficiency and use of renewable energy. The goal of such taxation is to more consistently take into consideration the environmental effects of energy use and other steering measures such as the emissions trading system and efforts to promote the use of renewable energy. This would mean, for example, emphasizing energy taxation in the sectors outside emissions trading and discontinuing subsidies for electricity generation insofar as they will be covered by new subsidy instruments such as the feed-in tariff system.

§2. Windfall Profits

697. Windfall profits and their possible taxation have been discussed in Finland since the beginning of emissions trading. However, tax on windfall profits has not been introduced to date.

698. The Working Group for Developing the Finnish Tax System assessed whether windfall profit tax should be introduced in 2010, but gave no suggestion for such a tax.

699. The working group discussed that the windfall tax would be a state-wide real estate tax targeting nuclear power and hydropower plants. Wind power, small-scale hydropower and joint production of heat and electricity would be excluded from tax.

700. Windfall profits result from the effect of emissions trading on the wholesale price of electricity as the price of electricity produced by technologies that produce emissions is raised due to the costs of emissions trading. The wholesale price per hour in the Nordic markets is based on the costs of the power plant with highest variable production costs (so-called *marginal production technology*). The market mechanism, in turn, guides the power plants to be used in such a way that the electricity generated in a plant with the lowest variable production costs is preferred to that generated in a plant with higher costs; that is, the running order of the different plants is based on variable production costs. In Finland, electricity generated from coal presents this marginal production technology. Therefore, the market price is based on the variable production costs of plants using coal to generate electricity. The producers that use hydro and nuclear power, as well as other energy sources, to generate electricity receive the same price for the electricity they produce (including the market value of emission rights). As a result of this margin cost pricing system, economic benefits will accrue to the production technologies with lower variable production costs – which in the Nordic markets are hydro and nuclear power plants in particular. It is this economic benefit that would be the target of windfall profits taxation.

701. The energy industry has criticized the suggested windfall profits tax, stating that it would increase the price of electricity, since not all companies supplying electricity use the wholesale price as a basis for their prices, but instead base their prices partly on the production costs or the costs of acquiring electricity. In addition, the indirect price increase would happen through investments. According to critics, the real estate tax that the nuclear and hydropower producers are currently paying is substantially higher than what the other production forms are required to pay, and the 2006 increase in the real estate tax was partially based on the competition benefit received by the hydro and nuclear power producers due to climate policy.

§3. International Energy Agency Report

702. The International Energy Agency (IEA) carried out a review on Finland in 2013.[306] One of the IEA's conclusions was that Finland's energy policies are generally advanced, balanced and sound, but that four areas should be given particular attention: supply security, energy efficiency, contribution to EU level sustainability criteria discussion and gas market integration. Overall, the link between energy policy goals and objectives and the policies and measures that address these goals was noted in positive terms, but a longer-term approach was suggested. No detailed recommendations concerning energy taxation were presented, nor were any details of the energy taxation scheme criticized in the report.

306. International Energy Agency, 'Energy Policies of IEA Countries, Finland 2013 Review'. A previous review was carried out in 2007.

Part VI. Interaction Between Energy Law and Competition Law

703. This part examines the interaction between sector-specific energy law and the general competition law as well as the application of this general competition law in the energy sector. Several issues emerge in this context: the structure, competitiveness and the particularities of the Finnish energy markets; the dynamics between the two sets of legal rules governing the functioning of the energy markets; and the jurisdiction of the competition law authorities over the energy markets, in particular when compared to the jurisdiction of the EA. In addition to the general structure of the markets, the cooperative company structure typical in the Finnish electricity market and its relevance to competition will briefly be examined. Finally, some of the energy market related case law from the FCCA and the Market Court will be discussed.[307]

704. The first chapter will first briefly analyse the structure of the Finnish electricity and natural gas markets. As these issues have been examined in more detail in the parts concerning electricity and gas markets, the chapter will provide only a brief overview of the elements that are of direct relevance for the competition law assessment of energy markets.

705. The focus and emphasis of this part will primarily be on the electricity market for two reasons. First, the consumption of natural gas as an energy source in Finland is limited and decreasing; and second, the Finnish natural gas market continues to be isolated and non-competitive despite the recent legal developments.

307. For purposes of clarity, the competition authority will be consistently referred to as the FCCA even for case law that dates back to a time when the FCCA was still called the Finnish Competition Authority (FCA). Similarly, a reference to the Energy Authority (EA) will be used even for cases that were issued at a time when the Energy Authority was still called the Energy Market Authority (EMA).

Chapter 1. The Structure of the Finnish Energy Markets

706. As discussed in detail in Part I, the Finnish electricity markets were liberalized much earlier than in most European countries and the number of active market participants is comparatively high. In recent years, the total number of companies producing electricity has increased to approximately 150.[308] In contrast, electricity is produced by approximately 400 power plants around Finland, which is over a hundred less than a decade ago.[309] Joint and cross-ownership of generation capacity is a common ownership structure in the electricity market.

707. In 2017, there were seventy-three retail suppliers, fifty-five of which offered their products nationwide.[310] Furthermore, there were seventy-seven distribution network operators, twelve regional high-voltage distribution network operators and one TSO under the supervision of the EA.[311]

708. Within Finland, the three largest generation companies have a combined market share of approximately 50% of the total installed generation capacity.[312] However, Finland was interconnected to other Nordic countries, Russia and Estonia by 5,250 MW of transmission capacity at the end of 2016.[313] Because of this, Finland has access to the competitive benefits of an integrated market, which decreases the level of concentration of the national market. On a retail level, it has been estimated that the combined market share of the three largest companies in the market for small and medium-sized customers is 35%–40%.[314] Over recent years, the rate of supplier switching has increased and supply contracts are increasingly based on hourly consumption data.[315]

709. The Finnish natural gas market remains isolated and non-competitive. The retail supply of natural gas only represented approximately 8% of the total consumption in 2016 and consumption continues to decrease.[316] Unlike the electricity markets, the Finnish gas markets are not characterized by joint and cross-ownership. Instead, the natural gas markets are characterized by strong vertical integration. As was seen in more detail in Part II, the wholesale supplier Gasum Oy is the only importer of natural gas in Finland. It is also the operator of the transmission system and it is integrated into and involved in retail supply and distribution operations.

---

308. National Report 2017 to the Agency for the Cooperation of Energy Regulators and to the European Commission, no. 1469/401/2017, 12 Jul. 2017, 7–8.
309. *Ibid.*
310. *Ibid.*, 9–10.
311. *Ibid.*, 12.
312. *Ibid.*, 7–8.
313. *Ibid.*, 7.
314. *Ibid.*, 9–10.
315. *Ibid.*
316. National Report 2017 to the Agency for the Cooperation of Energy Regulators and to the European Commission, no. 1469/401/2017, 12 Jul. 2017, 12–13.

710. Due to the lack of competition in the natural gas market, Finland has been able to apply certain exemptions from the EU energy law regimes. However, the construction decision for a new pipeline between Finland and Estonia was made in 2016. Upon completion, the pipeline will allow the development of a regional gas market in Finland and in the Baltic States, facilitate European market integration and introduce competition to the market. The New Natural Gas Market Act, which has been extensively discussed above in Part II, will also fundamentally change the approach to competition in the Finnish natural gas market.[317] In accordance with this Act, the Finnish gas market will be opened to competition at the beginning of 2020.

317. The New Natural Gas Market Act (maakaasumarkkinalaki, 587/2017).

Chapter 2. Regulating the Energy Sector Through Competition Law

711. The Finnish energy markets are not regulated solely by sector-specific energy market legislation. General competition law has a significant role to play in addressing anticompetitive behaviour in the electricity and gas markets.

712. The legal regimes for both sector-specific energy rules and competition reflect the underlying assumption that free competition can provide efficiencies that benefit the consumer. A difference between the two is that, while the objective of the general competition law is the promotion of a competitive market economy, the objectives of sector-specific energy regulation are wider. These objectives include, for example, security of energy supply and the protection of the environment as well as reasonable and equitable service principles in the operation of electricity and natural gas systems.[318] Nevertheless, the underpinning assumption is that a competitive energy market is the most efficient instrument to achieve these diverse objectives.

713. A second difference between the two legal regimes is that, save for the merger control provisions, general competition law is primarily based on *ex post* regulation, whereas the sector-specific laws are typically based on *ex ante* regulation.[319] This need for *ex ante* regulation is founded on the fact that the energy sector is network dependent and control of the network means control of virtually the entire market. Therefore, negative measures such as removing special and monopoly rights are not enough to ensure effective functioning of the energy market. In order to have an effectively functioning internal market, positive action is necessary. This requires *ex ante* regulation or, as has been said, 'regulating *for* competition'.[320] This is the general rationale for the existence of sector-specific regulation.

714. Finally, it is clear that the sector-specific legal instruments for energy, mainly the Electricity and Natural Gas Market Acts are *lex specialis* by nature, whereas competition law operates on a general level and applies to most sectors of the economy without distinction. In principle, this means that sector-specific legal instruments for energy would prevail if a conflict between competition law and energy law were to arise. However, in practice, these two areas of law generally have a mutually supportive role in the energy sector.

---

318. Section 1 of the Electricity Market Act; s. 1 of the Natural Gas Market Act.
319. However, *see* arguments on the special nature of EU competition law in the energy sector in Leigh Hancher and Adrien de Hauteclocque, 'Manufacturing the EU Energy Markets: The Current Dynamics of Regulatory Practice', 11(3) *Competition and Regulation in Network Industries* (2010), 307–334.
320. Peter D. Cameron, 'The Internal Market in Energy: Harnessing the New Regulatory Regime', 30(5) *European Law Review* (2005), 631–638, at 637.

715. The relationship between the sector-specific rules over general competition law was discussed in case law by the Competition Council (predecessor of the Market Court) in 2001. In its decision concerning Helsingin Energia and Kuopion Energia, the Competition Council expressed its opinion on the application of the Electricity Market Act and the Act on Competition Restrictions (480/1992, no longer in force) to excessive pricing.[321] The Council found that the mere fact that a company's pricing is not considered reasonable within the meaning of the Electricity Market Act is not alone sufficient to declare the pricing incompatible with competition law. However, prices considered reasonable under the Electricity Market Act cannot be considered unreasonable under general competition law. In other words, the threshold for unreasonable pricing is lower in sector-specific energy rules and, therefore, pricing is more likely to be considered unreasonable under the rules of the Electricity Market Act. The same rules are in place in the New Natural Gas Market Act and, as a consequence, the same logic may be applied analogously to the natural gas market.

716. The overall objective of the Competition Act (kilpailulaki, 948/2011, as amended) is to ensure and protect functional economic competition from harmful restrictive practices.[322] The facilitation of functional competition in the markets and the protection of economic freedoms to the benefit of the consumers should particularly be taken into account when applying the Competition Act.[323]

717. Finnish competition law operates in close connection with EU competition law. This interrelationship is explicitly acknowledged in the Competition Act, which states that in addition to the rules established in the Competition Act, Articles 101 and 102 TFEU will also apply when the identified restriction on competition may affect trade between the EU Member States.[324] By contrast, the rules of the Competition Act apply alone in cases which may not affect trade between the Member States. However, many of the substantive provisions of the Competition Act closely follow the wording of the corresponding EU provisions.[325] In practice, this results in the extension of the application of EU rules to purely national cases which do not have an effect on trade between the Member States. This extension is best demonstrated by sections 5, 6 and 7 of the Competition Act, which address vertical and horizontal cooperation between undertakings (Sections 5 and 6) and abuse of dominant position (Section 7).

---

321. Competition Council Decision no. 151/690/1999 on 18 Jun. 2001 (kilpailuneuvoston Helsingin kaupunkia / Helsingin Energiaa koskeva päätös, Dno 151/690/1999, annettu 18.6.2001); Competition Council Decision no Dno 173/690/2000 on 18 June 2001 (kilpailuneuvoston Kuopion kaupunkia / Kuopion Energiaa koskeva päätös, Dno 173/690/2000, annettu 18.6.2001); and Finnish Competition Authority, April 2002, OECD, Committee on Competition Law and Policy, 'Annual Report on Competition Policy Developments in Finland March 2001– March 2002.'
322. Section 1 of the Competition Act.
323. Section 1 of the Competition Act.
324. Section 3 of the Competition Act.
325. Compare the wording of s. 5 of the Competition Act and 102 TFEU for example.

718. Section 5 of the Competition Act prohibits all agreements between undertakings, decisions by associations of undertakings, and concerted practices by undertakings which have as their object the significant prevention, restriction or distortion of competition or which result in a significant prevention, restriction or distortion of competition. In particular, section 5 of the Competition Act prohibits agreements, decisions, or practices which:

- directly or indirectly fix purchase or selling prices or any other trading conditions;
- limit or control production, markets, technical development, or investment;
- share markets or sources of supply;
- apply dissimilar conditions to equivalent transactions with other trading parties, thereby placing them at a competitive disadvantage; or
- make the conclusion of a contract subject to acceptance by the other party of supplementary obligations which, by their nature or according to commercial usage, have no connection with the subject of such a contract.

719. However, the prohibitions laid down in section 5 do not apply agreements, decisions, or practices which:

- contribute to improving the production or distribution of goods or to promoting technical or economic progress;
- allow consumers a reasonable share of the resulting benefit;
- do not impose on the undertakings concerned restrictions which are not indispensable to the attainment of these objectives; and
- do not afford such undertakings the possibility of eliminating competition in respect of a substantial part of the products in question.[326]

720. Within the context of the Finnish electricity market, sections 5 and 6 of the Competition Act are particularly interesting with regard to the common structural solutions of cross- and joint ownership. Joint ownership, particularly in the form of cooperative companies, is a common form of financing investments in electricity generation capacity in Finland. These so-called *Mankala companies* do not aim to make a profit but rather supply their shareholders with electricity at a cost-based price. In other words, the shareholders only cover the investment and operation costs of the power plants in proportion to their shares. For the shareholders, the low-cost, non-taxable supply of energy replaces the annual monetary return from the investment.[327]

721. This company structure was first developed in the 1940s to allow small companies to invest in generation capacity, which was sorely needed after the war, particularly to supply the Finnish industrial forestry and to allow market access to

326. Section 6 of the Competition Act.
327. Supreme Administrative Court cases KHO:1963-I-5, 21 May 1963 and KHO:1968-II-521, 20 Jun. 1968.

new players that alone did not hold the necessary resources to invest in new generation capacity. The driving motivation for this approach was the fact that the shareholders needed increasing amounts of electricity for their operations. As the initial investments required for powers plants were in most cases too large to be undertaken by any of the shareholders alone, they decided to pool their resources and create a separate company for the production of electricity. The shares of the new company were divided equally, and the shareholders were entitled to equal amounts of energy, coupled with an obligation to pay an equal portion of the costs.[328]

722. Joint ownership of power plants, particularly through the Mankala approach, may potentially have adverse effects on the competitiveness of the market. Joint ownership may potentially allow competing shareholders to agree on fixed prices or output or to share markets for example.[329]

723. Despite the potential adverse effects on competition, the compatibility of the Mankala model with competition law has never been tested in case law by the courts. However, such an approach would be evaluated under sections 5 and 6 of the Competition Act or, if there are potential effects on cross-border trade, under Article 101 TFEU. In order to fall within the application of either provision, certain criteria must be met.

724. First, it is clear that in order to be caught by the definition for prohibited agreements, the parties concluding these agreements must be in competition with one another or at least have the potential to compete in the same market.[330] Second, the cooperation between these parties cannot be considered incompatible with competition law if none of the parties alone would be able to carry out the economic activity that the cooperation establishes.[331] This criterion is particularly relevant in terms of the Mankala model the purpose of which is to pool resources that none of the parties could alone generate. Although this interpretation is specifically laid down by the Commission on Article 101 TFEU and not on the Competition Act, it seems the national competition authority FCCA has taken an identical approach.[332]

328. Pohjolan Voima 60 vuotta, *Pohjoisen vesiltä monipuoliseksi energiayhtiöksi* (Helsinki: Edita, 2003), 144 (with a summary in English), p. 145.
329. Communication from the Commission, Guidelines on the applicability of Art. 101 of the Treaty on the Functioning of the European Union to horizontal cooperation agreements, OJ C 11, 14.1.2011, pp. 1–72, para. 3.
330. Communication from the Commission, Guidelines on the applicability of Art. 101 of the Treaty on the Functioning of the European Union to horizontal cooperation agreements, OJ C 11, 14.1.2011, pp. 1–72, para. 10.
331. Communication from the Commission, Guidelines on the applicability of Art. 101 of the Treaty on the Functioning of the European Union to horizontal cooperation agreements, OJ C 11, 14.1.2011, pp. 1–72, para. 30.
332. FCCA statement no. 589/14.00.20/2010 on the construction of nuclear power and the mankala-principle (Kilpailuviraston lausunto eduskunnan talousvaliokunnalle 4.6.2010, Dnro 589/14.00.20/2010).

725. If the horizontal cooperation in the form of joint-ownership fulfils the criteria laid down above, it may fall within the scopes of section 5 or Article 101(1) TFEU. However, exemptions from the prohibitions laid down in both section 5 and Article 101(1) TFEU are possible on the basis of very similar criteria. In essence, these criteria require that the positive effects of the cooperation outweigh the negative.[333] While this company structure has certain anticompetitive aspects and in all the probability also decreases the competition in the markets, it also has certain positive effects.

726. First and most obviously, it has the potential of balancing the typical dominance of state-owned energy companies. Unlike the situation in many other EU Member States, the state-owned company Fortum – while still being dominant in the Finnish markets, though not in the Nordic markets – does not have an excessively dominant position, which leaves room for a degree of competition between the cooperative energy companies and Fortum.

727. Second, Mankala companies have been active investors in the Finnish electricity market, in terms of both generation capacity and transmission capacity. Third, the Mankala model allows the shareholders more long-term predictability in their power procurement. The flipside of the coin is, of course, the possible foreclosure and exchange of sensitive commercial information, especially since participation in the Mankala companies might be restricted through the articles of association. In terms of the foreclosure, in particular, the overall market structure and the web of similar solutions are highly important from a legal point of view. Despite the potential negative effects, it seems as though the European Commission has demonstrated a positive interest in this type of company structure in its search for the solution to a possible investment gap in the EU energy markets.[334]

728. Overall, the compatibility of Mankala companies with competition law can only be determined on a case by case basis and will strongly depend on the details of the arrangement and the market structure within which the arrangement is adopted.

729. Interestingly, some guidance on a possible EU approach may be sought from the EDF/Exeltium case.[335] This case concerned a contractual arrangement between EDF and Exeltium, under which EDF was to supply significant volumes of electricity to the consortium on a very long-term basis. As Exeltium is a consortium of a number of large industrial electricity consumers in France, it bears certain similarities to the Mankala companies in Finland.[336] It seems that in that case, the key

333. Section 6 of the Competition Act and Art. 101(3) TFEU.

334. Communication from the Commission, Nuclear Illustrative Programme, COM(2016) 177 final, p. 6.

335. European Commission Press Release, 'Commissioner Kroes Welcomes Amendments in EDF/Exeltium Announced Framework' (MEMO/08/533), issued 31 Jul. 2008.

336. However, there are also significant differences between the two situations. First, the EDF/Exeltium case deals with a vertical contractual situation, whereas the cooperation through the Mankala companies is primarily of horizontal nature. Second, one of the key concerns in the EDF/Exeltium case

concerns of the Commission included the existence of resale restrictions and the existence of an effective opt-out for the members wishing to contract with other suppliers.

730. One significant aspect of the EDF/Exeltium case was that, even though the Commission accepted this arrangement, it did specifically note that it accepted only this particular contract, as the competition concerns were in this case, when viewed in isolation, addressed through certain arrangements. The Commission continued that this contractual arrangement would be taken into account in the overall analysis of the foreclosure of French electricity market, implying that the situation might change.[337] This is well in line with the Commission practice that emphasizes the overall effects of all relevant factors, such as the existence of a web of similar agreements, on the markets.

731. In addition to regulating vertical and horizontal cooperation between undertakings and agreements with an adverse effect on competition, the Competition Act aims to limit abuse by undertakings of a dominant position. This objective is particularly relevant in the energy markets, which are traditionally highly concentrated. Section 7 of the Competition Act prohibits any abuse by one or more undertakings or association of undertakings of a dominant position.

732. Such abuse may, in particular, consist of:

- directly or indirectly imposing unfair purchase or selling prices or other unfair trading conditions;
- limiting production, markets or technical development to the prejudice of consumers;
- applying dissimilar conditions to equivalent transactions with trading parties, thereby placing them at a competitive disadvantage; or
- making the conclusion of a contract subject to acceptance by the other contract party of supplementary obligations which, by their nature or according to commercial usage, have no connection with the subject of such a contract.

733. Merger control is one of the primary ways to control the emergence of undertakings of a dominant position and minimize the potential of abuse of such a position. The merger control rules of the Competition Act apply to mergers if two cumulative conditions are met. First, the combined turnover of the merging parties exceeds EUR 350 million and, second, the turnover recovered in Finland exceeds EUR 20 million for at least two of the parties.[338]

---

was certainly the maintenance of the dominant position of EDF. This aspect is not present in cases dealing with Mankala companies. These differences must be kept in mind in any comparisons.

337. Adrien de Hauteclocque, *Market Building Through Antitrust. Long-Term Contract Regulation in EU Electricity Markets* (Edward Elgar, 2013), p. 89.

338. Section 22 of the Competition Act.

734. The market structure and the development of the geographical market definition, within which market dominance is evaluated, were at the heart of one of the most significant merger cases of the FCCA and the Market Court in the electricity sector.[339] The original commitments imposed by the FCCA were finally overruled by the Market Court, which demonstrates the difficulties of defining a relevant market.

735. The conditional approval of the transaction in which Fortum Power and Heat Oy acquired control in E.ON Finland Oyj dates back to June 2006.[340] According to the assessment of the FCCA, the negative effects of the acquisition were to be felt in the electricity production and wholesale markets in Finland.[341]

736. The FCCA found that 'due to the restraints in the electricity transmission capacity, the geographical scope of the electricity production and wholesale market is national part of the time. During this time, Fortum holds a dominant position in these markets. The demand and competing supply of electricity met by Fortum do not effectively reduce Fortum's opportunities to affect the wholesale price level of electricity during these times in particular'.[342] Therefore, without the imposition of conditions that would result in divestiture of some of the generation capacity,[343] the dominant position of Fortum would have been strengthened, as both parties in the transaction were active in the relevant product markets (the production and wholesale markets). Very significantly, the conditions imposed by the FCCA were temporary in nature. This – undoubtedly correct – approach was based on the idea that the situation in the Finnish markets would change significantly with the completion of the new nuclear power plant (Olkiluoto III) and the new interconnector (Fenno-Skan II) between Finland and Sweden.[344]

339. FCCA Decision no. 52/81/06 2 Jun. 2006 and the overruling judgement of the Market Court no. 123/08, 14 Mar. 2008.
340. FCCA Press Release, 'FCCA Clears Fortum's E.ON Finland Acquisition, Subject to Conditions', issued 2 Jun. 2006. This case tied up most of the FCCA's energy-related expertise for all of 2006. For this, *see FCCA 2007 Year Book*, at 6 and 24–26.
341. As the wholesale electricity price is largely set by the Nordic Nord Pool electricity exchange, the FCCA had, according to its decision, cooperated extensively with Nord Pool in investigating the price formation in the integrated Nordic markets.
342. FCCA Press Release, 'FCCA Clears Fortum's E.ON Finland Acquisition, Subject to Conditions', issued 2 Jun. 2006.
343. The FCCA required Fortum to: (1) lease its share in the Meri-Pori coal-fired power plant until 30 Jun. 2010, (2) offer to the Finnish market an annual 1 TWh of so-called virtual capacity until 31 Mar. 2011, (3) sell its peat condensate power plant at Haapavesi and (4) sell its combined power and heat production plant and gas turbine power plant in Hämeenlinna. The acquirer(s) of this capacity had to be pre-approved by the FCCA.
344. Finnish Competition Authority Press Release, 'FCCA Clears Fortum's E.ON Finland Acquisition, Subject to Conditions', issued 2 Jun. 2006. The idea was undoubtedly that the new generation capacity in Finland would decrease the amount of electricity imported from other Nordic countries. Fenno-Skan 2, in turn, would increase cross-border transmission capacity and thus eliminate some of the congestion on the Finnish-Swedish border.

737. The parties appealed the decision to the Market Court, where it was overruled.[345] In essence, the Market Court concluded that the FCCA had adopted an incorrect definition of the geographical market. According to the Market Court, the temporary cross-border congestion issues did not change the fact that the relevant geographical market was at least Finland and Sweden. For most hours, the cross-border interconnectors were not congested and even when they were, these congestion periods were not predictable enough to be abused by a dominant market player. Considering the small market share of Fortum in the geographical market of Finland and Sweden, Fortum did not hold a dominant position prior to or after the transaction.

345. Market Court case no. 123/2008, 14 Mar. 2008.

Chapter 3. The Dynamics Between the FCCA and the EA

738. As mentioned in the Introduction to this book, the Finnish energy markets are not regulated solely by the EA and sector-specific energy market legislation. The FCCA, as the general competition and consumer authority, has a significant role to play in addressing anticompetitive behaviour in the electricity and gas markets. It also has certain specific tasks with regard to consumer contracts in the electricity and natural gas markets. The division of competencies and tasks between the EA and the FCCA is established in both sector-specific energy law instruments and legal instruments on general competition law.[346] However, there are still issues in which the competences of the institutions overlap. This is undoubtedly a result of the fact that their objectives and tasks are very similar.

739. While the objectives of the EA and the FCCA partially overlap, there are significant differences between the two institutions. These differences became more defined after the gradual revision of the relevant legislative acts since 2011. In particular, the revision of the Electricity and Natural Gas Market Acts and the adoption of the Energy Authority Act and the Act on Monitoring the Electricity and Natural Gas Markets shifted the overall division of tasks and powers from being shared between both the institutions to the EA. While the FCCA still has primary jurisdiction in merger control, for example, the overall regulatory oversight of energy markets now falls to the EA. The interrelation and division of tasks between these two institutions are briefly examined next. However, as the tasks and objectives of the EA have already been analysed in detail above, this chapter will not repeat the information here but will rather start by examining the tasks of the FCCA. After the tasks of the FCCA have been established, the relationship between the two institutions will be discussed.

740. Energy is not specifically addressed in the Competition Act or in the Act on the Finnish Competition and Consumer Authority and the FCCA does not have any energy-specific tasks. However, the powers conferred upon the FCCA apply in most sectors of the economy, including the energy sector.

741. The fundamental objective of both institutions is to facilitate and maintain competitive energy markets. While the EA does this pursuant to the sector-specific legal instruments,[347] the FCCA's jurisdiction in the energy markets is based on the

346. Most notably the Electricity Market Act and the Natural Gas Market Act (sähkömarkkinalaki, 588/2013, as amended and maakaasumarkkinalaki, 587/2017), the Competition Act (kilpailulaki, 948/2011, as amended), the Act on the Finnish Competition and Consumer Authority (laki kilpailu- ja kuluttajavirastosta, 661/2012, as amended), the Energy Authority Act (laki Energiavirastosta, 870/2013, as amended) and the Act on Monitoring the Electricity and Natural Gas Markets (laki sähkö- ja maakaasumarkkinoiden valvonnasta, 590/2013, as amended).

347. Electricity Market Act (sähkömarkkinalaki, 588/2013) and the Natural Gas Market Act (maakaasumarkkinalaki, 587/2017), the Energy Authority Act (laki Energiavirastosta, 870/2013) and the Act on Monitoring the Electricity and Natural Gas Markets (laki sähkö- ja maakaasumarkkinoiden valvonnasta, 590/2013).

Competition Act and the Act on the Finnish Competition and Consumer Authority (laki kilpailu- ja kuluttajavirastosta, 661/2012, as amended).

742. The FCCA was established to ensure the functioning of the markets and to implement competition and consumer policy. The general objective of the FCCA is to ensure compliance with EU competition law and to enforce the provisions of the Competition Act.[348] The legislative framework confers the FCCA with powers to ensure the objectives of the competition rules.[349] Generally, the FCCA may prepare proposals and initiatives to promote competition, eliminate regulations and provisions that restrict competition and improve consumer policy and consumer protection. It also handles the responsibilities mandated to it by the Competition Act and supervises compliance with decisions made under the Competition Act.

743. The most essential market supervision powers conferred upon the FCCA include the power to investigate and decide cases relating to vertical and horizontal cooperation between undertakings (cartels) and abuse of a dominant position.[350]

744. The FCCA also has competences with regard to the supervision of competition in economic activities carried out by public authorities or bodies under the control of public authorities. The FCCA may remove a practice or a structure by these entities that prevent, restricts, distorts or has the potential to distort competition or is incompliant with the requirement of market-based pricing.[351] Such a removal should primarily be carried out through negotiations with the relevant public authorities or bodies under the control of these authorities.[352]

745. Furthermore, merger control is at the heart of the FCCA's competence. Mergers, which exceed the thresholds identified in the chapter above, must be notified to the FCCA after the conclusion of the agreement, acquisition of control, or the announcement of a public bid but prior to the implementation of the transaction.[353] A merger may also be notified to the FCCA when the parties are able to demonstrate their intention to conclude a merger with sufficient certainty.[354]

746. Based upon a proposal of the FCCA, the Market Court may prohibit a merger, order it to be dissolved or attach conditions on the implementation of a merger.[355] Imposing these limitations requires that the resulting concentration causes a significant impediment to effective competition in the Finnish markets or in a substantial part of them, in particular as a result of the creation or strengthening

348. Section 1 of the Act on the Finnish Competition and Consumer Authority (laki kilpailu- ja kuluttajavirastosta, 661/2012).
349. Section 2 of the Act on the Finnish Competition and Consumer Authority.
350. Chapter 4 of the Competition Act and s. 2 of the Act on the Finnish Competition and Consumer Authority.
351. Section 30a of the Competition Act.
352. Section 30a of the Competition Act.
353. Section 23 of the Competition Act.
354. Section 23 of the Competition Act.
355. Section 25 of the Competition Act.

of a dominant position.[356] Defining the relevant market in which to evaluate dominant position is, however, subject to interpretation as was demonstrated in the Fortum case.[357]

747. Finally, the FCCA may impose penalties for the infringement of competition law and approve commitments submitted by undertakings or associations of undertakings involved in a suspected infringement of competition law.[358]

748. The overlap in the FCCA's and the EA's jurisdictions requires a legal framework for close cooperation. This cooperation includes rules on the exchange of information, rules on the transfer of decision-making powers and rules on the coordination of sanctions for example.

749. Public authorities in Finland have a comparatively strong tradition of cooperation and openly sharing information between authorities to enable the effective functioning of public decision-making.[359] In addition to this general administrative approach, sector-specific energy legislation and competition law both include provisions on the cooperation and information sharing between the FCCA and the EA.

750. In accordance with section 39 of the Competition Act, the FCCA has the right to submit to the EA confidential documents that it has obtained or drafted in the process of carrying out its tasks. Such a right, however, extends only to what is necessary to carry out the tasks of the EA.

751. This right to share confidential information is mutual. According to section 28 of the Act on Monitoring the Electricity and Natural Gas Markets, the EA has the right to submit the FCCA with confidential documents that the FCCA needs to effectively carry out its tasks. The EA, however, cannot submit confidential documents it has obtained from a foreign public authority or from an international institution without the consent of these foreign entities.[360]

752. Under section 27 of the Act on Monitoring the Electricity and Natural Gas Markets, the EA has the right to conduct supervisory cooperation with the FCCA in matters that fall within the competence of the EA. When requested, the EA may also assist the FCCA in matters related to the supervision or inspection of an electricity or natural gas undertaking.[361] The EA and the FCCA have a tradition of mutual cooperation even before this provision entered into force in 2013.[362] The objective

356. Section 25 of the Competition Act.
357. Market Court case no. 123/2008, 14 Mar. 2008.
358. Chapter 3 of the Competition Act.
359. Act on the Openness of Government Activities (laki viranomaisten toiminnan julkisuudesta, 621/1999); s. 10 of the Administrative Procedure Act of Finland (hallintolaki, 434/2003).
360. Section 28 of the Act on Monitoring the Electricity and Natural Gas Markets.
361. Section 27 of the Act on Monitoring the Electricity and Natural Gas Markets.
362. Joint memorandum between the FCCA and the Energy Authority (yhteistyömuistio 26.1.2006), available at https://www.kkv.fi/.

of the cooperation was to increase the effectiveness of operations by the two institutions. This meant both the exchange of information and the use of accumulating expertise resulting from the work carried out by the two institutions.[363]

753. Because of the overlapping objectives between the EA and the FCCA, there are matters that may fall within the competence of both institutions. For example, network operators typically always hold a dominant position, the abuse of which falls within the competence of the FCCA. Overseeing the reasonability of network tariffs, however, falls within the competence of the EA.[364] To address these kinds of situations, the EA may transfer the competitive elements a matter to be decided by the FCCA.[365] If a matter to be handled by the EA relates to a procedure that may constitute an infringement of the provisions of the Competition Act that address restrictions on competition, the EA may transfer the matter to be decided by the FCCA insofar as restrictions on competition are concerned.[366] Such a transfer decision is not open to an appeal.[367]

754. In general, the EA supervises compliance with matters regulated through the Electricity and Natural Gas Market Acts.[368] However, consumer contracts in electricity and natural gas markets make an important exception to this rule. The Consumer Ombudsman, which operates under the FCCA, supervises the legality of access contracts, distribution contracts and electricity and natural gas supply contracts from the point of view of protecting the consumer.[369]

755. The Consumer Ombudsman has the power to conduct inspections, negotiate voluntary abandonment of consumer practices by undertakings that are incompliant with consumer law and issue decisions that prohibit such practices.[370] Furthermore, the Ombudsman may assist a consumer in managing an individual

363. Joint memorandum between the FCCA and the Energy Authority (yhteistyömuistio 26.1.2006), available at https://www.kkv.fi/.

364. *See* Energy Authority, Decision on the methodologies for calculating electricity network income between 2016 and 2013, no. xxx/430/2015, 30 Nov. 2015 (Sähkön jakeluverkkotoiminta ja sähkön suurjännitteinen jakeluverkkotoiminta – Vahvistuspäätös) and Energy Authority, Decision on the methodologies for calculating natural gas network income between 2016 and 2013, no. xxx/430/2015, 30 Nov. 2015, no. xxxx/530/2015 (Verkonhaltijan verkkotoiminnan tuoton määrittämistä koskevien menetelmien vahvistaminen neljännelle 1.1.2016 – 31.12.2019 ja viidennelle 1.1.2020 – 31.12.2023 valvontajaksolle). There is an abundant body of case law, where an electricity undertaking has challenged the Energy Authority's decision on the level of reasonable profit for network operators. *See*, for example, Market Court case no. 15/47, 28 Jan. 2015 and Market Court case 12/503, 21 Dec. 2012 (electricity) and Market Court case no. 17/247, 5 May 2017 (natural gas).

365. Section 32 of the Act on Monitoring the Electricity and Natural Gas Markets.

366. Section 41 of the Electricity Market Act; s. 4 of the Natural Gas Market Act.

367. Government bill on the regulation on electricity and natural gas markets (HE 20/2013 vp., hallituksen esitys eduskunnalle sähkö- ja maakaasumarkkinoita koskevaksi lainsäädännöksi), p. 172.

368. Section 106 of the Electricity Market Act and s. 88 of the Natural Gas Market Act.

369. Section 106 of the Electricity Market Act and s. 88 of the Natural Gas Market Act.

370. Chapter 2 of the Act on the Finnish Competition and Consumer Authority. For case law, *see* Market Court case no. 15/405, 10 Jun. 2015.

matter if such a matter is important to the application of the law and its management is in the best interests of consumers, or if an undertaking has failed to comply with a decision.[371]

756. Both the EA and the FCCA may impose sanctions on undertakings for in compliance with the law. To avoid dual sanctioning in overlapping matters, section 16 of the Act on Monitoring the Electricity and Natural Gas Markets states that the EA may not impose sanctions on a matter in which a decision on sanctions has already been issued by the FCCA.

371. Section 13 of the Act on the Finnish Competition and Consumer Authority.

Conclusion

757. This book has examined and explained various aspects of Finnish energy law and energy markets. It has covered the markets and the regulation of electricity, natural gas, coal and oil. In addition, the interaction between various branches of law, including tax, environmental and competition law, has been examined in much detail. The emphasis of and relations between various parts largely mirror the significance of the respective areas of the energy markets and their regulation.

758. This brief conclusion will highlight the particularities of the Finnish energy markets and Finnish energy law. These two items are obviously interrelated in the sense that the particularities of the markets are mirrored in the particularities of the regulations. As such, this conclusion will be organized thematically to include electricity, natural gas, oil and coal. The effect of other branches of law will be highlighted only where necessary.

759. The liberalization of the Finnish electricity markets took place earlier than in most EU Member States. Today, again at the forefront of all the EU Member States, Finland is pushing the boundaries of its electricity markets from national to international. Following the proactive approach and the investments by national TSOs, cross-border congestion is becoming less serious and less frequent. Unlike in most other areas, the geographical electricity markets are no longer national but cover at least Finland and Sweden. Finland is also an integral part of what is often considered to be the most competitive market in the world, the Nordic electricity market driven by the Nord Pool power exchange. These factors have significant effects in terms of security of supply and competitive conditions.

760. However, while the Finnish electricity market is fairly competitive, cross-ownership is a common phenomenon. In addition, the cooperative companies continue to pose a challenge for the regulators. On the one hand, this company structure carries certain efficiency gains, as it enables large-scale investments, including nuclear generation. On the other hand, it has the clear potential to reduce competition in the Finnish markets.

761. The Third Energy Directive did not come without consequences for the Finnish electricity markets. The most visible and concrete effect has been the ownership unbundling of the TSO. While the ownership unbundling obligation became obsolete in most cases, it had the effect of requiring a significant change in the ownership structure of Fingrid. Currently, the State owns 12.33% of the shares of the company.

762. A distinctive feature of the Finnish electricity markets is its continued reliance on nuclear power. The decision-making procedure relating to this mode of power generation is divided into administrative and political phases. While the administrative phase is largely a straightforward assessment of the applicants and their projects, the political phase is more problematic. Its very national approach however argued on the basis of the Treaty[372] as opposed to a wider EU approach is likely to raise discussion at some point in the future.

763. Finland has final storage capacity for its nuclear waste and has regulated this aspect intensively. The final repository will be located in the proximity of the nuclear power plants at Olkiluoto, and the waste will be stored deep in the Finnish bedrock. Here the issue of free movement of nuclear waste and the use of Finnish territory and technology by the other EU Member States has raised concerns. However, due to the very specific nature of nuclear waste, which differentiates it from most other types of wastes, these concerns are unfounded.

764. Where the Finnish electricity markets may be well advanced in an EU comparison, this is not the case with the natural gas markets. Finnish gas markets are currently completely dependent on a single pipeline bringing natural gas from Russia. The extent of the gas market in Finland is very limited, in terms of both total use and geographical coverage, and the majority of the gas is consumed by industry, the power sector being the second major consumer of natural gas. This isolation, coupled with the fact that a single company is dominant in all the market segments, does not provide the preconditions necessary for efficient competition to emerge. This market isolation is about to come to an end in January 2020 when the Balticconnector-pipeline from Finland to Estonia will be completed and the Finnish natural gas markets will be opened and joined together with the European Gas Markets. However, before this opening of the natural gas market happens, the Finnish markets enjoy an exemption from many aspects of the EU energy acquis.

765. In the oil markets, the role of the state company, Neste Oil, has traditionally been very much interlinked with the internal and external policies of the State. It has, in particular, been an instrument for the State in its efforts to find the balance between its policy towards Russia and towards Western Europe and the US.[373] Like oil, all the coal used in Finland is imported, primarily from Russia, but also from other countries. Another Finnish particularity is its significant use of peat for CHP production. Peat accounts for approximately 4% of all power production in the country. Peat is also used for security-of-supply purposes, and peat-based condensing power generation benefits from a feed-in tariff.

372. *See* Art. 176a(2) of the Treaty of the Functioning of the European Union.
373. This has been discussed in much detail in Markku Kuisma, *Kylmä sota, kuuma öljy – Neste, Suomi ja kaksi Eurooppaa* (Helsinki: WSOY, 1998).

766. Today, following the international trends and the concerns over climate change, the main challenge for the Finnish oil and coal industry, and more generally for the entire energy industry, is the transition from the traditional fossil fuels to a more sustainable energy mix, even though in an international comparison, the Finnish energy mix already includes a significantly large proportion of energy from renewable and zero-emission energy sources. Here the traditional use of hydropower, both in Finland and in other Nordic countries, and the increased use of nuclear generation will help in responding to the future challenges.

Selected Bibliography

Cameron, Peter D., 'The Internal Market in Energy: Harnessing the New Regulatory Regime', 30(5) European Law Review (2005).

de Hauteclocque, Adrien, Market Building Through Antitrust. Long-Term Contract Regulation in EU Electricity Markets (Edward Elgar, Cheltenham, UK, Northamton, MA, USA, 2013).

EU Energy Law – Volume 1, The Internal Energy Market. 4th ed. (Claeys & Casteels, Deventer (Netherlands) – Leuven (Belgium), 2016).

Guimaraes-Purokoski, Alice, Vertikaalinen toimivallanjako EU-oikeudessa – Tutkimus yhteisön toimivallan kehittymisestä energia-alalla sekä julkisen palvelun velvoitteiden ja yleispalvelun sääntelystä sähkön sisämarkkinoilla (Helsinki: Suomalainen Lakimiesyhdistys, 2009).

Hancher, Leigh and de Hauteclocque, Adrien, 'Manufacturing the EU Energy Markets: The Current Dynamics of Regulatory Practice', 11(3) Competition and Regulation in Network Industries (2010).

Kärkkäinen, Seppo & Rajala, Arto, Pitkien tukkusähkösopimusten vaikutukset sähkön vähittäismyynnin kilpailutilanteeseen (Helsinki: Edita, 1999).

Kuisma, Markku, Kylmä sota, kuuma öljy – Neste, Suomi ja kaksi Eurooppaa (Helsinki: WSOY, 1998).

Kuusiniemi, Kari (ed.), Uusi ympäristönsuojelulainsäädäntö (Helsinki: Edita, 2001).

Kuusiniemi, Kari 'Arvojen muutos ja ympäristölakien tulkinta teoksessa Oikeuden tavoitteet ja menettelyt, Muistokirja Hannu Tapani Klamille', in Turun yliopiston oikeustieteellisen tiedekunnan julkaisuja A. juhlajulkaisut N:o 12, ed. Ari-Matti Nuutila (Helsinki: Edita, 2003).

Lappalainen, Vesa, 'Proposed Finland-Russia Interconnector Rejected', OGEL 1 (2007), <www.ogel.org>.

Poesche, Jurgen, Ökologisches Energierecht in der Europaischen Union (Helsinki: Helsinki University Press, 2008).

Pohjolan Voima 60 vuotta, Pohjoisen vesiltä monipuoliseksi energiayhtiöksi (Helsinki: Edita, 2003).

Pöyhönen, Juha (ed.), An Introduction to Finnish Law (Helsinki: Kauppakaari 2002).

Talus, Kim, 'Competition Law Country Report' (Finland) at <www.concurrences.com>.

Vihervuori, Pekka, Environmental Law – Finland (Kluwer Law International, Wolters, USA).

Selected Bibliography

Viitanen, Klaus, 'Compulsory Purchase as an Administrative Procedure', 3rd FIG Regional Conference, Jakarta, Indonesia, 3–7 October 2004.
Wiwen-Nilsson, Tove; Håkansson, Malin & Wärnsby, Mikael, Sweden – Energy Law (The Hague: Kluwer, 2005).
World Energy Outlook OECD 2017.

Index

The numbers here refer to paragraph numbers.

Index

www.ingramcontent.com/pod-product-compliance
Ingram Content Group UK Ltd.
Pitfield, Milton Keynes, MK11 3LW, UK
UKHW020140290926
15471UKWH00003B/609

9 789403 505039